Tips for Success on the Verbal Sections

General tips

- ✔ Use roots, prefixes, and suffixes to determine the gist of an unfamiliar word.
- ✔ Guess quickly if you are stumped. The computer won't let you go on until you've made a guess; answering a few questions incorrectly hurts your score less than not finishing a section.

Antonym tips

- ✔ Create an approximate definition of the word in your mind.
- ✔ Predict the obvious opposite.
- ✔ Remember that words have more than one meaning.

Reading Comprehension tips

- ✔ Choose positive or neutral answers to the Reading Comprehension questions, not negative ones.
- ✔ Roman numeral and negative/exception questions are often tricky and time-consuming; guess quickly on them and go on.
- ✔ Don't choose an answer simply because it's true; make certain that it answers the question correctly.

Analogy tips

- ✔ Create a sentence that shows the relationship between the two words and then use that sentence on each answer choice.
- ✔ Use roots, prefixes, and suffixes to help define unfamiliar words.
- ✔ Beware of answers with inverse relationships (for example, part to whole when the question was whole to part).

Sentence Completion tips

- ✔ Read the entire sentence to get its gist before looking at the individual blanks.
- ✔ Search for key connector words (such as because, although, and however) that may change the meaning of the sentence from what you'd expect.
- ✔ Predict whether the blanks need positive or negative words.

This test is rated PG — Proctor Guarded.

Proctors have been genetically altered to have eyes in the backs of their heads; they'll catch you if you peek at this cheat sheet during the GRE. Learn it, and then burn it.

The GRE® Test For Dummies, 5th Edition

Cheat Sheet

Tips for Success on the Math Sections

General tips

- Lose the calculator (not allowed); the proctor will provide scratch paper.
- The GRE tests algebra, geometry, and arithmetic, not calculus or trigonometry.
- Memorize formulas before you take the test. The GRE doesn't provide them.

Quantitative Comparison tips

- Triple-check your answer before hitting the CONFIRM button, as the answers to the QC questions are often not the obvious, first-response answer.
- Remember that the answer choices are the same for every question. Choose A if Column A is greater than Column B; B if Column B is greater; C if the two columns are equal; and D if insufficient information is given. E is not a choice.
- If the columns seem to be equal, do the required calculations to *prove* that they are.
- Play the *what-if* game by plugging in 1, then 2, 0, –1, –2, and ½. If the answer *depends* on what you plug in for the variable, choose D.

Problem Solving tips

- Note what the question specifically asks for: perimeter, area, length, degree, fraction, percentage, and so on.
- Before you begin working on the problem, read the answer choices. You may be able to estimate and answer without working out the solution.
- Plug answer choices into the question to see which one works. Do the easy choices first; you may not have to do the hard ones.

Tips for Success on the Analytical Writing Section

Present your perspective on an issue

- Answer the question specifically, making your opinion known to the readers in the introductory paragraph.
- Use all 45 minutes to create a 3 to 5 paragraph essay, giving supporting reasons and examples for your perspective (and anticipating and addressing counterarguments).
- Create a final paragraph that summarizes, not merely repeats, the points of the essay.

Analyze an argument

- Identify the assumptions the writer is making and discuss how reasonable those assumptions are.
- Provide outside counterexamples or supporting information to strengthen or weaken the argument.
- Avoid giving your opinion on the topic; the point is to discuss how well argued the essay is as written.

Tips for GRE CAT Success

- The first five or so questions in each section are critical; take your time to answer those correctly.
- You cannot skip and go back to a question, but guess quickly and go on when you are stumped; you benefit from answering every question more than you lose by missing a few.
- Keep an eye on the clock and sprint to the end, being sure to fill in something for every answer before time runs out.

Wiley, the Wiley Publishing logo, For Dummies, the Dummies Man logo, the For Dummies Bestselling Book Series logo and all related trade dress are trademarks or registered trademarks of Wiley Publishing, Inc. All other trademarks are property of their respective owners.

For Dummies: Bestselling Book Series for Beginners

The GRE® Test

FOR

DUMMIES®

5TH EDITION

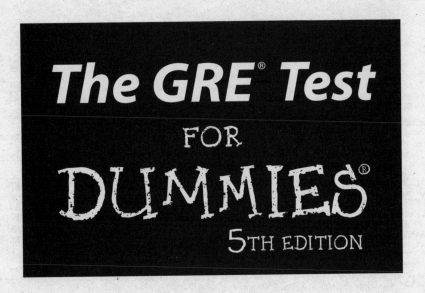

The GRE® Test

FOR

DUMMIES®

5TH EDITION

by Suzee Vlk

Wiley Publishing, Inc.

The GRE® Test For Dummies® 5th Edition

Published by
Wiley Publishing, Inc.
909 Third Avenue
New York, NY 10022
www.wiley.com

Copyright © 2002 by Wiley Publishing, Inc., Indianapolis, Indiana

Published simultaneously in Canada

For general information on our other products and services or to obtain technical support, please contact our Customer Care Department within the U.S. at 800-762-2974, outside the U.S. at 317-572-3993, or fax 317-572-4002.

Wiley also publishes its books in a variety of electronic formats. Some content that appears in print may not be available in electronic books.

Library of Congress Control Number: 2002108091

ISBN: 0-7645-5473-5

Manufactured in the United States of America

10 9 8 7 6 5 4 3 2

5B/SS/QY/QS/IN

About the Author

"I'm not a complete idiot. Parts of me are missing."

Although more likely to admit to being a mortician, used-car salesperson, or guinea pig for Army experiments, **Suzee Vlk** has been a test-prep specialist since 1975, working her way through graduate business school and law school by teaching courses in GMAT, GRE, LSAT, SAT, and ACT preparation. She found the paranoia and take-no-prisoners mind-set required for doing well on the GRE a big help in developing cutthroat tactics to use in the boardroom or courtroom.

Today Suzee is president of Suzee Vlk Test Prep (no ego involved in that company name!) and has taught thousands of students in dozens of courses at universities and private corporations, including "mature" adults who have been out of school for a decade (or two or three) and international students from countries all over the world. (All victims have, so far, survived.) She has written material used in GRE and SAT preparation software and videos (starring in one set of videos when she was younger and blonder). Her prep books for the GRE and other standardized exams have been published worldwide.

Suzee currently specialized in one-on-one tutorials and teaches GRE prep tricks and traps to all levels of students from those who are struggling to remember the basics ("Let's see: A triangle has three sides, or is it four?") to whiz kids who will probably be her boss one day. Her students have not only been accepted at graduate business progams in colleges and universities nationwide, including such dream schools as Harvard and Stanford, but they also have done well enough on their GREs to be awarded scholarships (to the unbounded joy of their parents, who can now spend what's left of their kids' education funds on sailboats, flashy sports cars, and other midlife crisis toys).

Suzee lives by the following motto, which she is delighted to share with you:

"Madness takes its toll. Please have exact change ready."

Dedication

This book is dedicated to Dr. Regis Weiss, my oncologist, who will be in my thank-you prayers every night for the rest of my long, long, loooooonnng life.

Author's Acknowledgments

After years of having California students groan at my puns, make rude hand gestures in response to my scintillatingly clever quips, and threaten to storm out of the classroom if I tell my geometry jokes one more time, it's wonderful to get the chance to inflict my dysfunctional humor on a worldwide, unsuspecting audience. The decline of civilization begins here.

Thanks to my agents, Bill Gladstone and Matt Wagner of Waterside Productions in Cardiff, California, for getting me this opportunity. A panegyric and paean for my project editor, Marcia Johnson, my acquisitions editor, Kathy Cox, and copy editor Mike Baker, not only for their erudition but also for their effervescence and ebullience that didn't flag even under deadlines. Special thanks to Barb Terry for the iron fist in a velvet glove (and for laughing at most of my jokes). Many thanks also go to Kristin Cocks, Jennifer Ehrlich, as well as all past editors of previous editions.

Thanks to independent college counselor Jill Q. Porter of La Jola, California, for her up-to-the-minute insights about what college and university programs seek and to Larry Asmus and all the other specialists in their various fields who helped me write test questions.

And thanks as always to my students over the years, those wonderful young and not-so-young adults who have had enough faith in me to use my tricks and tips and enough kindness to let me share their joy in the good scores hat result. You all keep this fun.

Publisher's Acknowledgments

We're proud of this book; please send us your comments through our Dummies online registration form located at www.dummies.com/register/.

Some of the people who helped bring this book to market include the following:

Acquisitions, Editorial, and Media Development

Project Editor: Marcia L. Johnson
   (Previous editions: Sherri Fugit, Colleen Rainsberger, Barb Terry, Jennifer Ehrlich)

Acquisitions Editor: Kathy Cox

Copy Editor: Mike Baker

Technical Editor: David Herzog

Editorial Manager: Jennifer Ehrlich

Editorial Assistant: Nivea C. Strickland

Production

Project Coordinator: Regina Snyder

Layout and Graphics: Karl Brandt, Joyce Haughey, Jacque Schneider, Betty Schulte, Erin Zeltner

Proofreaders: Laura Albert, Andy Hollandbeck, Arielle Carole Mennelle, Susan Moritz

Indexer: Sherry Massey

Special Help: Melissa Bennett

Publishing and Editorial for Consumer Dummies

Diane Graves Steele, Vice President and Publisher, Consumer Dummies

Joyce Pepple, Acquisitions Director, Consumer Dummies

Kristin A. Cocks, Product Development Director, Consumer Dummies

Michael Spring, Vice President and Publisher, Travel

Brice Gosnell, Publishing Director, Travel

Suzanne Jannetta, Editorial Director, Travel

Publishing for Technology Dummies

Andy Cummings, Acquisitions Director

Composition Services

Gerry Fahey, Vice President of Production Services

Debbie Stailey, Director of Composition Services

Contents at a Glance

Cartoons at a Glance

By Rich Tennant

page 77

page 7

page 267

page 35

page 185

page 139

Cartoon Information:
Fax: 978-546-7747
E-Mail: richtennant@the5thwave.com
World Wide Web: www.the5thwave.com

page 167

Table of Contents

Introduction

Welcome to *The GRE® Test For Dummies,* 5th Edition. Don't take the title personally. Being a dummy is good; it just means you're normal. Unfortunately, the GRE is anything *but* normal. As I've learned in more than two decades of fighting the GRE wars, the GRE has no connection to the Real World. When you were given the dire news that you had to take the GRE to get into graduate school, you probably flashed back to the SAT (lovingly known as Sadists Against Teenagers) that you had to take to get into college. Although the two tests share some similarities (both exams are the leading causes of ulcers, migraines, and decisions to become a Bora Bora beachcomber), they do have some differences.

The primary dissimilarity has to do with your familiarity with the material. In high school, instructors often "teach to the test." They know that their students are going to take the SAT, know the kids themselves, and teach them what will be on the test and how to take the exam. In college, you're on your own. Your professors may not have any idea who you are ("The kid in the *I'm only here for the beer* T-shirt who sits in the upper row of the lecture hall? In my mind I call him Bud, but I don't know him at all"), and they almost certainly are not going to take time away from class to discuss the tricks and traps on the GRE. In addition, you have spent the last few years of college working on the courses specific to your major: invertebrate biology, lifestyles of the upper Botswana natives, or maybe sociological and psychological implications of domestic dissonance. It's been a long, long time since you've taken basic algebra, geometry, and arithmetic (found in the math portions of the exam) or vocabulary and writing (found in the verbal and analytical portions of the exam). And what about those of you who are no longer in college? I, for one, entered college in the days of parchment and quills but didn't get around to taking the GRE until the era of laptops and battery packs. No doubt about it; you need some help. And a specialist is in the best position to provide the skills you need. Think of this book as a SWAT team that you can call in when the situation gets desperate.

Like a SWAT team, this book aims to deal with the crisis efficiently, do the job, save the day, and get you out as quickly as possible. I know that you have a life you'd like to get back to. The goal of this book is to help you to learn what you need and can use on the GRE — period. No extra garbage is thrown in to impress you with esoteric facts; no filler is added to make this book the fattest one on the market. If you need a doorstop, go pick up the New York City telephone directory. If you need a quick 'n' easy guide to surviving the GRE, you're in the right place.

About This Book

It's Us versus Them. Who are They? The creators of the GRE, those gnomes in green eyeshades. The next time you're trying to get away from a *soporific dolt* (sleep-inducing blockhead) at a party, answer the question, "So, what do you do for a living?" with the response, "I create questions for the GRE." That conversation stopper is guaranteed to send any *paramour manqué* (would-be sweetie) running and screaming into the night.

In *The GRE Test® For Dummies,* I show you how to approach each type of question, recognize the traps that are built into the questions, and master the tricks that help you to avoid those traps. The book is full of Gotchas! that I (a test prep tutor since the Dawn of Time) have seen students fall for repeatedly. In this book, you learn to think the GRE way (don't worry; it's not permanent) to identify the point behind the various styles and types of questions and to figure out what each style and type is trying to test. This book also gives you a review of the basics (from math formulas to common roots, prefixes, and suffixes useful for improving your vocabulary), along with a laugh or two to make learning the material as painless as possible.

If you only use this book to prop open a window or as a booster seat for a toddler, you won't get the most out of it. I suggest two alternatives:

- ✔ **Fine-tune your skills.** Turn to specific sections for specific information and help. The organization of this book makes it very easy to find the type of math question you always have trouble with, suggestions for answering reading questions without having finished the passage, and tricks for guessing. If you are in college classes or in a career in which you use this jazz every day (maybe you're a math major at school or teach high school English classes) and need just a nudge in one or two areas, you can work through those sections only.

- ✔ **Start from scratch.** Read through the whole book. Actually, I'd like you to follow this approach. No matter how well you do on a section, you can improve. It's a common mistake to believe that you should work on your weakest sections only. The 50 points you gain in your mediocre section by skimming through the suggestions in this book are just as worthwhile as the 50 points you get by grunting, groaning, and sweating through your most difficult area. If you have the time, do yourself a favor and read the book from cover to cover. Besides, you don't want to miss any of my jokes, now do you?

The GRE® Test For Dummies is simple and straightforward enough for first-time GRE victims, er, students that they can understand the entire exam and do well right out of the starting gate. But it's also detailed and sophisticated enough that veterans — those of you who have taken the exam once or twice before but aren't resting on your laurels (sounds painful, anyway) — can learn the more complicated information you need to get those truly excellent scores.

Note to nontraditional students: I'm aware of the fact that some of you are not 21-year-old college seniors taking this exam to go into graduate school right after college. You may have been out of college so long that your *children* are 21-year-old seniors! Maybe you've just decided to go back to grad school after a long career or after raising a family, and you need help getting back into the math and verbal stuff that you had in what seems like another lifetime. I sympathize with you; it's tough to deal with nonagons, quadratic equations, and analogies again. Don't despair; you can get outside help, especially in math, which is one of the first things to fade when people get away from school. Call a community college (or even a high school; the math on this exam doesn't exceed what is taught in upper-division high school math classes, depressing as that may seem to you as you're sweating through it). Ask for help in finding a tutor or for suggestions on finding a quick review course in your area. You also can call your local library for assistance.

Pardon Me for Having a Life: Who Has Time for This?

You have school or work, sports or other hobbies, family responsibilities, and oh yes, something that vaguely resembles a social life. How on earth are you going to fit in studying for the GRE?

Time required to go through the GRE lectures

Buying this book was brilliant. (Okay, so your roommate, your spouse, or some significant other bought it and tossed it at you with the snide comment, "Hey, you can sure use all the help you can get." Whatever.) How much time should you take to go through this book? I suggest 24 hours.

Each subject (Antonyms, Analogies, Sentence Completions, Reading Comprehension, Quantitative Comparisons, Problem Solving, and Analytical Writing) includes a chapter on the format, approach, and tricks and traps for that particular type of question. Following each lecture, I include a quiz chapter featuring a sampling of questions that tests what you learned in that lecture. The detailed answer explanations point out the traps you may have fallen for and the tips that you should have used to avoid the traps. You learn which questions to guess at quickly (they're either too hard or too time-consuming) and which to double-check. You should spend about two hours per lecture, including the quiz — you're looking at 14 hours total here. The book also includes a three-part math review; each section (geometry, algebra, and arithmetic) should take roughly one hour, for a total of three hours.

Time required to go through the practice GREs

At the end of the book are two full-length GREs. Each exam takes two and a fourth hours to complete and about another hour to review. My thinking that you should take an hour to review the exam does not reflect a lack of confidence in your *erudition* and *sagacity* (knowledge and wisdom). I'm not saying that you're so *inept* and *bungling* (unskilled) that you're going to miss a *plethora* (abundance) of questions. My suggestion is that you review *all* the answer explanations — even those for the questions you answer correctly. You'll learn some good stuff from the explanations; you'll review formulas, find shortcuts, and see more tricks and traps. I'll exaggerate and say that the whole test and review should take you three and a half hours. The following table gives you what I think is a reasonable timetable.

Activity	*Time*
7 lectures at 2 hours per lecture	14 hours
2 exams at 3½ hours per exam (including review)	7 hours
3 math review chapters at 1 hour per chapter	3 hours
Time spent laughing hysterically at author's jokes	5 minutes
Time spent composing letter complaining about author's crummy jokes	5 minutes
TOTAL	24 hours, 10 minutes

No one expects you to read this book for 24 hours straight. Each unit is self-contained. The answer explanations may remind you of things from other units because repetition aids learning and memorizing, but you can read through each unit separately.

Are you ready? Stupid question. Are you resigned? Have you accepted your fate that you're going to take the GRE no matter what and that you may as well have fun studying for it? Take a deep breath, turn the page, and go for it. Here's hoping that, for you, GRE comes to stand for Genius Rocks Exam!

How This Book Is Organized

This book is divided into seven parts. Each one focuses on a separate aspect of preparing for the GRE, but together they lay the foundation for improving your test scores.

Part 1: An Aerial View: Putting the GRE into Perspective

In this part, you get some perspective on the GRE as a whole. I introduce you to what's on the exam, what you need to know to do your best on the test, and what the scores look like.

Part II: A Word to the Wise: Verbal Questions

The verbal portion of the GRE tests your vocabulary (with Antonyms, Analogies, and Sentence Completion questions) and reading skills (with Reading Comprehension passages and questions). In this part, I put you through the paces so that these questions (I hope) become second nature to you.

Part III: Two Years of Math in 60 Pages: The Dreaded Math Review

I know that all those geometry formulas, algebra rules, and arithmetic concepts you learned once upon a time still lurk back in the dim, dark recesses of your mind. The job of the three math-review chapters in this part is to force all that information front and center, where you can make good use of it.

Part IV: Your Number's Up: Math Questions

The bits of wisdom imparted to you in Part IV allow you to do your best on the two types of math questions found on the GRE — Quantitative Comparisons and Problem Solving.

Part V: Getting into Analysis: Analytical Writing

The newest portion of the GRE, Analytical Writing, asks you to craft two essays on topics presented to you. Part V gives you tips on how to overcome writer's block and get started, as well as what the readers reward you for writing . . . and what causes them to scream in anguish.

Part VI: It All Comes Down to This: Full-Length Practice GREs

What good is all this brilliance if you can't show it off? Part VI lets you take two full-length exams to make sure you can practice what I've preached.

Part VII: The Part of Tens

At last, the good stuff! This part has fun — but useful — information such as ten stupid things you can do to mess up your GRE and ten relaxation techniques you can try before and during the GRE.

Icons Used in This Book

To help you to get through this book more quickly, I include some icons that flag the particularly important stuff. If you need to work on your vocabulary, for example, flip through the book to find the Vocabulary icons and then make a list of the accompanying words and their meanings. The icons look like this.

This icon marks sample problems that appear in the lectures.

Be wary of the important stuff that this icon points out to you. If you skip these sections, I accept no responsibility for what may happen to you.

This icon points out information pertaining to international students and suggestions that can make life easier for those of you for whom English is a second or third language. International students, please see welcoming comments to you in Chapter 1.

As you stumble through your GRE preparation, these little commandments are things you should never forget.

This icon directs you to tips that should make taking the GRE go much more smoothly. These tips alone are worth the price of this book. Trust me.

The test makers throw in some nasty traps that may get you if you don't think about the questions carefully. Learn the tricks marked by this icon, and you'll be amazed at how easily you can outsmart the GRE.

This icon points out the big words (useless in the Real World and therefore almost inevitably on the GRE) that you may not know. (Let's face it: Some of the vocab words on the GRE are so tough that you practically have to be constipated to pronounce them!) Learning those words and their definitions is sure to help you on the GRE. The words themselves are in a special typeface — *like this* — and their meanings appear next to them. (You'll fix these words even more successfully in your memory if you try to use them in your real life. Call your roommate or your children *indolent, lethargic,* and *listless* when they don't jump up to do the dishes right after dinner; promise your professor you'll be *diligent, meticulous,* and *painstaking* in your lab assignment.)

Part I

An Aerial View: Putting the GRE into Perspective

The 5th Wave   By Rich Tennant

"Okay — now that the paramedic is here with the defibrillator and smelling salts, prepare to open your test booklets..."

In this part . . .

1 know, I know — the only aerial view you'd like to have
of the GRE is the one you see from 10,000 feet up as
a jet takes you far, far away from this exam. Use the info
in this book correctly and you can ace the GRE, go to a
top grad school, get a great job — and then buy your own
private jet and buzz the office of that college guidance
counselor who told you your best chance at a good life
would be to marry rich. Hey, it's something to aim for
(the goal, not the college counselor!).

You're probably eager to get right into studying for the
GRE (or maybe not), but take a few minutes to go through
this introductory material. It's good strategy to find out
everything you can about your enemy before going into
battle.

Chapter 1

Know Your Enemy:
What the GRE Looks Like

In This Chapter

▶ Understanding the format: Number and types of questions

▶ Scoring the exam

▶ Breaking the tension: Using the intermission wisely

Unlike traditional, standardized paper and pencil tests, which feature a roomful of test-takers sweating and fretting together in a lecture hall, the GRE is now totally computer-based. No, you don't get to take the test on your home computer with a dictionary in one hand and a tropical drink with a paper umbrella in the other (sorry if I got your hopes up only to dash them cruelly). The GRE is offered at designated technology centers (many of them are Sylvan Learning Centers) throughout the world on most days of the year during most business hours. This schedule means that if you're not a morning person, you don't have to worry about getting up at the crack of dawn and trudging across town to attempt to make your lethargic brain cells function at 8:00 a.m. You can take the test at any hour you personally consider civilized, such as later in the afternoon or even in the evening. For information on signing up for the GRE, see the current GRE Registration Bulletin. (You can pick up this bulletin at a college admissions office, request one from 1-800-537-3160, or download it from the Web at *www.gre.org*.)

For each section of the GRE, the difficulty level of the questions is tailored to your abilities. You have a *bespoke* (custom-tailored) exam. Each section of the exam begins with a question of average difficulty (500 level). If you answer this question correctly, the computer elevates you to the 580 level or so and gives you a question more difficult than the first. If you answer this second question correctly, the computer will place you at about 640, and you will get a question commensurate with that ability level. As long as you keep answering questions correctly, your score goes up, and you get more difficult questions. Later questions do not cause as dramatic a jump in your score as the first few questions cause. When you miss a question, your score goes down, and you get an easier question. Eventually, you get to a level at which you are answering about half of the questions correctly. At that point, the computer only adjusts your score by about ten points at a time. (Test-takers scoring at or near 800 may never get to the point at which they are missing half the questions; those poor souls scoring at or near 200 may never achieve a level at which half of their answers are correct.)

Looking at the Breakdown
(To Avoid Having One!)

The GRE consists of four scored sections: one 30-minute verbal subtest, one 45-minute quantitative (math) subtest, one 45-minute essay, and one 30-minute essay. Typically, you get 30 verbal questions, 28 quantitative questions, and two essay topics with the number of each question type (such as Analogies and Quantitative Comparisons) proportional to what appeared on the old pencil-and-paper version of the test.

Table 1-1 provides a quick overview of what the GRE is all about, how many questions it torments and delights you with, and how much time you get to complete each section. The sections of the test may be arranged in any order. (For the scoop on the unscored sections of the test, flip to "When Your Answers Don't Count: The Unscored Sections," later in this chapter.)

Table 1-1	GRE Breakdown by Section	
Section	**Number of Questions**	**Time Allotted**
Verbal	30	30 minutes
Math	28	45 minutes
Analytical Writing	2	75 minutes
*Unidentified unscored	28 to 35	30 to 60 minutes
*Identified unscored	Test-maker's surprise	

*Not always given, but be prepared for the worst.

Table 1-2 shows another way to look at the GRE: by the approximate number of each type of question.

Table 1-2	GRE Breakdown by Question Style (Not Including the Unscored Section)
Type of Question	**Number of Questions**
Antonyms	9
Analogies	7
Sentence Completions	6
Reading Comprehension	8
Quantitative Comparisons	14
Problem Solving (Data Interpretation)	14
Perspective on an Issue	1 topic
Analysis of an Argument	1 topic

These different question types are mixed throughout the section in which they belong. For example, you may get two analogies, two sentence completions, and two antonyms to start off your verbal section. Next, you may see some reading comprehension questions, then more analogies, and so on. The math section could feature three quantitative comparisons, two problem-solving questions, two data interpretation questions, four more quantitative comparisons, and so on.

Be sure to use your time wisely. Because you cannot go back and change your answers, you must be as accurate as possible on each section's first five questions (average difficulty) to ensure that you get harder questions for the rest of the exam! Sound bizarre? Strange, but true. You *want* harder questions because the level of difficulty you reach determines your score. If you slip up and miss one early question, you can still reel off a series of correct answers, show that your mistake was a fluke, and get to the harder questions. However, if you miss a handful of early questions, the computer determines that these questions are too difficult for you and gives you easy questions. You may answer all these easy questions correctly, but your test will be over by the time the computer raises the difficulty level to the high-score range.

On the GRE, the first five questions of the verbal section and the first five questions of the math section are the most important. You get a much higher score if you answer the first five questions correctly and miss all the rest than if you miss the first five questions and answer all the others correctly.

Everyone Wants to Score

You don't have the Ferrari yet. (If you do, and you are a single, eligible male, please write to me care of the publisher. . . .) You don't have the six-digit paycheck yet. (If you do, please see the previous parenthetical comment.) It's rough being 21 (or 25 or 30). You need something to boast about. How about your GRE scores? GRE scores are to would-be graduate students what salaries are to people in the Real World. Students brag about them, exaggerate them, and try to impress others with them.

When you finish the test, you have the option of seeing your score or canceling it. You cannot, however, decide to cancel your score after you see it, so think carefully about how well you feel you've done. Finding out your score at the end of the testing session is one of the things students like about the computerized testing. Instead of waiting two to four weeks to get scores in the mail, you can get your good news immediately! Schools still have to wait a little while, generally receiving the scores within 15 days.

Figuring out your score

With the GRE, you get three separate scores: verbal, math, and analytical writing. Although you can get unofficial verbal and math scores immediately after you've taken the test, you have to wait to get your analytical writing score in the mail.

- **Verbal score:** The verbal score (called verbal ability) ranges from 200 to 800. You get 200 points for showing up at the technology center and staring at the computer.

- **Math score:** The math score also ranges from 200 to 800.

- **Analytical writing score:** The analytical score ranges from 0 to 6. Two graders each assign you up to 6 points; the two scores are averaged.

Different schools have different ways of using the analytical writing scores from the exam. Previously, the analytical writing section was an entirely separate test and not part of the General GRE. Not every school required that you take that test. But as of October 1, 2002, analytical writing is included in the General Test. (Check out the chapters in Part V to find out how to improve your writing score.) Schools are still deciding how much weight to give your essays and how to use the score. Contact each school directly to find out its individual policy.

Knowing how your score measures up

On a recent GRE, the averages (that is, half the students taking the exam were above these scores, half were below these scores) were as follows: verbal 480 and math 570. The analytical writing section was not previously part of the General GRE. Averages change according to which GRE you take. For example, the average of students taking the exam in April may be slightly different from the average of students taking the exam in June. Your individual goals should depend on which grad schools you are applying to and what GPA (grade-point average) you have. There is no such thing as a passing or failing score — only what you need to get accepted to the program that you have your heart set on.

Playing the guessing game

You may have no choice but to guess. The computer doesn't budge until you choose an answer. Unlike paper-and-pencil tests, on which you can move around and choose questions more to your liking, the computer requires you to mark an answer before you go on to the next question. So, if you are completely stuck, don't waste time agonizing. Guess quickly and move on. Which oval should you fill in? Any. There is no truth to the *scurrilous* (obscenely abusive) rumors that the correct answers on the exam more often correspond to any particular oval. (Remember that on the computer screen, the ovals are not marked A, B, C, D, and E; they are left blank.) Every answer has the same probability. It doesn't matter which oval you choose.

Be sure to answer all the questions. You are penalized more for an unanswered question than for a wrong answer, so make sure that you get to the end, even if it means guessing wildly in the last minute or so.

Discovering the number of correct answers you need for specific scores

Here are rough estimates of how many questions you must answer correctly to get certain scores on each section. Keep in mind that these numbers change from exam to exam.

Verbal scores

To get a 400, you need 14 out of 30 questions correct (about 47 percent).
To get a 500, you need 18 out of 30 questions correct (about 60 percent).
To get a 600, you need 22 out of 30 questions correct (about 73 percent).
To get a 700, you need 25 out of 30 questions correct (about 84 percent).

Math scores

To get a 400, you need 11 out of 28 questions correct (about 38 percent).
To get a 500, you need 15 out of 28 questions correct (about 51 percent).
To get a 600, you need 19 out of 28 questions correct (about 66 percent).
To get a 700, you need 23 out of 28 questions correct (about 81 percent).

Analytical Writing scores

There is no particular "number correct" in this section because you have two essays to write. Please see Chapter 18 for more information on how the essays are scored.

When Your Answers Don't Count: The Unscored Sections

So what's the story with these "unscored" sections? (Some people refer to them as _experimental_ or _equating_ sections.) Why does the GRE often feature sections that don't count? One of the two unscored sections is not identified as such — the test-makers are using you as a guinea pig, trying out new questions on you, double-checking that all questions on the GRE are fair. You are an unwilling — and unwitting — participant. You're obviously unwilling — who would want to prolong this agony? You're unwitting, because you don't know which section is experimental. (The test-makers wouldn't find out too much about their new questions if you could sit back and refuse to do your best, knowing that your unwillingness will not hurt your score.)

The experimental, or uncounted, section can be verbal or math, and you will have absolutely no idea which section is uncounted. Well, you may have _some_ idea: If the test has two verbal sections, you can deduce that one of them is an experimental section — but which one? Don't try to outsmart the test-makers. The GRE has rooms full of men and women whose only task in life is to create these mind-warping questions. You, as a normal person, don't stand a chance of outsmarting them; why even try? Just do your best on every section.

If you want to give your brain a break, you may be able to do so on an "identified experimental section." The GRE sometimes tells you about an experimental section, which you do not need to take, at the end of the test. If you feel like playing with the computer and helping out ETS (Educational Testing Service), you can go ahead and answer the questions, but you have no obligation to do so.

Add it all up, and you realize that the part of the test that determines your future takes two and a half hours. (That's right. Two hours and thirty minutes of this test may be roughly as important as four years of college.) You may spend up to three and a half hours or so dealing with test material, depending on how many experimental sections you get. Keep in mind, though, that you will probably be at the testing center for approximately four and a half hours. You get some breaks (discussed in the next section), and you'll have to go through some procedures (such as getting comfortable with the computer via a tutorial, receiving scratch paper, and finding out your score) before and after the test. In other words, kiss an entire morning or afternoon goodbye.

Gimme a Break! The GRE Intermissions

You have the option of taking a ten-minute break between the second and third sections of the GRE. Depending on whether your bladder is the size of Rhode Island or Texas, you may or may not spend most of your break in the bathroom. Do yourself a favor: Don't drink or eat too much during the break. There's nothing worse than sitting there crossing and uncrossing your legs during the test as your eyeballs slowly turn yellow.

Between other sections of the test, you get a one-minute break — just enough time to stand up and stretch a bit. You don't have time to leave your seat and come back before the test resumes. If you absolutely, positively have to go to the restroom and leave the computer during the test, the clock keeps ticking.

You may want to take some munchies to eat and water to drink at the big break, but make sure that the snacks are light and nutritious. Sugar makes you high for a few minutes and then brings you way down. You don't need to crash right in the middle of a quadratic equation ("Doughnut Disaster: Film at 11:00 . . ."). Take a handful of peanuts, some trail mix, or anything light that won't send all the blood from your brain down to your stomach for digestion. Life is hard enough without trying to figure out how to find the interior angles of a nonagon using your stomach instead of your brain.

I wish it were all Greek to me: A welcome to international students

Students from all over the world take the GRE to attend American graduate schools. I've taught GRE prep courses to students from Brazil, Taiwan, the Ivory Coast, Egypt, Japan — all over the globe. When I got my own graduate degree, my courses were enriched by the contributions of students from Korea, Hong Kong, Saudi Arabia, the Netherlands, China, and Mexico. To all of you readers from other nations, welcome!

As international students, you have strengths and weaknesses that are different from those of American students; therefore, the focus of your study should be different as well. Here are my suggestions to help you to get the most out of this book and to help you do your best on the actual GRE:

1. Concentrate on the questions that test vocabulary in the Antonyms and the Analogies portions. You probably have an advantage over American students on these questions, believe it or not — especially if your native tongue is a Romance language such as Spanish or French. Romance languages are Latin-based and commonly use words that are uncommon in English. Take, for example, *bibliophile*. A Spanish speaker knows *biblio* means book (*bibliotéca* means library) and can figure out this "hard" word pretty easily. (A bibliophile is a book-lover.)

   One more thing: Because you've studied English, you're used to memorizing vocabulary (unlike American students who haven't taken vocabulary tests since junior high school). Although you probably can't dramatically change your basic reading comprehension level in a few hours, you *can* dramatically add to your vocabulary. You, more than American students, need to keep and learn the vocabulary lists suggested throughout this book.

2. Forget about the Reading Comprehension portion. The reading passages in the GRE are long, hard, and booooring. They are difficult enough to understand for people who grew up speaking and reading English and are totally demoralizing for people who didn't. My suggestion is that you not take reading comprehension too seriously. Take your time on the first passage, reading it slowly and carefully. Then scroll through the passage thoroughly to answer the questions. It's probably a good idea to make quick guesses when you get to the other passages.

3. Concentrate on the math, especially geometry. Although you do get separate verbal and math scores, some colleges concentrate on your overall or combined score. Doing extremely well on math can compensate for weaker verbal skills. I suggest that you pay particular attention to the geometry problems. They are rarely "word problems" — questions that require a lot of reading. Geometry problems usually feature figures that you can easily understand and use to answer the questions — even if English is not your strong suit.

4. Go, Go, Go! I've said it before and I'll say it again: The GRE penalizes you more for unanswered questions than for wrong answers. Be sure to fill in an answer for every question, even if you have to guess wildly. You must finish the exam.

Chapter 2

Knowledge Is Power: Getting the Advantage

Question: What do standardized tests really test?

Answer: They test how well you take standardized tests!

The GRE is not an IQ test; it's not a measure of your worth as a human being; and it's not a predictor of whether you'll be so successful that you'll make Bill Gates look like a pauper. The GRE tests how well you take a test because test-taking skills determine how well you'll do in grad school. (A logical premise when you think about it, isn't it?) In this chapter, I provide you with some of the general strategies that can help you on the exam as a whole. I wonder whether Bill Gates ever knew these strategies?

Beating the Clock: Tips on Timing

The computer provides you with a stopwatch — an on-screen clock — to time each section. (One of my students told me that with that image of the clock ticking away, she kept looking for Mike Wallace and Morley Safer!) You have the option of removing the clock from the screen. If that ticker makes you nervous, by all means, get it out of sight (the computer tutorial at the beginning of the session tells you how to do so).

Professionally, I definitely recommend that you hide the clock when you begin each section. Why? You should do whatever it takes to get the first five questions right (I talk about the importance of those first five questions in Chapter 1). Bring the clock back when you finish the first several questions, or at least check the clock every fifteen minutes or so. Because the early questions count more than later ones, if you've answered fewer than half the questions when half of your time has expired, you're still doing okay. *Note:* The clock comes on and stays on during the last five minutes; you can't banish it from that point on. This clock serves to remind you that you may have to sprint to the finish soon.

Answer ALL the questions, even if you have to make wild guesses to do so. When it comes to scoring your test, you're not penalized for wrong answers. In fact, blank answers (as in not finishing the entire test) hurt your score more than wrong answers.

Scratching like a Crazed Chicken

You are not allowed to bring in a grease pencil and do scratch work on the computer screen! (Don't laugh! I've had more than one student ask me about doing so!) The test proctor will give you blank scratch paper (you cannot bring in your own) before the test begins. Test-takers usually know that they should use this paper for such traditional scratch work as mathematical calculations, but you can use this paper in another key way: Use the general instruction time (before the exam officially starts, a few minutes during which you can go through a computer tutorial) to write down any key strategies and formulas that will help you get through the exam. You may not bring such memory aids into the testing center, but you may certainly write them down just before you start tackling the questions.

Packing Your Bags on Test Day

Take your brain down from the shelf, dust it off, and take it to the exam with you. In addition, take along a few more items:

- **Authorization voucher from ETS:** You can request that a voucher be mailed to you when you register for the test. Some testing sites may send you notices in the mail; others may simply give you a confirmation number, which you must mention when you show up for the exam. Have the information with you.

- **Map or directions:** Be sure that you know in advance how to get to the testing site. Drive there a few days prior to your test and check out how long the drive takes you, where to park, and so on. One of my students had to take the test at a center in the middle of a downtown area. On the day of the test, she couldn't find any parking and was totally stressed out before she even got to the testing site. The last thing you need the day of the test is something more to worry about.

- **Photo ID:** You must have identification with three key elements:

  - A recognizable photo (something that shows you as the haggard, sleep-deprived person you are after studying for this test, not as the perky, cheerful person you vaguely remember having been a month or so ago).

  - The name you registered under (if your driver's license lists you as Steven Boyd Brown, don't sign up under your nickname of "Boatman" or "Bubbles" or whatever your friends call you).

  - Your signature.

  Usually, a driver's license, passport, employee ID, or military ID is acceptable. A student ID alone is usually not enough, although it is acceptable as a second form of ID in case there is some confusion with the first form. Note that a social security card or a credit card is not acceptable identification.

- **Clothes:** You signed up for the special Nude GRE, you say? Well, everyone else should remember to take a few extra layers. Testing centers may be boiling hot or freezing cold. It's the pits to sit there for hours either shivering with hands so cold they can't hit the computer keys or sweating all over your keyboard from the heat. Dress in layers and be prepared for anything.

You Can't Take It with You

Besides your dreams, hopes, goals, and aspirations, leave these other things at the door of the GRE testing room:

- **Books and notes:** Forget about last-minute studying. You aren't allowed to take books or notes into the testing room. If you don't know the material by that time, you never will. (One student asked me whether he could take in a dictionary. You gotta give the guy credit for hope, but somehow I think he missed the point of the verbal questions.)

- **Scratch paper:** You are not allowed to bring in your own scratch paper (with handy notes prepared ahead of time). The proctor will give you scratch paper when you arrive at the testing center. (If you run low, request some more from the proctor during the one-minute breaks between sections.) You'll have plenty of room to do calculations and scribbling. (I understand, however, that ETS owns the copyright to all last will and testaments written during the exam.)

- **Calculator:** You are not allowed to use a calculator during the exam. Those of you who grew up before calculators were common and learned your times tables have a definite advantage here over those young whippersnappers who can't add 2 + 2 without dragging out the calculator. Don't think that because your watch has a calculator, you can bend this rule — NO mechanical or digital calculating devices are allowed.

- **Test aids:** You may not bring in a radio, cassette, or CD player with headphones, a cell phone, or a personal computer (like a laptop or a hand-held device). In other words, leave the electronics at home. The most you can bring is that good, old-fashioned, #2 pencil.

Isn't that special? Unique circumstances

Dare to be different. If you have a special circumstance, those GRE testers are usually willing to accommodate you. For example, if you have a learning disability (no, that doesn't include being bored and frustrated), you may be able to get additional testing time. Following is a brief list of special circumstances and what to do about them.

- **Learning disabilities:** These circumstances can range from attention deficit disorder to dyslexia and all sorts of other things. To find out whether you qualify for a disabilities waiver of any sort, contact the Office of Disability Policy of the Educational Testing Service Corporate Headquarters, Educational Testing Service, Rosedale Road, Princeton, NJ 08541; phone 609-921-9000; fax 609-734-5410; Internet: www.ets.org; e-mail: etsinfo@ets.org.

- **Physical disabilities:** Pay attention: I'm about to say something nice about ETS here, a once-in-a-googol-plex occurrence for me. ETS tries very hard to accommodate everyone. Those folks who need special arrangements can get Braille or large-print exams, can have test readers or recorders, can work with interpreters, and so on. You can get the information about what the ETS considers to be disabilities and how the disabilities can change the way you take the GRE in the GRE Information and Registration Bulletin.

- **Financial difficulties:** Until you ace the GRE, get into a top-notch graduate school, and come out with a smokin' brain ready to make your first million before your 30th (40th? 50th?) birthday, you may have a rough time paying the GRE fees. Fee waivers are available. Note that this waiver applies only to the actual GRE fee, not to miscellaneous fees such as fees for the test disclosure service, hand-grading service, and so on. Your college counselor can help you obtain and fill out the appropriate request forms. (If you're not currently in college, a counselor or financial-aid specialist at the closest college or university may still be glad to help you. Just call for an appointment.) The GRE is inflicted upon rich and poor alike.

Déjà Vu All Over Again: Repeating the Test

Should you repeat the test? Before you make that decision, ask yourself the following questions:

✔ **Am I repeating the test to get a certain minimum qualifying score or just to satisfy my ego?** If you have your heart set on a particular graduate school that requires a minimum GRE score, you may want to take the test again and again and again until you get that score. If you're taking the test only because your ego was demolished when you didn't score as well as your friends, you should probably think twice before putting yourself through all that trauma again.

✔ **Am I willing to study twice as hard, or am I already burned out?** If you put your heart and soul into studying for the exam the first time, you may be too pooped to pop (*enervated,* as we didactic dames like to say) for the second exam. Scores don't magically go up on their own; you have to put in a lot of effort.

✔ **What types of mistakes did I make on the first test?** If you made mistakes because of a lack of familiarity with either the test format (you didn't understand what to do when faced with a Quantitative Comparison question) or substance (you didn't know the vocabulary words or were baffled by the geometry problems), you're a good candidate for repeating the test. If you know what you did wrong, you can fix it and improve your score.

However, if your mistakes were due to carelessness or a lack of concentration, you are very likely to make those same types of mistakes again. If you truly, honestly, sincerely, and without *dissembling* (lying) feel that you can sit in the test room and stay focused this time and not make the same stupid mistakes, go for it. But chances are, if you're the type of test-taker who either always makes a lot of careless mistakes or rarely makes them, you're not going to change your whole test-taking style overnight.

✔ **Were there extenuating circumstances beyond my control?** Maybe your nerves were acting up on the first exam, you were feeling ill, or you didn't get enough sleep the night before. In that case, by all means, repeat the exam. You're bound to feel better the next time.

✔ **Did I not finish?** If you did not reach a lot of questions, take the test again. (You may take the test only once during each calendar month, but a smart test-taker can schedule her testing so that she takes the exam on, say, October 31 and then again on November 1.) This time, fill in something for every question. Remember that you lose more points for not reaching a question than you do for answering the question incorrectly.

Can repeating the exam hurt you? Not really. Most schools look only at your highest score. Find out from the individual schools you're interested in whether this is their policy; it isn't the case for every school. If you are on the borderline, or if several students are vying for one spot, sometimes having taken the exam repeatedly can hurt you (especially if your most recent score took a nosedive). On the other hand, an admissions counselor who sees several exams with ascending scores may be impressed that you stuck to it and kept trying, even if your score went up only a little bit. In general, if you're willing to take the time to study and take the repeat seriously, go for it.

GRE score reporting is cumulative; that is, all the scores you obtain for five years are sent to the schools you designate. You cannot, I repeat, CANNOT send scores from only one exam date. For example, if you do great in October, take the exam again in April, and blow it big time, you cannot tell ETS to ignore the April *debacle* (a sudden collapse, a rout) and send just the October scores. All scores are part of your permanent record.

Experience Counts: Using Older Scores

What if you took the GRE years and years ago when you thought you were going to go to grad school and then elected to take a job or start a family instead? Between October 1, 1974, and September 30, 1985, ETS promised students that scores would be valid for 20 years. Never one to go back on its word, ETS (noted for its *veracity,* or truthfulness) agrees to send those scores out if you so desire . . . but will do so with a note to the schools to be extra careful in looking at such old scores. But the good news is, if you liked your scores from as long ago as two decades, you may be able to get away with sending those and not taking the exam again at all. If that's so and you're waving me goodbye at this point, adios and good luck to you. For the rest of you who can't escape my company so quickly, read on.

Chapter 3

Starting with the Easy Stuff: Analogies

In This Chapter

▶ Understanding the format of an analogy

▶ Building your vocabulary with prefixes and suffixes

▶ Answering an analogy question with the correct two-step approach

▶ Recognizing the nasty and vile traps built into analogies

▶ Identifying and avoiding stupid (trap) answers

ANSWER: The shiny red bike you got for your tenth birthday. Your first kiss from someone who wasn't related to you. Analogies.

QUESTION: Name three of the best gifts you've ever received.

Analogies are a gift. Manna from heaven. Freebies. For most students, analogies are the place to rack up the points big time. The number of analogies on the computer-based GRE can vary, but you almost certainly have at least seven.

The great thing about analogies is that they are doable. Some of the Reading Comprehension passages are ridiculously hard. Some of the Sentence Completion questions are so long you may be tempted to take a snooze in the middle of them. But analogies are great. You read 12 words, apply a few tricks, and you're outta there.

If Only All Relationships Were This Easy: The Format

Some people look at analogies and wonder, "Where's the question?" Even though analogies can be quite simple (with practice), the format is bizarre. Here's an example of what you see. (*Note:* When you take the test, the answer format will be a bit different. The answer choices are accompanied by ovals without letters in place of A, B, C, D, E.)

PIG : STY ::

(A) teenager : rubble

(B) roommate : bathroom

(C) bird : nest

(D) swine : house

(E) barnacle : barn

You see two words in uppercase letters. The five answer choices each consist of two words in lowercase letters. Not a lot of reading here. When you get good at analogies, you can zoom through them faster than you can finish a pint of ice cream.

Your job is to identify the *relationship* between the question words and then choose a pair of answer words that expresses the *same* relationship.

Approaching Perfection

When you see an Analogy question, you should take this very straightforward, two-step approach:

1. **Use both words in a *descriptive* sentence.**

   Make a sentence using the words. Avoid something vague and useless such as "has." For example, do *not* say, "A pig *has* a sty." That sentence tells you nothing — you have no idea what the relationship between a pig and a sty is. Pretend that a Bulgarian exchange student comes up to you and says, "Excuse me, please. What is the connection between a pig and a sty?" If you answer that a pig *has* a sty, the Bulgarian may go away thinking that a sty is a curly tail, a snout, or a big stink. But if you say, "A pig *lives in* a sty," your Bulgarian buddy now understands the relationship. A good sentence paints a mental picture: You can actually see the scene in your mind.

2. **Apply the *exact* same sentence to each answer choice.**

   Go through each of the answer choices using your sentence.

   (A) *A teenager lives in rubble.*

   Maybe you flash back to your teenage years and recall having to wade through the *detritus* (trash, rubble) of your bedroom to get to the door, but this is the GRE. The test-makers assume that all of you were sweet little kids who obeyed your parents, respected traffic signals, and didn't ever use the middle finger of your hand for pointing or otherwise gesticulating. By the way, *rubble* is the ruined remains of a building, such as knocked-down bricks and junk. If you forget this word, think of Barney Rubble from the Flintstones. He's short, like a knocked-down pile.

   (B) *A roommate lives in the bathroom.*

   It may seem like it sometimes, but it ain't so. Any answer that is funny, witty, or charming is almost certainly the wrong answer. (The GRE has nooooooo sense of humor; count on it.) If you think that an answer is funny — or desperately *trying* to be funny — you can be sure that it's wrong.

   (C) *A bird lives in a nest.*

   Sounds pretty good, but you have to go through all the answer choices, just in case. Just like not marrying the first person you kiss, don't immediately choose the first answer that looks good. Something may come along later that makes you happier.

   (D) *A swine lives in a house.*

   If you choose this answer, remind me not to come to your home! The trap here is that a pig (from the question) and a swine are much the same. Be careful: Just because words are connected in *meaning* does not mean that the answer is right. The *relationship* between the words is being tested. For example, the question may be about perfume, and the correct answer may involve sweat socks. No connection.

   (E) *A barnacle lives in a barn.*

   If you don't know what a barnacle is, you may be tempted to choose E, but C is the right answer. A *barnacle* is a creature that lives in the water (not in a barn) and often attaches itself to the bottoms of ships. You scrape the barnacles off the ship periodically to clean the ship's hull. *Correct Answer:* C.

Just Because You're Paranoid Doesn't Mean They're Not Out to Get You: Traps, Tricks, and Tips

Face it — this is why you really bought this book. You want to know about those little traps built into the questions sitting there waiting to pounce on unsuspecting victims. What time bombs, ready to go off in your face, have the test makers created? Here are a few, with suggestions for how to deal with them.

Turn a verb into an infinitive

No, an infinitive is not the latest Japanese import car. An *infinitive* is the "to" form of any verb: to drink, to burp, to party. When an analogy features a verb, turn it into an infinitive and the sentence practically writes itself.

GIGGLE : LAUGH ::

To giggle is *to laugh* a little bit.

YELL : TALK ::

To yell is *to talk* loudly.

RUN : WALK ::

To run is *to walk* rapidly.

Notice that I'm adding another word on the end. Usually this word is an adverb to answer the "How?" question. How do you laugh when you giggle? A little bit. How do you talk when you yell? Loudly. How do you walk when you run? Rapidly. Saying "To giggle is to laugh" is not enough. You want to fine-tune the sentence; tweak it a little bit to clarify the relationship between the words. That Bulgarian exchange student is counting on you.

Identify the part of speech of the question word

Sometimes your sentence is easier to write if you know which part of speech — noun, verb, or adjective — a difficult word is. You find out by looking at the word's counterparts in the answer choices. That is, if you want to know which part of speech the first word in the question is, look at the first words in the answers. If you want to know which part of speech the second word in the question is, look at the second words in the answer choices.

DASHIKI : TAILOR ::

(A) shovel : professor

(B) table : singer

(C) garment : jock

(D) cake : baker

(E) book : poseur

Don't know what the word *dashiki* means? You're not alone; it's a pretty hard word. Not to worry. You know by looking at the first words in the answer choices — shovel, table, garment, cake, and book — that *dashiki* must be a noun and is a thing. (Remember that nouns are persons, places, or things.) Your very simple sentence should be: "A dashiki is a thing of a tailor." That's all you can do for now. Go through each answer choice.

(A) shovel : professor — Although it can get deep in the classroom sometimes, a shovel is not standard equipment for a professor.

(B) table : singer — A singer may stretch herself out on a table during a Las Vegas lounge act while doing a sexy, sultry number, but a table is not normally associated with a singer.

(C) garment : jock — This is a trap answer. You may be tempted to choose it because a tailor (from the question) deals with garments. However, you've already learned that the meanings of the question words are not necessarily related to the answer; the *relationship* between the pairs of words is important. Had the question said GARMENT : SEAMSTRESS or even GARMENT : MODEL, it would have been a good choice. But a garment is not necessarily a thing of a jock.

(D) cake : baker — A cake is a thing of a baker. Yeah, this answer sounds pretty good. There is a logical connection. Try the next one to be sure, but D is probably right.

(E) book : poseur — This answer is put here to trap students who immediately assume that the hardest word in a question or any word they themselves don't know must be the correct answer. A *poseur* is someone with an attitude, a person who adopts an affected style. People who go around using words like poseur are often poseurs themselves.

The right answer is D. A *dashiki,* by the way, is a type of shirt, and a tailor creates a dashiki just as a baker creates a cake. You can get the question right without knowing what the word means. *Correct Answer:* D.

Look for the salient features of a word

The *salient* feature is what makes something stand out. The salient feature of a basketball player is his or her height. The salient feature of a genius is his or her intelligence.

MINNOW : FISH ::

(A) elephant : animal

(B) recluse : shy

(C) gnat : insect

(D) giraffe : quadruped

(E) votary : peremptory

The salient feature of a minnow is that it is a *small* fish. Although most of the answers are or may be synonyms (an elephant *is* an animal; a recluse *may be* shy), only C gives the salient or outstanding feature. A gnat is a *small* insect. Choice E features antonyms. A *votary* is a devoted follower (think of a votary as an elegant, grown-up groupie!). *Peremptory* means absolute, imperative, allowing no disagreement. The boss may be peremptory; the votary would more likely be *docile* (easily swayed; compliant). *Correct Answer:* C.

Back into it

QUESTION: Is it okay to make the sentence by using the words backward?

ANSWER: Sure, as long as you remember to use the answer choices backward as well. That is, don't say, "A tailor makes a dashiki," and then say, "A cake makes a baker."

Identify common relationships

Certain standard relationships are often found in the analogies. There are a *plethora* (a lot) of them; here are ten of the more useful ones.

1. **Opposites**
   BIG : LITTLE
   PULCHRITUDINOUS : UGLY

2. **Synonyms**
   HAPPY : GLAD
   PUSILLANIMOUS : COWARDLY

3. **Cause and effect**
   TICKLE : LAUGHTER
   OSSIFY : BONE

4. **Part to whole**
   TOES : FOOT
   TALON : EAGLE

5. **Position**
   FRAME : PICTURE (a frame goes around a picture)
   SHOULDER : ROAD (a shoulder is to the side of a road).

6. **Greater to lesser**
   OVERJOYED : HAPPY
   CATACLYSMIC : UNFORTUNATE

7. **Location**
   PIG : STY
   RABBIT : WARREN

8. **Purpose or function**
   PILOT : FLY
   PUGILIST : BOX

9. **Characteristic**
   BLEAT : SHEEP (a bleat is the sound a sheep makes)
   POD : WHALES (a pod is a group of whales)

10. **Member to group** *(or specific to general)*
    FORK : UTENSIL
    ISLANDS : ARCHIPELAGO (an archipelago is a group of islands)

Use roots, prefixes, and suffixes

My three favorite words. . . . Other women like "I love you," but I live for "roots, prefixes, suffixes." These three words can bump up your score significantly. If you know just a few basic roots, prefixes, and suffixes, you can write magnificent analogy sentences and avoid falling into traps.

Suppose that the question is

IMPECUNIOUS : MONEY ::

If you don't know *impecunious,* you may be tempted to make the words synonyms and simply say, "Impecunious *is* money." A tempting and logical answer may be reservoir : water, for example. Alas, once again you pay the price for giving in to temptation.

If you know that *-ous* means full of and *im-* means not, you can make a good sentence: "Impecunious is *not full of* money." That changes the whole picture. Now the right answer may be, for example, vacuum : air. A *vacuum* is *not full of* air. Note that a *reservoir* in fact *is* full of water — the opposite of your relationship sentence.

Although you can learn hundreds of prefixes and suffixes, I realize that you have a limited number of brain cells that you're willing to devote to this subject. Therefore, here is a list of ten commonly used prefixes and eight commonly used suffixes, with examples of each. Memorize them. Burn them into your brain. I get to some of the more common roots later on in Chapter 7. I don't want you to get overexcited by this stuff all at once.

Prefixes

1. **a- = not or without:** Someone *amoral* is without morals, like the sadist who designed this test. Someone *atypical* is not typical, like the students who wear pocket protectors and love to take tests. Someone *apathetic* is without feeling or uncaring, like most students by the time they finish the test and are leaving the exam room. ("The world is going to end tomorrow? Fine; that means I can get some sleep tonight.")

2. **an- = not or without:** An *anaerobic* environment is without oxygen (like the test room feels when a killer question leaves you gasping for air). *Anarchy* is without rule or government (like a classroom when a substitute teacher is in for the day).

3. **eu- = good:** A *eulogy* is a good speech, usually given for the dearly departed at a funeral. A *euphemism* is a good way of saying something or a polite expression, like saying that someone has passed away instead of calling her "worm meat."

4. **ben-/bon- = good:** A *benefit* is something that has a good result, an advantage. Someone *benevolent* is good and kind; when you have a date, a benevolent father lets you take his new car rather than your old junker. *Bon voyage* means have a good voyage; a *bon vivant* is a person who lives the good life.

5. **caco- = bad:** Something *cacophonous* is bad sounding, such as nails on a chalkboard.

6. **ne-/mal- = bad:** Something *negative* is bad, like a negative attitude. Someone *nefarious* is "full of bad," or wicked and evil, such as a nefarious wizard in a fantasy novel. Something *malicious* also is "full of bad," or wicked and harmful, such as a malicious rumor that you are really a 30-year-old undercover narc.

7. **im- = not:** Something *impossible* is not possible. Someone *immortal* is not going to die but will live forever. Someone *implacable* is not able to be calmed down; she's stubborn. Notice that *im-* can also mean inside (*immerse* means to put into), but that meaning is not as common on the GRE. First, think of *im-* as meaning not; if that doesn't seem appropriate, switch to Plan B and see whether the *im-* can mean inside in the context of the question.

8. **in- = not:** Something *inappropriate* is not appropriate, such as the language people may use in front of small children when studying for the GRE. Someone *inept* is not adept, not skillful. (Can you sue an inept surgeon who amputates the wrong leg? Nah, you wouldn't have a leg to stand on!) Someone *insolvent* has no money, is bankrupt, like most students after four years of college. *In-* can also mean inside (*innate* means something born inside of you) or beginning (the *initial* letters of your name are the beginning letters). However, the most common meaning of *in-* is *not.* Think of that one first; if it doesn't seem to work, try the others.

9. **ante- = before:** When the clock tells you that it's 5 a.m., the a.m. stands for *ante meridian,* which means before the middle, or the first half of the day. *Antebellum* means before the war. Tara in *Gone with the Wind* was an antebellum mansion, built before the Civil War. *Antediluvian* literally means before the flood, before Noah's deluge. Figuratively, it means very old; if you call your mother antediluvian, you mean that she's been around since before the flood. It's a great word to use as an insult because almost no one knows what it means and you can get away with it.

10. **post- = after:** When the clock tells you that it's 5 p.m., the p.m. stands for *post meridian.* It means after the middle, or the second half of the day. Something *postmortem* occurs after death. A postmortem exam is an autopsy.

Suffixes

1. **-ette = little:** A *cigarette* is a little cigar. A *dinette* table is a little dining table. A *coquette* is a little flirt (literally, a little chicken).

2. **-illo = little:** An *armadillo* is a little armored animal. A *peccadillo* is a little sin. (Do you speak Spanish? *Pecar* is to sin.)

Flash your friends: How to use flashcards

Go out and buy three packages of the largest index cards you can find: white and two other colors. Put all the roots, prefixes, and suffixes you learn that have negative connotations on cards of one color. For example, ne- means bad or not; put it on a brown card. Ben- means good; put it on a pink card. -ous means full of. It doesn't "feel" good or bad; it's neutral. Put it on a white card.

When you get to the exam, you may encounter the word nefarious. You know you've seen it before, but you can't for the life of you remember what it means. Then a little picture unfolds in front of your eyes: You see ne- on a brown card. Aha! If it's on a brown card, it must be something negative. Just knowing that much often helps you to get the right answer.

Say the analogy is NEFARIOUS : SAINT. Normally, you assume that the words are synonyms and say, "A saint is nefarious." However, remembering that ne- is on a brown card, which means that it is negative, makes you change the sentence to "A saint is *not* nefarious,"

because saints are generally considered pretty good. (I make no comments about the New Orleans Saints football team, strong though the temptation is.)

There is no right or wrong way to classify the roots. If you think that a root is positive, fine, it's positive. If you think that a root is negative, fine, it's negative. The whole purpose of flashcards is to help you associate the words. Go with whatever works for *you.*

Bonus! When you come across a word that incorporates the root, put that word on the card as an example. That way, you learn both the root and the vocabulary word: two for the price of one. If you're reading a newspaper article about a program that will have a *salubrious* effect on the economy, note that sal- means health (I cover that root later) and -ous means full of. You know immediately that the word means healthful. Put it on both the sal- card and the -ous card. You'll learn the vocabulary without realizing it.

3. **-ous = full of (very):** Someone *joyous* is full of joy. Someone *amorous* is full of *amour,* or love. Someone *pulchritudinous* is full of beauty, and therefore beautiful.

4. **-ist = a person:** A *typist* is a person who types. A *pugilist* is a person who fights (*pug-* means war or fight), a boxer. A *pacifist* is a person who believes in peace, a noncombatant (*pac-* means peace or calm).

5. **-ify (-efy) = to make:** To *beautify* is to make beautiful. To *ossify* is to make bone. (If you break your wrist, it takes weeks to ossify again, or for the bone to regenerate.) To *deify* is to make into a deity, a god.

6. **-ize = to make:** To *alphabetize* is to make alphabetical. To *immunize* is to make immune. To *ostracize* is to make separate from the group, or to shun.

7. **-ate = to make:** To *duplicate* is to make double. To *renovate* is to make new again (*nov-* means new). To *placate* is to make peaceful or calm (*plac-* means peace or calm).

8. **-ity = noun suffix that doesn't actually mean anything; it just turns a word into a noun:** *Jollity* is the noun form of jolly. *Serenity* is the noun form of serene. *Timidity* is the noun form of timid.

The Terminator: Eliminating Idiotic Answers

The first answer to eliminate is the backward one. Putting answers in reverse order is a common trap. If the question goes from greater to lesser (OVERJOYED : CONTENT), the answers almost certainly contain a trap that goes from lesser to greater (displeased : furious). Look for it.

Another good answer to eliminate is one that duplicates the *meaning* rather than the *relationship* between the words. The question may be PROFESSOR : EDUCATED. The words are synonyms. A good answer to eliminate is teacher : moronic. Even though a professor is a teacher and those words have the same meaning, the *relationship* between the trap answer words is antonymous, not synonymous.

Finally, forget about humor. Anything funny or trying to be funny is outta there. Correct answers are almost always dull and boring.

Déjà Vu Review

Before going on to the practice questions, review what you've discovered about analogy questions. Don't forget to use the simple two-step approach to answering an analogy question:

1. **Use both words in a *descriptive* sentence.**

2. **Use the exact same sentence on each answer choice.**

Even if you don't have a clue what the words in an analogy mean, you can often get the correct answer by using the following five tips. These tips help you to identify the relationship between the words well enough to make a reasonable guess.

- ✔ Turn a verb into an infinitive.
- ✔ Identify which part of speech — noun, verb, or adjective — the question words are.
- ✔ Use roots, prefixes, and suffixes.
- ✔ Look for the *salient features* of a word.
- ✔ Identify common relationships.

Ten words that Julia Roberts never hears

obese	rotund
corpulent	fleshy
flaccid	homely
drab	frowzy
unkempt	slovenly

Chapter 4

The Dirty Dozen: Analogy Practice Questions

● ●

Ready to practice what I've been preaching? Here are The Dirty Dozen Analogy practice questions to get you into the swing of things. This chapter is loaded with good vocabulary words. Don't forget to pay extra-careful attention to the words in this font: *vocabulary word.* Just consider this entire chapter stamped with a big ol' vocabulary icon!

1. PEANUT : SHELL ::

    (A) atom : proton

    (B) clock : dial

    (C) corn : husk

    (D) emollient : solid

    (E) enamel : tooth

Make a simple sentence defining the relationship between the words: "A peanut is surrounded by a shell." Corn is surrounded by a husk. *Correct Answer:* C.

Choice E is backward. The enamel is not surrounded by the tooth but vice versa. Keep your eyes open for a backward answer among the answer choices; those evil test makers frequently put one there to getcha.

2. HYMN : SONG ::

    (A) screech : whisper

    (B) waltz : dance

    (C) misnomer : correction

    (D) discussion : altercation

    (E) smile : reproof

A simple sentence is "A hymn is a type of song." A *waltz* is a type of dance. A *screech* is a loud noise, just the opposite of a whisper. Your tires screech when you take the corner wide in your rush to get to the GRE, having overslept that morning. (I know — I shouldn't even joke about such a thing!) In choice C, a *misnomer* is the wrong name — calling someone Tracy instead of Stacy, for example. It therefore is not a correction but a mistake. An *altercation* is a disagreement. Although it may be a discussion, the answer is not as close to being synonymous as choice B. In choice E, a *reproof* is a condemnation, a criticism. *Correct Answer:* B.

3. CHUCKLE : MERRIMENT ::

   (A) goose bumps : denial

   (B) blush : glee

   (C) scowl : perfidy

   (D) wince : discomfort

   (E) shout : fury

Make your sentence: "A chuckle indicates merriment" or "A chuckle is the result of merriment." *Merriment* is just what it looks like, happiness. The suffix *-ment* doesn't mean anything; it just turns a word into a noun such as in the case of content and contentment or argue and argument. A *wince* (an involuntary shrinking back or flinching) indicates discomfort. You wince when your Dearly Beloved says to you, "We *have* to talk." In choice A, *goose bumps* indicate cold or fright, not denial. Choice B could trap a careless reader who thinks that this answer fits because *glee* means happiness or merriment. In choice C, *perfidy* means disloyalty. Choice E is a "mebbe so, mebbe not" answer. A shout may indicate fury (you shout at the ATM when it gobbles up and shreds your bankcard), but the connection is not absolute. Always look for the *salient* or outstanding feature of the word. *Correct Answer:* D.

Choose an answer based on the *relationship* between the words, not on the meanings of the words. The question can be about houses and the answer about cantaloupes; the meanings of the words don't have to have any connection whatsoever.

4. COW : TERRIFY ::

   (A) praise : denounce

   (B) interest : fascinate

   (C) invigorate : exhaust

   (D) soothe : agitate

   (E) diminish : lessen

Okay, suppose that you have no idea what the word *cow* as a verb means. You can still get this question right by the process of elimination. The relationships between the answers in choices A, C, and D are all that of antonyms. Because they can't all be correct, they must all be wrong. You now know that *cow* and *terrify* are not antonyms. As quickly as that, you've narrowed the answers down to two, but can you narrow the answers down even further? The relationship between the words in choice B is lesser to greater; that is, interesting someone is less intense than fascinating that person. Because *terrify,* in the question, is such a strong word, it's unlikely that the first word, *cow,* is something even stronger. Just so you know, *to cow* means to intimidate, to browbeat. *Correct Answer:* B.

Words have more than one meaning. A test question may key into this fact. If your first response seems to make no sense in the context of the question ("Why would a cow terrify anyone?"), think of alternate meanings of the word or words.

5. XENOPHOBIC : STRANGERS ::

   (A) claustrophobic : Christmas

   (B) hydrophobic : fires

   (C) agoraphobic : open spaces

   (D) pyromaniac : animals

   (E) romantic : love

You may not know the word xenophobic, but you can deduce that *phobic* means fearful of because you know such relatively easy words as *hydrophobia* (fear of water) and *claustrophobia* (fear of closed spaces). Therefore, make the sentence: "Xenophobic is fearful of strangers." *Agoraphobic* means fearful of open spaces. An agoraphobe is often afraid to leave the house at all. When it's your turn to shovel the snow off the front walk, you may suddenly turn into an agoraphobe.

Choice A is a lame attempt at humor (and won't be found on the actual GRE, which contains no humor at all, lame or otherwise). Claustrophobic does not mean fearing Santa Claus and Christmas. Hydrophobic means fearing water, not fires. Someone who is a *pyromaniac* has a love of fire. Someone romantic has a love of love, not a fear of love. *Correct Answer:* C.

6. ELEGIAC : JOY ::

   (A) innocuous : harmful

   (B) phlegmatic : peace

   (C) implacable : tranquility

   (D) dynamic : energy

   (E) disparaging : insults

Something elegiac is not full of joy. An *elegy* is a sad or mournful poem. Something *innocuous* is not full of harm. (Figure this out using the roots: *In-* usually means not; *noc* means harm; *-ous* means full of: not full of harm.)

 Often, if you don't know a word, you make the "is" sentence: Elegiac is joy. But, in this case, I made the question an opposite to make you miss it and, therefore, help you to remember the word *elegiac* (sad or mournful). But you can still get this question correct because choice D, *dynamic,* does mean full of energy, and choice E, *disparaging,* does mean full of insults. Because two answers can't both be correct, they must both be wrong. Figuring that out should send you back to the drawing board to change your line of thinking from an "is" to an "is not" sentence.

Choice B, *phlegmatic,* means calm, composed. Now that you know this word, you can remain phlegmatic when you encounter it on the GRE and not panic. Choice C, *implacable,* means unchangeable, stubborn. An implacable toddler yells "NO!" no matter what the harassed parents suggest. (Do you see the roots? *im-* means not; *plac* means peace or calm; *-able* is able to be. Someone implacable is "unable to be calmed down," or just plain stubborn.) *Correct Answer:* A.

7. PECCADILLO : TRANSGRESSION ::

   (A) felony : crime

   (B) nibble : bite

   (C) alias : name

   (D) cacophony : noise

   (E) eructation : volcano

You know the suffix *-illo* means small or little. Make the sentence: "A peccadillo is a small transgression." You don't even have to know what the words mean to get a good sentence. (A *peccadillo* is a small wrong or fault. A *transgression* is a trespass or sin, a wrong.) A *nibble* is a small bite. In choice C, an *alias* is a different name, not a small name. In D, *cacophony* is a bad or harsh sound, such as my singing voice or the sounds of an orchestra warming up. The roots help you to define this word; *caco* means bad, *phon* means sound: bad sound. Choice E is my gift to you, a little comic relief. An *eructation* is a belch. Although a volcano may eructate, an eructation itself is not a volcano. *Correct Answer:* B.

8. PROGNOSTICATION : SOOTHSAYER ::

    (A) tumult : arbitrator

    (B) duplicity : idiot

    (C) fanaticism : zealot

    (D) adulation : adult

    (E) retrospection : prophet

Whoa! Suddenly these words have gotten terribly hard. Try saying: "Prognostication *is* sooth-sayer." Therefore, you are looking for two answer words that are synonyms or at least mean *nearly* the same thing.

Fanaticism is the state of being a fanatic (did you know that the word *fan,* like a rock star's groupie, comes from the word *fanatic?*), being really into something. *Zealous* also means very into something, enthusiastic, or involved. The words are synonyms. A zealot is one who is zealous.

You may have known the words for choice C but not for the other answers. Here's a quick review. You may be familiar with tumult in another form, *tumultuous,* which means wild, chaotic, or disorganized. An *arbitrator* is a mediator, a go-between in a fight or controversy. An arbitrator's job would be to stop the tumult, to calm things down and bring about a rational discussion. The words are closer to antonyms than synonyms.

By the way, a favorite ETS trick is to give you a common word in an uncommon form, just to confuse you and make your life miserable. For example, do you know this word?

    RUTH

Seeing it all by itself like that, you may swear that you'd never seen the word before. But you probably know it in another form:

    RUTHLESS

Ah, you know that *ruthless* means cruel, without pity or compassion. Work backwards. If ruth-less means *without* pity, ruth must mean *with* pity. *Ruth* is pity or compassion, kindness, and mercy. Ruth used to be a very popular girl's name.

The moral of the story? When you see a word that looks slightly familiar, knock it around a little bit. Change its form to see whether you can discover its meaning more easily. Tumult is just the noun form of the more common word, tumultuous.

In B, *duplicity* is the quality of being *dup,* or double, as in double-dealing, double-crossing, and double-talking. Benedict Arnold was noted for his duplicity. It has nothing to do with being an idiot. However, there is a trick here. A *dupe,* a person who has been double-crossed or swindled, is in fact rather idiotic. This would be an easy trap to fall for.

Choice D is silly. Adulation has nothing to do with being an adult. *Adulation* is hero worship, extreme admiration. You may have adulation for a war hero or for the person who discovers the cure for cancer.

The words in choice E are also closer to antonyms than to synonyms. *Retrospection* is a look back, a review. At my 16th birthday party, my parents showed home movies of me naked in the bathtub at 6 months, me crawling around on a rug at 7 months, and so on. They called it the Suzee Retrospective. I called it Death By Embarrassment. A *prophet* is supposed to prophe-sy or predict the future, not look back at the past. *Correct Answer:* C.

9. EXCULPATE : BLAME ::

   (A) demean : average

   (B) compromise : peril

   (C) proliferate : abundance

   (D) perturb : exasperation

   (E) exonerate : guilt

Just to keep you on your toes, I put in a question in which the right answer actually did have the same meaning as the question words. This situation is rare, but I always want to emphasize to you that my suggestions are tips, not rules. Never shut off your own brain in favor of mine. To *exculpate* is to remove the blame. Think of the roots: *ex-* means out of or away from; *culp* means guilt or blame; *-ate* means to make: To make away from the guilt or blame. When your roommate comes in breathing fire because someone has borrowed his car and put a big dent in it, you thank your lucky stars that you went to class with friends in their car that day and have witnesses to exculpate you. To *exonerate* is the same thing — to remove the guilt or blame. A defense attorney sends his or her investigators out looking for evidence to exonerate the client.

To *compromise* means to imperil, to put into danger. For example, a young girl who stays out all night long with her date — even though they are just talking — compromises her reputation. A government official seen fraternizing with lobbyists may be compromising her integrity, putting it into some question or doubt. As you learned with *cow* in Question 4, words may have more than one meaning. The first definition most people provide for *compromise* is to come to terms by mutual concession, to meet in the middle and agree. Because that meaning has no connection with peril, you need to wrack your brains for another, less-common meaning.

In choice C, to *proliferate* is to grow in number or size, to become more abundant. The most common meaning of *pro-* on the GRE is big or much; a proliferation is an abundance, very much. In choice D, *to perturb* is to exasperate, to annoy, or to harass. If you missed this question, you're probably perturbed and exasperated with yourself. *Correct Answer:* E.

10. DESICCATE : MOISTURE ::

   (A) sanction : restrictions

   (B) enervate : energy

   (C) swindle : chicanery

   (D) attenuate : attention

   (E) derogate : epithets

To *desiccate* is to dry out, to remove moisture. (Ever hear of desiccated liver tablets? Some health food stores sell them for people who don't want to eat liver and would prefer to ingest it in dehydrated or pill form.) You can figure out this relationship by knowing that *de-* means out of or away from: A desiccant moves moisture out of or away from something. To *enervate* is to devitalize, to remove the energy from, to weaken.

Choice A, to *sanction* is to restrict. You probably know about economic sanctions, in which a government prohibits businesses from working with companies in other countries. To sanction, therefore, is to add restrictions rather than to take them away. In choice C, to *swindle* is to cheat or trick, as in swindling someone out of his money. *Chicanery* is trickery in matters of law. To swindle is not to take away chicanery but to add to it. In choice D, to *attenuate* is not to take away attention (you didn't fall for such a cheesy trick, did you?) but to make slender, thin, or diluted. An *emaciated* person looks attenuated. In choice E, to *derogate* is to denounce or be critical of. An *epithet* is a descriptive term often used derogatorily or critically. *Correct Answer:* B.

11. TOADY : SYCOPHANT ::

    (A) recluse : pedant

    (B) heretic : leader

    (C) malingerer : prodigy

    (D) bluestocking : gymnast

    (E) miser : penny-pincher

If you don't know the words in the question, you're not alone. They are very difficult words put there in the hopes that you remember what to do when you don't have a clue: First, try making the words synonyms. Make the simple sentence: A toady is a sycophant. As it turns out, that's correct. Both a *toady* and a *sycophant* are over-flatterers, kiss-ups, and yes-men. A groupie to a rock star is a toady and a sycophant. A student trying to get the professor to turn a borderline A–/B+ into the A is a toady and a sycophant. In the correct answer, E, a *miser* (a cheapskate, someone stingy) is in fact a penny-pincher. A penny-pincher is a cheap person, one who "pinches" pennies and holds them securely, not letting them go or spending them.

Here are the definitions for the other words. A *recluse* is a hermit, a solitary person. You may have heard this word in another form, reclusive. A *pedant* is a teacher, especially one who is overly precise and didactic. A *heretic* is a rebel, particularly one who doesn't agree with the orthodox religion. Joan of Arc was burned at the stake as a heretic. A *malingerer* is one who pretends to be sick in order to get out of work. All of us have been malingerers on the morning of a big exam at school, swearing to a variety of symptoms that would kill an ox. A *prodigy* is a highly talented person (Mozart was a child prodigy). A *bluestocking* is a learned woman, especially one in literary circles. She has nothing to do with gymnastics. *Correct Answer:* E.

12. PUGILIST : BELLICOSE ::

    (A) benefactor : beguiling

    (B) chatterbox : taciturn

    (C) narcissist : charismatic

    (D) scholar : erudite

    (E) imbecile : obsequious

A *pugilist* is a boxer, one who fights (the root *pug* means war or fight, and *-ist* is a person). *Bellicose* is like belligerent: hostile, argumentative, and fighting. The test sentence is: "A pugilist is bellicose." If you don't know the words and assume that they are synonyms, you are right. A scholar is in fact *erudite,* which means well-educated or scholarly. In choice A, a *benefactor* is a person who does good, one who brings *benefits* (to use a more common form of the word). He or she probably would not be *beguiling,* which means tricking or confusing. In choice B, a *chatterbox* is just what it looks like, one who chatters or talks a lot. *Taciturn* means not talkative, or "of few words." A chatterbox is not taciturn.

Have you heard of a tacit agreement? It's an unspoken agreement. Try to think of more common or familiar forms of the word. If you can remember how you use those in context, you can often get a "good enough" definition for a difficult word.

In choice C, a *narcissist* is a person overflowing with self-love, someone who thinks that he or she is just the most wonderful thing around. Although the narcissist may think that he or she is *charismatic* (inspiring loyalty), 'tain't necessarily so. In choice E, an *imbecile* is a feebleminded person, a fool (what most of us feel like when we don't know all these words). An imbecile may or may not be *obsequious,* which means excessively flattering. Remember the toady and sycophant from a previous question? Now *they* would be obsequious. *Correct Answer:* D.

Part II
A Word to the Wise: Verbal Questions

The 5th Wave   By Rich Tennant

REAL LIFE APPLICATION OF CORRECT ANTONYM IDENTIFICATION

"Let's see - your listed salad dressings are 'Vinaigrette', 'Creamy Garlic', and 'Hydrochloric Acid'. Hmm - I think I'll go with the 'Hydrochloric Acid'."

In this part . . .

One of the sections on the GRE is the Verbal section, which contains 30 questions. The verbal questions come in four styles: Antonyms (finding words that are opposites), Analogies (far and away the easiest for most people), Sentence Completions (good ol' fill-in-the-blanks, the same stuff you've been doing since kindergarten), and Reading Comprehension (dull and deadly). Each question style has a chapter of its own in this part. You learn the format of the question (what it looks like), an approach to the question (where to begin and an organized plan of attack), and the various tricks and traps built into the questions (with, of course, suggestions for recognizing and avoiding such traps). Vocabulary-building material features roots, prefixes, and suffixes. Following each lecture chapter is a chapter that includes particularly wicked practice questions followed by detailed answer explanations that show you what you should have done, how to make the best use of your time, and what you should have guessed at randomly.

Remember: You must answer a question before the computer lets you go on to the next question. Because you can't go back and change your answers after you've hit the Confirm button, you want to be sure of each answer, but you also need to work quickly enough to get through all the questions.

What to Do When You Ain't Got a Clue

Suppose that you look at a word and think it looks more like an inkblot test than like any vocabulary word you've ever seen. The word may be *cadging*. Not a clue, right? (And no, it's not a typo or a misspelling of *cage*.) What do you do next? You have three options:

1. **Dissect and define the term using roots, prefixes, and suffixes.**

   As I point out in Chapter 3, roots, prefixes, and suffixes are the real key to vocabulary on the GRE. Unfortunately, you haven't learned a root, prefix, or suffix for *cadging*. Proceed to Step 2.

2. **Eliminate answer choices that are synonyms of each other.**

   Suppose that choice A is *bubbly* and choice D is *effervescent*. Both words mean exuberant or joyful. Because two answer choices cannot both be correct, they must both be wrong.

3. **Bail out! Choose an answer and leave the scene as quickly as possible.**

   Suppose that you have no idea what the word means. It has no identifiable root, prefix, or suffix. No two of the answer choices mean the same thing. There's no way to narrow the answers down. What happens now? Guess and go. Choose something, anything, and go on to the next question.

The biggest mistake that you can make on an antonym question is to waste time. The longer you sit there, staring at the word, scratching your head, and waiting for heavenly revelation, the more the test-makers in their dark cubbyholes chortle with glee at your struggling in the *quagmire* (bog) they designed for you. Get through an Antonym question quickly: You either know it, or you don't know it, and then you're outta there. Think of an Antonym question as a blind date. You can tell in the first few minutes whether something is happening or not. (P.S. *Cadging* means begging or scrounging. GRE students often cadge notes from friends for classes.)

Bad Things Come in Small Packages: Tricks, Traps, and Tips

How, you wonder, can there be tricks and traps in a one-word question? Read 'em and weep.

Ignore the synonym

You may be lucky enough to encounter a very difficult word that you just happen to remember. Suppose that the question word is *pulchritudinous*. If you have already gone through the analogies portion of this book, you remember that *pulchritudinous* means beautiful. Choice A is *beautiful*. You are so pleased with yourself for remembering this hard word that you choose A ("Ah, there it is!") and go on your merry way. It isn't until you're boasting to your friend later that afternoon about having remembered *pulchritudinous* that your mistake dawns on you: You were supposed to choose the *antonym*, not the synonym. In short: If you see a word in the answer choices whose meaning is the same (or nearly the same) as the question, ignore it. The test-writing gnomes put it there just to ruin your day.

Use roots, prefixes, and suffixes

As I mention throughout this material, roots, prefixes, and suffixes (RPS) can save you when you have to wade through this polysyllabic pit. If you have not yet learned the prefixes and suffixes in Chapter 3, I strongly suggest you do so now. You can analyze even the most difficult word by using roots. Even if you can't get the exact definition, you can get a general idea of the word well enough to choose it or lose it.

Suppose that the question word is *abjure*. You don't know what it means, but you recall that the prefix *ab-* means away from. A queen abdicates a throne, or goes away from a throne. One of the answer choices is embrace. To embrace something is to take it as your own, to accept it, as in embracing the principles of democracy. If you trust your roots-sense and choose this answer, you can get a hard question correct in just a few seconds. (To *abjure* is to renounce or reject.)

Memorize connotation cards

I talk in Chapter 3 about creating flashcards for the roots, prefixes, and suffixes. You should have those cards completed by now and should be ready to move on to a more sophisticated type of flashing: *connotation cards*.

Notice that I'm not wasting your time or mine by giving you a list of a thousand words. It would be useless for you to sit down and try to memorize so many. You'd get to a point where each new word would *supplant* (displace, push out) a previous word. So how *can* you cram the most vocabulary into the least brain space? Memorize groups of words by their connotation.

A *connotation* is an association or idea, an implication. It's what the word means to you — how you remember it. Use index cards to cluster words by their connotations. For example, on one side of a card, write *fat,* and on the other side, write *thin*. Every time you encounter a word that has one of these meanings, put it on the card. On the fat side, you may have corpulent, fleshy, rotund, and obese. On the thin side, you might have emaciated, attenuated, svelte, and lanky.

Suppose you get to the exam and you see the word *svelte* but can't for the life of you remember what it means. In your mind's eye, you see the word on the *fat/thin* card. Voilà! Or on second thought: Ooops! Wait a minute: Does *svelte* mean fat, or does it mean thin?

Write words on one side in red ink and words on the other side in black ink. Write all the *thin* words in bright red ink. Write all the *fat* words in black ink. During the exam, you can remember that *svelte* is a red word on the *fat/thin* card, so it must mean thin. You'll be surprised how many questions you can get correct without knowing precise definitions, just hazy general concepts.

Don't anticipate and misread

The GRE often features some pretty bizarre-looking words. My favorite is *froward* (stubborn). At least once a year, some student calls me, overjoyed at having "conquered" the GRE: "Suzee, you won't believe it. The GRE had a typo. One of the antonyms said *froward* instead of *forward.* However, the answer choice *backward* was there, so I had no trouble figuring it out." No, no, a thousand times, no! The GRE has no typos. The GRE has no spelling errors. The GRE has no heart. It's very easy to see what you want to see rather than to read what's actually shown on the screen. Double-check that you have read the word correctly, not rewritten the test to match your preconceptions.

Peroration (A Summing Up)

An Antonym question requires a simple, two-step approach:

1. **Define the word.**
2. **Choose the opposite.**

Antonyms are small but deadly. Remembering the following can help you get through these questions efficiently:

- ✔ Use roots, prefixes, and suffixes.
- ✔ Eliminate answer choices that are synonyms of each other.
- ✔ Look for and avoid the answer choice that is a synonym of the question word.
- ✔ Learn vocabulary words in clusters using connotation cards.
- ✔ Don't anticipate and misread unusual words (such as *froward*).

Chapter 6

Unattractive Opposites: Antonym Practice Questions

You say you've been using a dictionary for a pillow for the last six weeks, believing some of the words and their definitions would penetrate your skull by osmosis? Here's a chance to test your theory. (Consider this chapter to have one big, looming Vocabulary icon attached to it.)

1. CHANGING

    (A) lightweight

    (B) cautious

    (C) immutable

    (D) delicious

    (E) soft

You can get this question correct by the process of elimination. The opposite of changing is *not changing,* or *unchanging.* You know that lightweight, cautious, delicious, and soft do not mean "not changing," which narrows the answers down quickly to the correct one. Use your roots to define **immutable.** *Im-* means not; *mut* means change. Im-mut-able literally means not changeable, or unchanging. *Correct Answer:* C.

2. RECUPERATE

    (A) sicken

    (B) invent

    (C) operate

    (D) elongate

    (E) balance

To **recuperate** is to regain your health. The opposite is to sicken. Choice C has a small trap in it. A person recuperating may have been operated on, but just because an answer choice seems connected to the question word (both *recuperate* and *operate* have to do with health) does not mean the choice is correct.

Did you use your common sense to eliminate choice B? What word could possibly be the opposite of *invent*? As far as I know, no word means "uninvent." If you can't think of a logical opposite for a word, then it probably is not an antonym of the question. *Correct Answer:* A.

3. OPAQUE

   (A) old-fashioned

   (B) angry

   (C) improper

   (D) outdated

   (E) transparent

Something *opaque* is not clear, not see-through. It blocks the light (*op* means block or against). Something transparent is clear, does not block the light. Did you notice that you can eliminate choices A and D because they are synonyms of each other? If two words mean the same (or nearly the same) thing, they can't both be correct and therefore must both be wrong. *Correct Answer:* E.

4. LOQUACIOUS

   (A) elegant

   (B) quiet

   (C) overweight

   (D) excited

   (E) incapable

Loq means speech or talk; *-ous* means full of or very. Someone loquacious is full of talk, or very talkative. The opposite is quiet. *Correct Answer:* B.

Most of my students are quite loquacious in telling me that their biggest problem is vocabulary. They just plain can't remember pages and pages and pages of words. My suggestion is always the same: Concentrate on learning roots, prefixes, and suffixes, which can expand your vocabulary exponentially. In this book, you can find lists of roots, prefixes, and suffixes in Chapters 3 and 7.

5. SKEPTICAL

   (A) fast-acting

   (B) punctual

   (C) depressed

   (D) credulous

   (E) effervescent

If you are *skeptical,* you are dubious or doubtful. You are looking for a word that means not doubtful. Eliminate the words you do know — choices A, B, and C. *Credulous* can be defined using the roots: *cred* means trust or belief; *-ous* means full of or very. Someone credulous is full of trust, naive, and gullible — just the opposite of skeptical. *Effervescent* means bubbly. When an *Effer*dent (a brand-name, denture-cleaning tablet) is put into a glass of water, it bubbles. *Correct Answer:* D.

6. VIABLE

   (A) solid

   (B) moribund

   (C) vital

   (D) integral

   (E) irreplaceable

If you chose C, you fell for the trap. *Vital* means essential, critical. Just because it has a *vi* like the question word does not mean vital is the right answer (and anyway, you are looking for antonyms, not synonyms). Choices C, D, and E are similar enough in meaning that selecting one over the others would be hard. You can't have three right answers, so eliminate them all.

Viable means capable of working, developing adequately, or livable. A plan for learning several new roots like *vi* (meaning life) daily is viable (it can be done). *Moribund* means near death or extinction. A company that is bankrupt and firing employees may be described as moribund. *Correct Answer:* B.

7. SALUBRIOUS

    (A) unhealthy

    (B) serendipitous

    (C) dour

    (D) rapid

    (E) monumental

Salubrious means healthful, wholesome, or salutary (*sal* means health, *-ous* means full of). Unhealthy is as logical an opposite as you're ever going to find. Choice B, *serendipitous,* means fortuitous, or a happy, lucky occurrence. It would be serendipitous to walk out your front door and find a hundred-dollar bill on your doorstep. Choice C, *dour,* means gloomy. Finding out that the hundred-dollar bill you so serendipitously found on the sidewalk features a picture not of Ben Franklin but of Alfred E. Newman will leave you dour. *Correct Answer:* A.

8. IRASCIBLE

    (A) mendacious

    (B) serpentine

    (C) phlegmatic

    (D) fatigued

    (E) tepid

Irascible means hot-tempered, easily angered. Choice C, *phlegmatic,* means slow, having a stolid temperament, not easily excited to action. Choice A, *mendacious,* means lying, dishonest, or untruthful. Don't confuse the adjective mendacious, meaning dishonest, with the noun *mendicant,* a beggar. A mendicant may be mendacious when he tells you how he's going to spend the quarter you just gave him. Choice B, *serpentine,* means like a snake, twisting or turning. The road to Pike's Peak is a serpentine road. Choice E, *tepid,* means lukewarm. A tepid response to a marriage proposal should send you to your lawyer's office to get a prenuptial agreement. *Correct Answer:* C.

9. FRANGIBLE

    (A) refulgent

    (B) histrionic

    (C) unbreakable

    (D) unfriendly

    (E) masculine

Frangible means breakable. The opposite, amazingly enough, is unbreakable. Choice A, *refulgent,* means shining, radiant, and gleaming. Choice B, *histrionic,* means theatrical, hysterical, and dramatic. *Correct Answer:* C.

10. PALLIATE

   (A) laud

   (B) appraise

   (C) exacerbate

   (D) befriend

   (E) mitigate

To *palliate* is to soften, lessen, or assuage. You can palliate an insult by smiling to take the sting out. Choice C, *exacerbate,* is to make more severe, to aggravate. You exacerbate a fight when you slam the door in your opponent's face. Choice A, to *laud,* is to praise. (Think of app*laud.*) Choice D, to *befriend,* is to make a friend of. (*Be* is a prefix meaning *completely;* however, you can basically ignore this prefix. To befriend someone is simply to "friend" him.) Choice E, *mitigate,* is the same as palliate. To mitigate is to lessen or decrease, to make less severe. You may have heard of "mitigating circumstances." Hot wiring and stealing a car is a felony that can land you in prison; taking the car because your wife is in labor and you have to get to the hospital pronto is a mitigating circumstance (but if you take *my* car, you have *unmitigated* gall!). *Correct Answer:* C.

11. CONDIGN

   (A) incapable

   (B) inevitable

   (C) inconsistent

   (D) unremitting

   (E) undeserved

Condign means deserved or appropriate. A condign punishment for those of you who do not laugh at my jokes is to spend eternity listening to your parent's old record albums. The opposite (logically enough) is undeserved. *Correct Answer:* E.

12. SALACIOUS

   (A) wholesome

   (B) rustic

   (C) noxious

   (D) merry

   (E) puissant

Salacious means lustful, lecherous, lewd — the opposite of wholesome. Choice B, *rustic,* means rural, appropriate for the country. A rustic outfit would be plus fours and a shooting stick. Choice E, *puissant,* means strong, influential, powerful.

Did you fall for the trap answer, C? *Sal-* means health; *-ous* means full of. No one can fault you if you thought salacious meant "full of health." However, the word for that is *salubrious.* Choice C, *noxious,* means poisonous. It is a good antonym for salubrious but not for salacious. *Correct Answer:* A.

No, no, don't panic. Of course, this section is hard for you. But I have news for you: It's just as hard for native English speakers. It's true! Your average American has no more idea of the meanings of *prolix* (verbose and long-winded) and *salubrious* than you do. Everyone is equal when it comes to needing to learn roots, prefixes, and suffixes.

Chapter 7

Finish What You Start: Sentence Completions

• •

In This Chapter

▶ Drawing a blank: What Sentence Completion questions look like

▶ Cutting away the deadwood: Dissecting and simplifying the sentences

▶ Sweeping away the trash: Eliminating wrong answers

• •

Sentence Completion questions are the blind dates of the GRE. What you see is not necessarily what you get . . . or what you want. Looks can be deceiving. Don't judge a book by its cover. Beauty is only skin deep. Let's see, have I left out any other trite, banal, hackneyed clichés? The point of all this babbling is that Sentence Completion questions can be sneaky, tricky, duplicitous, and worse than they look. Fortunately, there are ways to beat the questions at their own game.

Recognizing Sentence Completion Questions

A Sentence Completion question consists of one sentence with one or two blanks. Your job, should you choose to accept it, is to fill in those blanks. Usually only one word goes in each blank; occasionally, however, the blank requires a few words or a short phrase instead. Here is an example:

Disgusted at having to spend the entire weekend studying for the GRE instead of going hang gliding, Faye - - - - her book across the room with such - - - - that it soared high into the sky, causing three of her neighbors to call the UFO hot line.

   (A) tossed ... gentleness

   (B) hurled ... ferocity

   (C) pitched ... glee

   (D) carried ... gloom

   (E) conveyed ... reluctance

The key word in this example is *disgusted,* indicating strong, negative emotions. Only choice B offers two words that match the tone of *disgusted. Correct Answer:* B.

Looking at the Empty Sentence

Do you look at Sentence Completion questions and draw a blank? (Sorry, I couldn't resist.) Knowing where to start is a great confidence builder and time saver. Try the following steps.

1. **Read the entire sentence for its gist.**

2. **If possible, predict words to fit the blanks.**

3. **Insert the answer choices.**

The following sections explain these steps.

Read the entire sentence

Although this may seem obvious, many people read until they get to the first blank and then head for the answers. The problem is that the sentence may change in midstream, messing everything up. Note, for example, the big difference between

> Having been coerced by her mother into accepting a blind date, Mitzi was ---- *because* Marty turned out to be ----.

> — and —

> Having been coerced by her mother into accepting a blind date, Mitzi was ---- *although* Marty turned out to be ----.

In the first example, you may want to say something like this:

> Having been coerced by her mother into accepting a blind date, Mitzi was *ecstatic* because Marty turned out to be *gorgeous*.

In the second example, you could say the following:

> Having been coerced by her mother into accepting a blind date, Mitzi was *content* although Marty turned out to be *mediocre*.

How you fill in the blanks depends on the middle term — in this case the conjunction *because* or *although*.

Keep in mind that the purpose of Sentence Completion questions is to measure your ability to recognize words and phrases that logically and stylistically complete the meaning of the sentences.

If possible, predict words to fit the blanks

Notice the careful hedge, "if possible." You can't *always* predict words. But it's amazing how often you can get close. Consider the following example:

> Hal was ---- when his new computer arrived because he realized he'd have no excuses now for not finishing his homework.

You can predict that the word should be something negative such as *depressed, sad,* or *unhappy.* (If your vocabulary is up to the task, you can also predict negative words such as *lachrymose, dolorous,* and *lugubrious.*)

Did you predict something positive such as *happy* or *glad?* If you did, you probably headed for the answers before you read the entire sentence. What did I just tell you in the preceding section? Tsk, tsk.

Insert the answer choices

Don't try to save time by hurrying through Sentence Completion questions. You just need to plug and chug. Plug in every answer choice and chug through the whole darned sentence again. Occasionally, you can eliminate answers because you know the word *must* be positive, but that answer choice is negative. After you eliminate everything you can, you must insert the remaining answers into the blanks and read through the sentences that result. Try the following example:

As a public relations specialist, Susan realizes the importance of ---- and ---- when dealing with even the most exasperating tourists.

   (A) dignity ... etiquette

   (B) fantasy ... realism

   (C) kindness ... patience

   (D) courtesy ... compassion

   (E) truth ... honesty

Because the two blanks are connected by *and,* the words in those blanks should be synonyms (or almost synonyms). They may not need to mean exactly the same thing, but they certainly should not be opposites. They should be on the same wavelength. That means you can eliminate choice B because *fantasy* and *realism* are opposites. That's the only answer, however, that you can eliminate immediately. The others are all close enough in meaning to fit together.

This leaves you with no choice but to plug and chug. Insert every answer and see which one makes the most sense. The right answer here is choice C. Choice A looks pretty good, but you don't "treat someone with etiquette." *Etiquette* is a system of rules for manners. Choice D also looks pretty good, but treating someone who is *exasperating* with compassion is not as logical as treating the person with patience. Choice E is very tempting until you plug it into the sentence. *Truth* and *honesty* are synonyms, but they don't fit as well in the context of the sentence as do *kindness* and *patience. Correct Answer:* C.

Forget about taking a lot of shortcuts. After you eliminate the obviously incorrect answers, take your sweet time going back and inserting every remaining answer into the sentence. Sentence Completion answers aren't right or wrong so much as good, better, or best. Sometimes all the answers seem to "sorta fit;" your job is to choose the one that fits best.

Blowing Sentences Away: Dynamite Traps 'n' Tricks

Let me introduce you to the nasty little gremlins lurking in the Sentence Completion questions and give you some suggestions for dealing with them. The basic steps to take are as follows:

   1. **Look for key connecting words that may change the meaning of the sentence.**

   2. **Predict positive or negative words to fit in the blanks.**

   3. **Don't waste time scratching your head over questions with vocabulary that is totally unfamiliar to you: Make a guess and go on to the next question.**

The following sections explain these steps.

Connections count

Changing *and* to *or* or *because* to *however* can change everything, as this example shows:

> Buzz was content to - - - - *and* - - - - on his weekend, answering to no one but himself, doing exactly as he liked.

Perhaps you would fill the blanks with *rest ... relax*. You know that the concepts are synonyms. Now check this out:

> Buzz was content to - - - - *or* - - - - on his weekend, answering to no one but himself, doing exactly as he liked.

The *or* changes everything. You may fill the blanks with *sleep ... party* or perhaps *work ... play*. You know that the concepts must be opposites here.

Some common connecting words are:

although	and	because
but	but for	despite
either/or	however	in spite of
moreover	nonetheless	or
therefore		

Whenever you see the preceding words, your antennae should go up, putting you on the alert for a plot twist — a trap of some sort.

Use your crystal ball

Sometimes the sentences are so long and *convoluted* (twisting or turning) that you can't make heads or tails of them. In that case, dissect the sentence. (A sentence so confusing probably makes you bloodthirsty or *sanguinary* enough to want to dismember something right about then.) Isolate just a bit of the sentence around the blank and try to predict whether that blank requires a positive or negative word. Consider the following:

> "Blah blah blah blah blah blah blah blah blah blah blah," Frances cursed - - - -.

Because people rarely curse or swear nicely, you can predict that the blank must be filled with a negative word. Maybe Frances curses *harshly, rudely,* or *viciously* (or *stridently, stentorianly,* or *fulminatingly*). You can eliminate answer choices such as *sweetly, kindly,* or *courteously* (as well as *benignly, amiably,* or *decorously*).

Guess and go!

Many times you can get the right answer in Sentence Completion questions by the process of elimination. You may have a hazy idea what type of word (positive or negative) or words (antonyms or synonyms) go into the blank or blanks. But what happens if you can't eliminate any answers because you don't know what any of the words mean? Hit the road, Jack. Get outta there fast. If you are making a wild guess anyway, why spend time deliberating over it? Guess and go!

A vocabulary helper bonus

You are no doubt delighted to know that roots, prefixes, and suffixes (RPS) help you immensely on the Sentence Completion vocabulary, just as they do on the Analogies and Antonyms sections. If you don't know what the words mean, use your RPS to figure them out (see Chapter 3 and the "Getting Back to Your Roots" section in this chapter for more on RPS). For example, consider the following sentence:

> Jane refused to eulogize Donald, saying that she thought he was a - - - - fellow.

Obviously, the entire sentence depends on the meaning of eulogize. If it means something bad, Jane refused to bad-mouth Donald and thought that he was a swell fellow. If it means something good, Jane refused to say anything good about Donald, thinking he was a bad fellow. Which is it? As you may recall, *eu* (along with *ben*

and *bon*) means good. You also probably picked up the suffix *-ize,* which means to make. And *log* means speech or talk. You can reason that *to eulogize* means to make good speech or talk. If she refused "to make good speech or talk" about Donald, she didn't like him. Fill the blank with a bad word, such as *rotten, terrible,* or *disgusting.*

Try this one:

> Ashamed of his obvious trembling and - - - - when confronted by the farmer's wife, Blind Mickey told his two good friends, "I thought I was a man, but I'm just a mouse."

You need a word here that means fear. The right answer may be trepidation. You can figure out the word if you know that the root *trep* means fear.

Although she usually was of a cheerful nature, Patty was - - - - when she heard the history professor assign a paper that would be due the first day back after Spring Break.

(A) ebullient

(B) indolent

(C) supercilious

(D) enigmatic

(E) lugubrious

Okay. You know that the blank needs to be filled with a word that means sad, gloomy, or glum. So far so good. But then you get to the answer choices, and life as you know it ceases to exist. You don't know *any* of those words. You can't get this one right except by randomly guessing. Fill in something, anything, and zoom on to the next question.

Leaving you hanging on this sentence would be too vicious, even for me. After all, I'm only an *unofficial* test-maker, a tyrant-in-training, as it were. The correct answer is E. *Lugubrious* means sad. As for the other words, *ebullient* means happy, overjoyed. *Indolent* means lazy, laid back. *Supercilious* means stuck-up, conceited. *Enigmatic* means mysterious, difficult to figure out. An *enigma* is a puzzle or a mystery, such as the enigma of how you ever let yourself in for something as soul leeching as this exam. *Correct Answer:* E.

Getting Back to Your Roots

Chapter 3 presents basic prefixes and suffixes. It's time now to increase your vast storehouse of knowledge by adding some of the important roots. The following is just a short list, but it is representative of what can greatly help you to figure out GRE *sesquipedalian* (foot and a half long!) vocabulary words.

If English is not your first language, vocabulary may be the hardest part of the exam for you. Using roots, prefixes, and suffixes can help you greatly.

- **som = sleep:** Take *Som*inex to get to sleep. If you have in*som*nia, you can't sleep. (The prefix *in-* means not.)

- **sop = sleep:** A glass of warm milk is a *sop*orific. So is a boring professor.

- **son = sound:** A *son*ic boom breaks the sound barrier. Dis*son*ance is clashing sounds. (My singing, quite frankly, is so bad that the governor declared my last opera a disaster aria!) A *son*orous voice has a good sound.

- **phon = sound:** *Phon*ics helps you to sound out words. Caco*phon*y is bad sound; eu*phon*y is good sound. Homo*phon*es are words that sound the same, such as *red* and *read*.

- **path = feeling:** Something *path*etic arouses feeling or pity. To sym*path*ize is to share the feelings (literally, to make the same feeling). Anti*path*y is a dislike — literally, a feeling against as in: No matter how much the moron apologizes, you still may harbor *antipathy* toward the jerk who parked right behind you and blocked you in, making you late for a date and causing all sorts of unfortunate romantic repercussions.

- **mut = change:** The Teenage *Mut*ant Ninja Turtles *mut*ated, or changed, from mild-mannered turtles to pizza-gobbling crime fighters. Something im*mut*able is not changeable, but remains constant. Don't confuse *mut* (change) with *mute* (silent).

- **meta = beyond, after:** A *meta*morphosis is a change of shape beyond the present shape.

- **morph = shape:** Something a*morph*ous is without shape. *Morph*ology is the study of shape. ("Yes, of course, I take my studies seriously. I spend all weekend on *morph*ology at the beach.")

- **loq, log, loc, lix = speech or talk:** Someone *loq*uacious talks a lot. (That person is literally full of talk.) A dia*log*ue is talk or conversation between two people. E*loc*ution is proper speech. A pro*lix* person is very talkative. (Literally, he or she engages in big, or much, talk.)

- **cred = trust or belief:** Something in*cred*ible is unbelievable, such as the excuse: "I would have picked you up on time, Sweetheart, but there was a 75-car pile-up on the freeway." If you are *cred*ulous, you are trusting and *naive* (literally, full of trust). In fact, if you're credulous, you probably actually feel sorry for my being stuck in traffic.

Be careful not to confuse the words *credible* and *credulous.* Something *credible* is trustable or believable. A credible excuse can get you out of trouble if you turn a paper in late. *Credulous,* on the other hand, means full of trust, naive, or gullible. The more credulous your professor is, the less credible that excuse needs to be.

- **gyn = woman:** A *gyn*ecologist is a physician who treats women. A miso*gyn*ist is a person who hates women.

- **andro = man:** Commander Data on *Star Trek: The Next Generation* is an *andro*id; he's a robot shaped like a man. Someone *andro*gynous exhibits both male (*andro*) and female (*gyn*) characteristics (literally, he/she is full of man and woman). For example, the character Pat on the TV show *Saturday Night Live* is androgynous.

- **anthro = human or mankind:** *Anthro*pology is the study of humans (not just men and not just women but humans in general). A mis*anthro*pe hates humans. (An equal-opportunity hater: He or she hates both men and women alike.)

- **pac = peace, calm:** Why do you give a baby a *pac*ifier? To calm him or her down. To get its name, the *Pac*ific Ocean must have appeared calm at the time it was discovered.

- **plac = peace, calm:** To *plac*ate someone is to calm him or her down or to make peace with that person. You placate your irate sweetheart, for example, by sending a dozen roses (hint, hint). Someone im*plac*able is someone you are not able to calm down — or someone really stubborn. If those roses don't do the trick, for example, your sweetheart is too implacable to placate.

- ✔ **pug = war, fight:** Someone *pug*nacious is ready to fight. A *pug*ilist is a person who li
  to fight — such as a professional boxer. (Did you ever see those big sticks that Mari
  train with in hand-to-hand combat — the ones that look like cotton swabs with a thy-
  roid condition? Those are called *pug*il sticks.)

- ✔ **bellu, belli = war, fight:** If you're *belli*gerent, you're ready to fight — in fact, you're
  downright hostile. An ante*bellu*m mansion is one that was created before the Civil War.
  (Remember that *ante-* means *before.* You can find this word in the prefixes section in
  Chapter 3.)

- ✔ **pro = big, much:** *Pro*fuse apologies are big, or much — in essence, a *lot* of apologies. A
  *pro*lific writer produces a great deal of written material.

  Pro has two additional meanings less commonly used on the GRE. It can mean *before,* as
  in "A *pro*logue comes before a play." Similarly, to *pro*gnosticate is to make knowledge
  before or to predict. A *pro*gnosticator is a fortune-teller. *Pro* can also mean *for.* Someone
  who is *pro* freedom of speech is in favor of freedom of speech. Someone with a *pro*clivity
  toward a certain activity is for that activity or has a natural tendency toward it.

- ✔ **gnos = knowledge:** A doctor shows his or her knowledge by making a dia*gnos*is (analysis of the situation) or a pro*gnos*is (prediction about the future of the illness). An
  a*gnos*tic is a person who doesn't know whether a god exists. Differentiate an *agnostic*
  from an *atheist:* An atheist is literally without God, a person who believes there is no
  god. An agnostic is without knowledge, believing a god may or may not exist.

- ✔ **scien = knowledge:** A *scien*tist is a person with knowledge. Someone pre*scien*t has
  forethought or knowledge ahead of time — for example, a prognosticator (a fortune-
  teller, remember?). After you learn these roots, you'll be closer to being omni*scien*t —
  all-knowing.

- ✔ **de = down from, away from (to put down):** To *de*scend or *de*part is to go down from or
  away from. To *de*nounce is to put down or to speak badly of, as in *de*nouncing those
  hogs who chow down all the pizza before you get to the party.

  Many unknown words on the GRE that start with *de* mean to put down in the sense of
  to criticize or bad-mouth. Here are just a few: demean, denounce, denigrate, derogate,
  deprecate, decry.

- ✔ **ex = out of, away from:** An *ex*it is literally out of or away from it — *ex*-it. (This is probably one of the most logical words around.) To *ex*tricate is to get out of something. You
  can extricate yourself from an argument by pretending to faint, basking in all the sym-
  pathy as you're carried away. To *ex*culpate is to get off the hook — literally to make
  away from guilt. *Culp* means guilt. When the president of the Hellenic Council wants to
  know who TP'ed the dean's house, you can claim that you and your sorority sisters are
  not *culp*able.

- ✔ **greg = group, herd:** A con*greg*ation is a group or herd of people. A *greg*arious person
  likes to be part of a group — he or she is sociable. To se*greg*ate is literally to make
  away from the group. *Se-* means apart or away from, as in *separate, sever, sequester,*
  and *seclusion.*

- ✔ **luc, lum, lus = light, clear:** Something *lum*inous is shiny and full of light. Ask the
  teacher to e*luc*idate something you don't understand (literally, to make clear). *Lus*trous
  hair reflects the light and is sleek and glossy.

- ✔ **ambu = walk, move:** In a hospital, patients are either bedridden (they can't move) or
  *ambu*latory (they can walk and move about). A somn*ambu*list is a sleepwalker. *Som-*
  means sleep; *-ist* is a person; *ambu* is to walk or move. A somn*ambu*list, therefore, is a
  person who walks or moves in his or her sleep.

Enough for now. You'll find no **paucity** (lack or scarcity) of roots to learn, but these should
provide you with a good foundation.

A fun word: Antepenultimate

Most people know that *ultimate* means *the last,* just as *Z* is the ultimate letter of the alphabet. But which letter is the antepenultimate? Give up? It's *X.* The ultimate is the last; the penultimate is the second to last; the antepenultimate is the third to last (literally, *before the second to last*). Therefore, if you have three younger brothers, you can introduce them as your antepenultimate, penultimate, and ultimate siblings.

A Sense of Completion: Review

Before you go on to the practice questions in the following chapter, take some time to review the following approaches and tricks, as discussed earlier in this chapter.

Approaches

1. **Read the entire sentence for its gist.**

2. **If possible, predict words to fit into the blanks.**

3. **Insert *every* answer choice into the blanks and reread the sentence.**

Tricks

- ✔ Look for key connecting words that may change the meaning of the sentence.
- ✔ Predict positive or negative words to fit in the blanks.
- ✔ Guess quickly on questions with answers that depend entirely on unknown vocabulary.

And, of course, you want to remember that using a few basic RPS (roots, prefixes, and suffixes) can help you to figure out the killer vocabulary.

A whale of an exam

QUESTION: What do the GRE and *Moby Dick* have in common?

ANSWER: They both feature the following vocabulary.*

prodigious	fathom	ruefully
blunder	fastidious	tyro
antediluvian	wretched	omnipotent
voracious	incensed	cadge
heinous	precipice	descry
effulgent	inert	leviathan
floundering	disparaging	sagacious
depict	incredulous	superficial
conflagration	dogged	indiscriminate

* Oh sure, you can probably think of other commonalities such as (1) no one ever finishes either one, and (2) they are leading causes of migraine headaches. But honestly, this is the real answer: All these GRE words are found in *Moby Dick.*

Chapter 8

Reality Check: Sentence Completion Practice Questions

*1*t's that time again — when you use it or lose it. Answering the following questions should reinforce what you learned in the preceding chapter about Sentence Completion questions.

1. Although dismayed by the pejorative comments made about her inappropriate dress at the diplomatic function, Judy - - - - her tears and showed only the most calm and - - - - visage to her critics.

   (A) obviated ... agitated

   (B) suppressed ... placid

   (C) exacerbated ... unfazed

   (D) monitored ... incensed

   (E) curtailed ... articulate

Look at the second blank first. Often the second blank is easier to predict than the first.

If Judy had a calm *and* (something) *visage* (a visage is a countenance, a facial expression), the (something) must go hand in hand with calm. Although it doesn't have to be an exact synonym, the second word can't be an antonym either. Look for a word that means calm. *Placid* means calm and tranquil as you know from the root *plac,* meaning peace. Check the rest of the second words. *Agitated* means upset or worried, just the opposite of what you're looking for. *Unfazed* may be good because it means not bothered by. (Erudite types are unfazed by seeing how that word is spelled, knowing that *unphased* is a trap often found on grammar exams.) *Incensed* means upset, burning mad (think of burning incense). *Articulate* means well spoken. Her visage, or facial expression, would not be well spoken, although Judy herself may be. So, you've narrowed the answers down to B and C based on the second words alone. Now check out the first words.

To *exacerbate* is to make worse. Words as hard as this one can exacerbate your headache. But if you choose this answer, you let your insecurity complex get the better of you. It's normal to think, "Oooh, big hard word; it must be the right answer." I'm not saying that these questions don't feature hard words, but the difficult words may be the trap answers, not the correct answers. *Suppress* means to hold back and fits the sentence perfectly. *Correct Answer:* B.

Take a quick look at some of the other vocabulary. To *obviate* is to prevent, as in your learning these words now obviates your falling for traps by choosing them later. To *curtail* is to shorten. (Think of cutting off the tail of a word when you cur*tail* it.)

Did you take note of the word *although?* A key word like that can change the meaning of the entire sentence. If it weren't there, you may think that Judy in fact burst out crying from the criticism rather than holding back.

2. Although there are those writers who carp and ---- about the current depressed state of our economy, many people insist that such writers don't speak for the common man (or woman) who believes in the ---- of the nation and the security of its future.

   (A) lampoon ... uniformity

   (B) grouse ... resilience

   (C) complain ... morbidity

   (D) laud ... strength

   (E) ridicule ... chaos

As I advise in Chapter 7, try to predict the words to fit into the blank or, failing that, predict the sense (positive or negative) of the words. You can predict here that the first word must be something bad (because the writers are carping, or griping, about a depressed economy) and that the second word must be something good (because the average man or woman believes in the future of the country). Eliminate all second words that are not good: *morbidity* (meaning gruesomeness) and *chaos* (meaning confusion and disorganization). Eliminate all first words that are not negative: *laud* (meaning to praise, as in to app*laud.*) Now you've narrowed the choices down to just two.

To *lampoon* is to ridicule (think of the satirical magazine, the *National Lampoon*). That may fit, but the second blank doesn't make much sense. Sure, it's good to believe in the uniformity, or unity, of a country, but that's not related to worrying about the depressed state of its economy. Choice B, *grouse,* is to complain or grumble. (The poet Dorothy Parker wrote a great stanza that says, "Cavil, quarrel, grumble, grouse/I ponder on the narrow house/I shudder at the thought of men/I'm due to fall in love again!") And *resilience* is elasticity, the state of springing back. The average person thinks the economy will stage a comeback. *Correct Answer:* B.

3. The speaker, ironically, ---- the very point he had stood up to make, and hurriedly sat down, hoping no one had caught his ----.

   (A) prognosticated ... summation

   (B) divulged ... information

   (C) refuted ... solecism

   (D) duplicated ... duplicity

   (E) ferreted out ... mistake

Predict that the second blank must be something negative because the speaker hoped no one had noticed it. That eliminates answers A (a *summation* is just what it looks like, a summary, and is not necessarily bad) and B (*information* is also neutral). Now try the sentence with the remaining answer choices inserted.

To *refute* is to disprove or show to be false. It would be *ironic* (the opposite of what is expected) if the speaker were to disprove the very point he stood up to make. A *solecism* is an inconsistency, a mistake. *Correct Answer:* C.

Take a moment to go through the other words to increase your vocabulary. (As you realize by now, you can narrow down many of the Sentence Completion questions to just two or three answers through the process of elimination. But to get the one, right answer you have to know the words.) To *prognosticate* is to predict. *Pro* means before; *gnos* means knowledge; *-ate* means to make. To prognosticate is to "make knowledge before," to predict.

If you chose A, you probably fell for the trap of looking only at the answer choices and not reinserting them into the sentence. Yes, something ironic is the opposite of what is expected, and a prognostication is the opposite of a summation, but that answer doesn't fit when reinserted into the sentence. Be sure to take your time and go back to the sentence with each answer choice. The Sentence Completion section is not a place to try to save seconds.

In choice B, to *divulge* is to reveal. That first word works, but the second does not. It's not ironic to divulge the very information you stand up to say; it's normal.

In choice D, duplicity is an interesting word. The root *dup* means double, but duplicity is not "doubleness" in the sense of two of something. *Duplicity* is deception, being two-faced. A traitor is noted for his or her duplicity. And in choice E, to *ferret out* is to search diligently, as a detective ferrets out clues to help his client. You ferret out the tips and traps scattered throughout these explanations to help you to remember them.

4. Although often writing of ---- activities, Emily Dickinson possessed the faculty of creating an eclectic group of characters ranging from the reticent to the epitome of ----.

   (A) questionable ... taciturnity

   (B) mundane ... effrontery

   (C) egregious ... discretion

   (D) horrific ... stoicism

   (E) commensurate ... composure

This is the first question in the batch that you may have wanted to make a wild guess at. The entire question depends on vocabulary, and all the vocabulary is very difficult. If you encounter a question of this sort on the exam, don't waste too much time on it. Make a quick guess and go on to the next question.

If you know that *reticent* means shy and holding back, you can predict that the second blank must be the opposite of that, something bold and forward. *Effrontery* is shameless boldness and audacity. You have effrontery when you ask your boss for a raise right after he or she chews you out for bungling a project and costing the company money. Effrontery is the only second blank that fits. *Taciturnity* is the noun form of the word *taciturn*, meaning quiet, not talkative, not forward. *Stoicism* is not showing feelings or pain. Only a stoic can look at words such as these without shrieking or ripping out her hair.

Turning to the first blanks, *mundane* means common, worldly. Mundane activities are day-to-day tasks, nothing exciting like winning a lottery or visiting Antarctica. *Egregious* means terrible or flagrant. An egregious mistake is right out there for the world to see. *Commensurate* means equivalent to or proportionate. Your score on this section will be commensurate with your vocabulary. *Correct Answer:* B.

5. Dismayed by the ---- evidence available to her, the defense attorney spent her own money (even though that would leave her nearly ----) to hire a private investigator to acquire additional evidence.

   (A) dearth of ... affluent

   (B) scanty ... insolvent

   (C) vestigial ... pecuniary

   (D) immense ... bankrupt

   (E) impartial ... penurious

Predict words to fit into the blanks. If the attorney is dismayed by evidence and hires an investigator to get *more* evidence, there must not have been much evidence to begin with. Predict the first word means not very much. *Scanty* means barely sufficient. A *dearth of* is a lack of. Those are the only two that fit for the first blank. *Vestigial* means not fully developed; for example, the tailbone of humans is a vestigial tail. *Immense* means large, just the opposite of what you want.

The words *even though* tell you that spending her own money to gather the extra evidence would have a negative effect on the attorney. She was nearly *insolvent,* or bankrupt. Choice A, *affluent,* means rich, wealthy, or — as a smart-aleck friend of mine says — financially over-supplied. That doesn't work — eliminate the choice.

In choice C, *pecuniary* means consisting of or pertaining to money matters. This could be a trick answer, as you know that the costs have to do with money as well. However, the first word definitely doesn't fit in this sentence. In choice E, *penurious* means poor, needy, or destitute. It fits the second blank, but the first blank doesn't work with this answer. *Impartial* evidence is neutral, neither good nor bad. *Correct Answer:* B.

6. Unwilling to be labeled - - - -, Gwenette slowly and - - - - double-checked each fact before expounding upon her theory to her colleagues at the convention.

   (A) precipitate ... meticulously

   (B) hasty ... swiftly

   (C) rash ... desultorily

   (D) efficacious ... haphazardly

   (E) painstaking ... heedlessly

The key here is pure vocabulary. You can probably predict the types of words you need, knowing that the first word must mean too fast and careless and the second word slow and careful. But if you don't have a clue what any of the words mean, don't waste time scratching your head over this one. Just guess and go.

Precipitate, hasty, and *rash* all mean overly quick, leaping before looking. Those fit the first blank. *Efficacious* means efficient and effective, something Gwenette wants to be labeled. *Painstaking* means meticulous, careful, and attentive to detail, another good thing to be. Dump choices D and E.

You know the second blank must be something good. *Meticulous* means careful with detail, paying careful attention. It is pretty much the opposite of *swiftly* (quickly), *desultorily* (aimlessly, not methodically), *haphazardly* (unsystematically, not methodically), and *heedlessly* (not paying attention). *Correct Answer:* A.

Even if you don't know the exact meanings of the words, you often have an idea whether they are positive or negative — whether they have good or bad connotations. If you sense that a word is bad when you need a good word, eliminate that answer choice. You'll be pleasantly surprised at how often your subconscious leads you to the correct answer.

If you didn't grow up in the United States, you may not be able to "sense" the meanings (good or bad) of words. In that case, it's even more important for you to make a *quick* guess and go on.

Chapter 9

Readings That Can Affect Your Future: Blood Pressure, Astrology, and the GRE

● ●

In This Chapter
▶ Covering the most common reading passages
▶ Figuring out whether the questions are worth your time
▶ Conjuring up tricks to save your sanity

● ●

Feared by more students than Monday's mystery meat in the college cafeteria, Reading Comprehension questions on the GRE comprise 8 out of the 30 verbal questions. The number can vary slightly, but in general, approximately 27 percent of your verbal score is determined by the Reading Comprehension questions.

For those of you used to taking pencil and paper tests, the reading passages on the computer can be quite a challenge. On a paper test, you have the option of skipping around and finding a passage you like (maybe you prefer a science passage to a humanities passage). You also have the option of skipping a question and coming back to it later. Those options are gone with the computerized GRE. You get only one reading passage at a time; you can't preview several and choose your favorite. Also, you must choose and confirm an answer before the computer will go on to the next question.

 On the computer, you'll probably have to scroll up and down to read and reread the passage. (For those of you not familiar with computers, *scrolling* means you use the mouse to push a bar on the right side of the screen up or down to move the text up or down on the screen.) Most likely, the entire passage cannot fit on the screen at once.

Why Do They Call It Reading Comprehension If I Don't Understand a Thing I've Read?

 The origin of the *misnomer* (wrong name) "Reading Comprehension" is a great topic for a *deipnosophist*. (A deipnosophist is one who converses eruditely at the dinner table. Don't worry; you don't have to know the word for the GRE. I just threw it in so you could sound smart to your friends.) For now, you don't care so much what the section is called; you just want to get through it. The following information presents an overview of the types of passages you may encounter, the best approach to each distinct type of passage, and tips and traps for answering the questions based on those passages. Start by seeing what a Reading Comp question looks like.

Which of the following best describes the tone of the passage?

(A) sarcastic

(B) ebullient

(C) objective

(D) saddened

(E) mendacious

All questions can be answered from information stated or implied in the passage. You aren't expected to answer questions based on your own knowledge, and you don't need to know anything special about science or humanities to answer these questions.

The Three Commonly Tested Reading Passages

In their torture chambers over the years (would someone please call Amnesty International?), the test-makers have decided to write passages based on biological or physical sciences, social sciences, and humanities. The following sections offer a preview of the passages to help you separate the devastating from the merely intolerable.

Beam me up, Scotty! Biological and physical science passages

A science passage is straightforward, giving you information on how laser beams work, how to build a suspension bridge, how molecular theory applies, and so on. Although the passage itself may be very booooooooring to read (because it is full of just facts, facts, and more facts), this type of passage is often the easiest passage for people because it has so few tricks and traps.

Reading tip

Time to talk reality here: You're not going to remember — and maybe not even understand — what you read in a science passage. It's all just statistics and dry details. No matter how carefully and slowly you read through it the first time, you're almost certain to need to go back through the passage a second time to find specific facts. You end up reading the passage twice. Why waste time? Zip through the passage, just to get a general idea of what it's about and where the information is. (Paragraph one tells how molecules combine; paragraph two tells how scientists are working to split the atom; paragraph three tells. . . .) You may want to jot down a one-or-two-word note on your scratch paper to summarize each paragraph: Molecules. Atoms. Research. No need to waste time understanding every nuance if you can get the answer right by going back and finding the specific fact quickly.

Science Bonus: What happens if you swallow a molecule of uranium? You get atomic ache!

Science passages are best for slow readers because you're not really *reading* the passages; you're skimming them. You don't have to understand what you read; just identify some key words.

Question tip

You can often answer science questions directly from the facts provided in the passage itself. They are rarely the inference type that requires you to read between the lines and really think about what the author is saying, what point he or she is trying to make, how she feels about the subject, and so on. Here's an example:

The author states that spices were used

   I. to improve the taste of food.

   II. for medicinal purposes.

   III. to preserve food before refrigeration.

   IV. as a substitute for cash.

  (A) I and III only

  (B) I, II, and IV only

  (C) I, II, and III only

  (D) II and III only

  (E) I, II, III, and IV

To answer the question, return to the passage and look for the specific answers — which should be easy to locate if you made those handy little notes during your first run-through (in this case, the notation may be *Purposes*).

It's not a disease: The social sciences passage

The GRE usually includes one social sciences passage. It may be about history, psychology, business, or a variety of other topics. In other words, the term *social sciences* is broad enough to include whatever the test-makers want it to include. The social sciences passage is often the most interesting passage you encounter. It may give you a perspective on history that you didn't know or provide insight into psychology or sociology that you can use to manipulate your friends. (Who says the GRE is useless?)

Reading tip

In many ways, social sciences passages are nearly the opposite of science passages. The questions here deal more with inferences and less with explicitly stated facts. Therefore, you must read the passages slowly and carefully, trying to understand not only what is said but also what is implied. Think about what you are reading.

Question tip

The questions that follow social sciences passages may not be as straightforward as those for a biological or physical science passage. You may not be able to go back to a specific line and pick out a specific fact. Instead, these questions ask you to understand the big picture, to comprehend what the author meant but didn't come right out and say. You may be asked why an author included a particular example or explanation. In other words, you're expected to be a mind reader. Whip out that crystal ball. Here's an example:

The author's primary motive in discussing Dr. Buttinski's theory was to

  (A) impress the reader with Dr. Buttinski's importance.

  (B) show that Dr. Buttinski overcame great odds to become a psychologist.

  (C) ridicule Dr. Buttinski's adversaries who disagreed with the theory.

  (D) predict great things for Dr. Buttinski's future.

  (E) evaluate the effect Dr. Buttinski's theory has had on our everyday lives.

Determining the author's motive involves as much reasoning as reading. No sentence specifically says: "Okay, listen up, troops. I'm going to tell you something, and my motive for doing so is blah, blah, blah." You need to read the passage slowly enough to develop an idea of why the author is telling you something and what exactly he or she wants you to take from this passage. Going back and rereading the passage doesn't do you much good; thinking about what you read does.

In the sample question provided here, every answer given probably would be true in the context of the passage itself. That is, the author probably thought Dr. Buttinski was important, probably believed that Dr. Buttinski had to overcome great odds to be a psychologist, and so on. Keep in mind, however, what the question is asking: *Why* did the author mention this specific thing? You must probe the author's mind.

Gimme a break, I'm only human: The humanities passages

Humanities passages may be about humans (well, duh!) or about art, music, philosophy, drama, or literature. The passages are usually positive, especially if they talk about a person who was a pioneer in his or her field such as the first African-American astronaut or the first female doctor. Think about this logically: If the GRE bothers with writing about someone, that someone must have been pretty darn great or done something noteworthy. Keep this sense of admiration, even awe, in mind as you answer the questions related to the passage.

Reading tip

Have fun with the passage. This is the only passage you may actually enjoy reading. You don't need to zoom through it to finish before you fall asleep as you have to with the science passages. You don't need to read it carefully for between-the-lines understanding as you must read the social sciences passages. You can read this passage normally. Pretend that you are reading an article in *People* magazine, for example.

Question tip

Although the humanities passages don't require meticulous between-the-lines reading, the questions are another matter. The questions following a humanities passage often require you to get into the mind of the author, to read between the lines and make inferences. While reading a passage about a particular person, for example, you are supposed to ascertain not just what the person accomplished but why he worked toward his goals and what mark he hoped to leave on the world. Here's an example:

It can be inferred from the passage that Ms. Whitecloud would be most likely to agree with which of the following statements?

(A) A good divorce attorney must take the broader view and in effect represent the marriage itself rather than either of the spouses.

(B) The job of a divorce attorney is similar to that of a psychologist, attempting to ascertain why the marriage failed and address that issue rather than just the legal issues.

(C) The most important function of a divorce attorney is to protect the interests of the children of the marriage.

(D) A divorce attorney's job is merely to represent the legal interests of his or her client and does not include becoming a "friend" to the spouses.

(E) A divorce attorney represents his or her success by how quickly the divorce is accomplished.

All or Nothing: Questions to Take Seriously; Questions to Laugh Off

Knowing how to approach the GRE Reading Comprehension passages is extremely important. Even more important than the passages themselves, however, are the questions following each passage. After all, the admissions officer at Harvard is not going to say to you, "Hey, tell me about that GRE passage you read about the curative properties of heavy metal music." The admissions officer is far more likely to ask, "How many questions did you answer correctly on the Reading Comprehension portion?" No matter how carefully you read the passage, no matter how well you understand it, you must be able to put that knowledge to work to answer the questions that follow those passages.

So just what kind of questions are you most likely to encounter in the Reading Comprehension portions of the test? The following sections describe the several basic question types you may face in the dark alleys of the GRE.

It's the attitude, dude: The attitude or tone question

The author's attitude may be described as . . .

The tone of the passage is . . .

These two questions are variations on a single theme. What is the tone of the passage or the attitude of the author? Nothing in the passage answers this type of question directly. You can't find any one line reading: "In my opinion, which, by the way, is sardonic, the importance of. . . ." You simply must reason this one out.

Table 9-1 lists the tone or attitude likely found in each type of reading passage.

Table 9-1	**Predominant Tones or Attitudes Found in GRE Reading Passages**	
Passage Type	*Tone or Attitude*	*Explanation*
Physical or biological sciences	Neutral or positive	A physical or biological science passage gives you just the facts. The author rarely evaluates the facts one way or the other and rarely expresses an opinion. After all, how opinionated can someone be about a color spectrum?
Social sciences	Positive or neutral	A social sciences passage may be about how some event unfolded or how some theory was developed. For example, a passage may talk about history, presenting the good events and downplaying the bad ones. Think positive, or at the very worst, neutral.
Humanities	Positive or neutral	If the passage is about an individual, it is probably positive, saying good and respectful things about that person and his or her accomplishments. If it is about the other topics of humanities, such as art, music, philosophy, drama, and literature, it may be either positive or neutral. Only very rarely does a humanities passage have a negative tone.

Do you notice a pattern here? Everything is either neutral or positive, positive or neutral. Because so many of the tones or attitudes of the Reading Comprehension passages are positive or neutral, certain words are often good to choose as answers to attitude or tone questions. With neutral passages, the term *objective* (which means neutral, not taking one side or the other, not subjective or opinionated) is often a correct answer. Don't simply turn off your own brain and choose *objective* automatically, of course, but it's a good guess if you're stumped for an answer. Think of a passage as neutral until proven otherwise.

The following list offers several common positive words. Each word is followed by a more unfamiliar term that has the same meaning:

Common Positive-Attitude Word	More-Difficult Word with the Same Meaning
Optimistic	Sanguine
Praising	Laudatory
Admiring	Reverential

You get the idea. Wrong answers — that is, negative answers — may include the words in the following list. ***Remember:*** These are words that you usually don't want to choose.

Common Negative-Attitude Word	More-Difficult Word with the Same Meaning
Ridiculing	Lampooning
Sarcastic	Sardonic
Belittling	Denigrating

The answer choices to an attitude or tone question often use quite difficult vocabulary. If you know from reading the passage that the author is delighted with something, which of the following would you choose to describe his attitude: *phlegmatic, dogmatic, ebullient, cantankerous,* or *lethargic?* The right answer is ***ebullient,*** which means bubbling over with enthusiasm or excitement — but how many people know that word? I mean, it's not as if your best friend asks you, "So, how are you today?" and your immediate response is, "Well, I'm ebullient, thanks; and you?" If you don't know the vocabulary in the answer choices, *quickly* make a wild guess and go on. It can be very frustrating to do so, because you know what kind of word you are looking for, but when you can't define the answer choices, all you're doing is wasting time. Guess and go.

What's the big idea: Main idea or best title

You can bet the farm (but, of course, only in states with legalized gambling) that you'll see a few main idea or best title questions; each Reading Comprehension passage usually has one. This type of question can assume any of the following forms:

> The main idea of the passage is . . .

> The primary purpose of the author is . . .

> The best title for the passage is . . .

The best place to find the main idea of the passage is in its topic sentence, which is usually the first or second sentence of the first paragraph. The topic sentence *may* be the last sentence of the passage, but such a structure is rare. Your game plan upon encountering one of these questions should be to head right back to the first or second sentence to locate a main idea.

Suppose that the passage begins as follows:

> The uses to which latex has been applied have exceeded the wildest fantasies of its creators.

What is the main idea of the passage: The uses of latex? The applications of latex? The many products made of latex?

After you've read the entire passage, all the darn answers in the main idea question may look pretty good. That's because they usually consist of facts stated in the passage. Just because something is true and just because it is discussed in the passage doesn't mean it's necessarily the main idea.

Really try or fly right by: How much time is it worth?

The main idea or best title question is worth a few minutes of your time. Go back and reread the first few sentences. Even if you don't have time to read the entire passage — or even get started on it — you can often hustle up an answer to this question by glancing at one sentence.

Because Reading Comprehension passages are almost always positive or neutral, the main idea/best title is almost always positive or neutral, too. Eliminate any negative answer choices right away.

The main idea of this passage is

(A) the submission and shame of the Native Americans.

(B) the unfair treatment of Native Americans.

(C) how Native Americans are taking charge of their own destinies.

(D) why Native Americans fail.

(E) the causes behind Native-American problems.

Because all the answers but C are negative, choose C. Humanities passages are often about people who have beaten the odds: inspirational pioneers and leaders. The passage is certain to be very admiring of those people. *Correct Answer:* C.

Don't pester me with details: The detail or fact question

One type of question very straightforwardly asks you about information explicitly stated in the passage. If a question begins with the phrase "According to the passage . . ." you've hit a detail or fact question — which is usually a very easy question to answer correctly. All you need to do is identify the key words in the question, return to the reading passage, and skim for those words. The answer is usually within a few sentences of those key words. Take a look at a few question examples:

> According to the passage, what two elements make up Drake's Elixir?

The key words are *Drake's Elixir.* Go back to the passage and find the exact answer.

According to the passage, why did Mr. Sanchez win a medal during the war?

The key words in this question are *Mr. Sanchez, medal,* and *war.* Go back to the passage and find the exact answer.

"According to the author" is not the same thing as "According to the passage." The two phrases may look the same, but author questions are often more difficult than passage questions and are not as straightforward. A question that asks you about the author may be more of a read-between-the-lines question than one about the passage — something you can answer only if you truly understand what you read. An "according to the passage" question, on the other hand, can often be answered even without reading the whole passage by skimming for the key words.

The power of positive thinking: Negative or exception questions

One type of GRE question is a trained killer: the negative or exception question. Here are a few ways this question may be worded:

Which of the following is *not* true?

Which of the following is *least* likely?

With which of the following would the author *disagree?*

All of the following are true *except* . . .

The questions are phrased in the negative, which makes them very tricky. You are actually looking for four correct answers and then by the process of elimination choosing the one that is not correct. It's easy to get confused and even easier to waste a lot of time. This is a good question to laugh off, to guess at randomly.

Toga! Toga! Toga! The Roman numeral question

A Roman numeral question looks like this:

The author mentions which of the following as support for her argument against unilateral intervention?

    I. economic considerations

    II. moral obligations

    III. popular opinion

(A) I only

(B) II only

(C) III only

(D) I and II only

(E) I, II, and III

Roman numeral questions are usually time-wasters. In effect, you have to go back and reread almost the whole passage to find whether I, II, or III was mentioned anywhere. A common trap is to find I and II mentioned close together and then have III mentioned far down the passage. Most people find I and II and then when III doesn't appear to be hanging around, choose I and II only, going down the tubes. (Hey, maybe the test-makers get bonus points for every student they snare with a trick, rather like a cop writing speeding tickets to meet his quota in a speed trap. Just a thought.) With a Roman numeral question, you have to make a commitment (did I just lose half my male readers?). You have to commit to rereading most of the passage just in case one of the concepts is floating around where you least expect it. If you are not willing (or able) to commit the time, forget about the question. Just make a random guess and go on.

Bonus: What do you call a pig who won't make a commitment? A hedge hog!

The Swing Vote: Extending the Author's Reasoning

You've learned which questions you should always do carefully and which questions you should usually guess at. The GRE has one more type of question that, although it has become increasingly rare, you need to be prepared to meet. This type of question asks you to extend the author's reasoning to another situation. The GRE may give a situation that is analogous, or similar to, the one described in the Reading Comprehension passage and then ask you to determine how the author's reasoning would or would not work in the new situation. The tone or attitude of this type of passage may be positive, neutral, or negative. Here's an example:

Which of the following would the author most likely feel would be a valid issue to appear on a referendum, based on his argument in the preceding passage?

(A) the right to die

(B) term limits for members of Congress

(C) expansion of the powers of the judiciary

(D) increased student involvement in college application processes

(E) tax rate increases

This type of question may be ridiculously easy or annoyingly difficult. If you understand the passage well and understand the author's reasoning, this question is simple. Sometimes you can answer this question without understanding the entire passage, as long as you have some general idea of the author's purpose in writing the passage.

Don't immediately choose an answer just because it refers to the topic discussed in the passage. For example, the passage may be about education. The trap answer to the previous question would be choice D. However, you are asked to extend the author's reasoning to an *analogous* situation. The situation can be about the right to die or about congressional term limits or about anything else.

Something up My Sleeve: Tricks for Making Life a Little Easier

Now that you know about the types of passages and primary types of questions, it's time for the fun stuff: the tricks.

Reading passages you'll never see on the GRE

- ✔ **Biological Science:** Cannibalism and You: The Science of Pigging Out at a Barbecue

- ✔ **Social Science (Psychology):** The End of Political Correctness: An Analysis of Howard Stern and Rush Limbaugh

- ✔ **Social Science (Behaviorism):** An excerpt from *Confessions from the Funny Farm,* Chapter Two: How the GRE Pushed Me over the Edge

- ✔ **Humanities:** The Developer of the Prefrontal Lobotomy: "Inspiration struck while I was studying for the GRE," says Famous Surgeon

---

Be positive or neutral, not negative

I will say this over and over until you are exasperated enough to cut off my air supply. Because most of the passages are positive or neutral, most of the correct answers are positive or neutral. Because the test-makers don't want to get sued for saying mean and vicious things about anyone, these men and women are generally sweet and charming (and probably go home, kick the dog, and evict a few widows and orphans just to get pent-up frustrations out of their systems after having to be so nice at work all day long). Be sweet and charming right back at 'em; choose positive, goody-goody answer choices.

Choose answers containing key words

The key words, often found in the topic sentence, are what the whole passage is about. The right answers usually feature those words. If the passage is about Chicano history, the right answer often has the words *Chicano history* in it. Don't immediately choose an answer *only* because it has the key words in it, but if you can narrow the answers down to two, choose the one with the key words.

Be wishy-washy, not dramatic

The test-makers realize that people have different points of view. They don't want to be *dogmatic* (narrow-minded), saying, "This is the right way, the only way. Zip your lip and don't argue." They want to hedge their bets, leave some space for personal interpretation. And, of course, they don't want to get sued. If you have two answers, choose the more moderate or wishy-washy of the two. Wimp out big-time.

Suppose that you have narrowed the answer choices to two:

(A) The author hates discrimination.

(B) The author is saddened by the discrimination and tries to understand its causes.

Choice B is the kinder, gentler, wimpier answer and would probably be correct.

Eponymous words

An **eponym** is a word derived from the name of a person. For example, the cardigan sweater got its name from the Earl of Cardigan (who would probably much rather be remembered for the garment than for his other claim to fame: He was the leader of the Light Brigade). Here are a few eponyms to add to your GRE vocabulary.

bowdlerize: To omit indecent words or phrases in a book or piece of writing (you bowdlerize a love letter before you let your roommate read it). Dr. Thomas Bowdler, an English physician, published in 1818 a ten-volume edition of Shakespeare's plays called The Family Shakespeare. He left out all the dirty parts. For example, instead of "Out, damn'd spot!" the line reads, "Out, crimson spot!"

boycott: You would think that Mr. Boycott started the practice of boycotting, wouldn't you? Just the opposite: He was the victim of the first boycott. Charles Boycott was a retired English Army captain who refused to lower rents to his farmer tenants after a few bad harvests and was accused of exploiting the poor. The locals harassed him, stealing his crops and refusing to sell his products in their stores, until he was hounded out of the county. Today, when you refuse to have anything to do with someone, you are said to boycott him.

Draconian: Extremely harsh and severe. When you tell your professor that dropping your grade one whole letter just because you turned in a report one day late is truly Draconian, you are harking all the way back to about 620 B.C. Draco was an Athenian who wrote a code of laws that made nearly every crime punishable by death, even laziness and, uh, urinating in public. The word Draconian came to apply to any laws that were just too darn cruel or strict.

maverick: An individualist, an unconventional person. Samuel Maverick, who lived during the 1800s, was a Texas rancher whose unbranded cattle roamed free. Maverick's neighbors refused to hand back his strays, claiming that because they were unbranded, there was no proof they were his. The word eventually evolved into meaning anything "without a brand," or unusual or unique.

Quisling: A traitor. Vidkun Quisling was a Norwegian politician who turned traitor in World War II, siding with Hitler. He was shot by a firing squad at the end of the war, but his name lives on to torment GRE-takers.

simony: The buying or selling of religious or sacred objects or privileges. Simon Magus (who is often described as a "reformed wizard"— great job description!) offered St. Peter and St. John money to give him their religious abilities. The word simony was especially popular in the Middle Ages, when people would sell pardons, indulgences, and the like.

Bonus! You probably already know these words, but did you know they are eponyms, too?

diesel: A type of engine, named for Rudolf Diesel, a German engineer.

mausoleum: A large tomb or memorial, named for King Mausolus, King of Calia in ancient Greece about 370 B.C.

nicotine: The (possibly) addictive stuff in tobacco, named for French diplomat Jean Nicot.

saxophone: A musical instrument, invented by and named after Adolphe Sax, a Belgian musician of the early to mid 1800s.

shrapnel: Fragments thrown out by a shell or a bomb, invented in 1802 by Lieutenant General Henry Shrapnel, an English army officer.

silhouette: Profile or shadow of a face, named after Etienne de Silhouette (1709–1767), a French finance minister.

The Final Paragraph: Review

You've picked up a lot in this chapter. Take a moment to review the key points before you jump into the practice exam in Chapter 10.

Approaches

- ✔ Identify the type of reading passage: biological and physical science, social sciences, humanities.

- ✔ Identify the type of question (for example, main idea or best title, detail or fact, negative or exception, Roman numeral, extending the author's reasoning) and decide how much time to invest in it.

Tricks

- ✔ Be positive or neutral, not negative.
- ✔ Choose answers containing key words.
- ✔ Be wishy-washy, not dramatic.

Chapter 10

Practice What I Preach: Reading Comprehension Practice Questions

● ●

*T*his section features two reading passages and nine questions. For now, don't worry about timing yourself. Try to identify each selection as one of the types of reading passages described in Chapter 9 (science, humanities, and so on) and use the tips I gave you for reading that type of passage. As you answer the questions, try to identify whether each question is attitude/tone, main idea/best title, Roman numeral, and so on and then try to recall any traps inherent to that type of question.

Passage 1

Line   Microbiological activity clearly affects the mechanical strength of leaves. Although it cannot be denied that with most species the loss of mechanical strength is the result of both invertebrate feeding and microbiological breakdown, the example of *Fagus sylvatica* illustrates loss without any sign of invertebrate attack being evident. *Fagus* shows little
(05) sign of invertebrate attack even after being exposed for eight months in either lake or stream environment, but results of the rolling fragmentation experiment show that loss of mechanical strength, even in this apparently resistant species, is considerable.

    Most species appear to exhibit a higher rate of degradation in the stream environment than in the lake. This is perhaps most clearly shown in the case of *Alnus*. Examination of
(10) the type of destruction suggests that the cause for the greater loss of material in the stream-processed leaves is a combination of both biological and mechanical degradation. The leaves exhibit an angular fragmentation, which is characteristic of mechanical damage, rather than the rounded holes typical of the attack by large particle feeders or the skeletal vein pattern produced by microbial degradation and small particle feeders. As the leaves
(15) become less strong, the fluid forces acting on the stream nylon cages caused successively greater fragmentation.

    Mechanical fragmentation, like biological breakdown, is to some extent influenced by leaf structure and form. In some leaves with a strong midrib, the lamina break up, but the pieces remain attached by means of the midrib. One type of leaf may break cleanly while
(20) another tears off and is easily destroyed once the tissues are weakened by microbial attack.

    In most species, the mechanical breakdown will take the form of gradual attrition at the margins. If the energy of the environment is sufficiently high, brittle species may be broken across the midrib, something that rarely happens with more pliable leaves. The result of attrition is that where the areas of the whole leaves follow a normal distribution, a bimodal
(25) distribution is produced; one peak composed mainly of the fragmented pieces, the other of the larger remains.

To test the theory that a thin leaf has only half the chance of a thick one for entering the fossil record, all other things being equal, Ferguson (1971) cut discs of fresh leaves from 11 species of leaves, each with a different thickness, and rotated them with sand and water in a
(30) revolving drum. Each run lasted 100 hours and was repeated three times, but even after this treatment, all species showed little sign of wear. It therefore seems unlikely that leaf thickness alone, without substantial microbial preconditioning, contributes much to the probability that a leaf will enter a depositional environment in a recognizable form. The results of experiments with whole fresh leaves show that they are more resistant to fragmentation than
(35) leaves exposed to microbiological attack. Unless the leaf is exceptionally large or small, leaf size and thickness are not likely to be as critical in determining the preservation potential of a leaf type as the rate of microbiological degradation.

1. Which of the following would be the best title for the passage?

    (A) Why Leaves Disintegrate

    ✓ (B) An Analysis of Leaf Structure and Composition

    (C) Comparing Lakes and Streams

    (D) The Purpose of Particle Feeders

    ✓ (E) How Leaves' Mechanical Strength Is Affected by Microbiological Activity

The main idea, main purpose, or best title is found in the topic sentence, which is usually the first sentence of the passage. The correct answer here is taken nearly word-for-word from the first sentence. Note that because the passage is talking primarily about leaves, that word needs to be in the title, which eliminates choices C and D right off. Choice A is too broad; there may be other causes of disintegration that the passage doesn't mention. Choice B is too specific. The passage mentions leaf structure but doesn't make that topic its primary focus. *Correct Answer:* E.

2. Which of the following is mentioned as a reason for leaf degradation in streams?

    I. mechanical damage

    II. biological degradation

    III. large particle feeders

    (A) II only

    (B) I and II only

    (C) I and III only

    (D) II and III only

    (E) I, II, and III

Paragraph two of the passage tells you that ". . . loss of material in stream-processed leaves is a combination of biological and mechanical degradation." Statement III is incorrect, because lines 12 and 13 specifically state that the pattern of holes is contrary to that of large particle feeders. *Correct Answer:* B.

3. The conclusion the author reached from Ferguson's revolving drum experiment was that

    (A) leaf thickness is only a contributing factor to leaf fragmentation.

    (B) leaves submersed in water degrade more rapidly than leaves deposited in mud or silt.

    (C) leaves with a strong midrib deteriorate less than leaves without such a midrib.

    (D) microbial attack is exacerbated by high temperatures.

    (E) bimodal distribution reduces leaf attrition.

Lines 31–33 tell you that it's unlikely that leaf thickness *alone* affects the final form of the leaf. You probably need to reread that sentence a few times to understand it, but this is the type of question you should take the time to be sure you answer correctly — a detail or fact question. Choice B introduces facts not discussed in the passage; there was no talk of leaves in mud or silt. Choice C is mentioned in the passage but not in Ferguson's experiments. Be careful to answer *only* what the question is asking; the mere fact that a statement is true or is mentioned in the passage means nothing if the question isn't asking about that point. Nothing appears in the passage about high temperatures, which eliminates choice D. (Did you know the word *exacerbated*? It means made worse — like this reading passage probably exacerbated your headache.) Choice E sounds pretentious and pompous — and nice and scientific — but again has nothing to do with Ferguson. To answer this question correctly, you need to return to the passage to look up Ferguson specifically, not merely rely on your memory of the passage as a whole. *Correct Answer:* A.

4. The tone of the passage is

   (A) mesmerizing.

   (B) biased.

   (C) objective.

   (D) argumentative.

   (E) disparaging.

You *had* to get this question correct. If you missed this question, please consider yourself totally humiliated. *Correct Answer:* C.

Most of the time, a science passage has a neutral, objective, unbiased tone. The author neither praises nor criticizes anything; he or she just gives the facts. *Biased* means prejudiced, having an opinion one way or the other, and is just the opposite of the correct answer. GRE passages are rarely argumentative, especially science passages. If you chose A or E, you let your insecurities get the better of you: "Oooh, big hard word. I don't know it. It must be the right answer!" *Mesmerizing* means hypnotic or captivating. You probably weren't held spellbound by this passage (if you were, hey, get a life!). By the way, do you know who Franz Mesmer was? He was called "the father of hypnotism." What we now know as hypnotism used to be called Mesmerism after Franz. (No extra charge for the fascinating facts.) In choice E, *disparaging* means in a degrading manner, speaking slightingly of. Disparaging is a negative answer, and as Chapter 9 says, GRE passages are rarely negative in tone.

5. The author most likely is addressing this passage to

   (A) gardeners.

   (B) botanists.

   (C) hikers.

   (D) mechanical engineers.

   (E) Adam and Eve.

The passage is talking about the microbiological activity affecting the strength of leaves. (You know this because you already answered a best title question on the topic — question number 1.) Although choosing D is tempting, given the topic of the passage, mechanical engineers are usually interested more in machines than in leaves. Botanists are the ones who would most likely read this passage. The advice is probably too technical for gardeners, choice A, and is waaaay too specific for hikers, choice C. Choice E was added for comic relief. (If anyone needed to know how and why leaves disintegrate, especially fig leaves, it would be Adam and Eve.) *Correct Answer:* B.

Passage 11

Line   Multinational corporations frequently encounter impediments in their attempts to explain to politicians, human rights groups, and (perhaps most importantly) their consumer base why they do business with, even seek closer business ties to, countries whose human rights records are considered heinous by United States standards. The CEOs propound that

(05) in the business trenches, the issue of human rights must effectively be detached from the wider spectrum of free trade. Discussion of the uneasy alliance between trade and human rights has trickled down from the boardrooms of large multinational corporations to the consumer on the street who, given the wide variety of products available to him, is eager to show support for human rights by boycotting the products of a company he feels does

(10) not do enough to help its overseas workers. International human rights organizations also are pressuring the multinationals to push for more humane working conditions in other countries and to in effect develop a code of business conduct that must be adhered to if the American company is to continue working with the overseas partner.

    The president, in drawing up a plan for what he calls the "economic architecture of our

(15) times," wants economists, business leaders, and human rights groups to work together to develop a set of principles that the foreign partners of United States corporations will voluntarily embrace. Human rights activists, incensed at the nebulous plans for implementing such rules, charge that their agenda is being given low priority by the State Department. The president vociferously denies their charges, arguing that each situation is approached

(20) on its merits without prejudice, and hopes that all the groups can work together to develop principles based on empirical research rather than political fiat, emphasizing that the businesses with experience in the field must initiate the process of developing such guidelines. Business leaders, while paying lip service to the concept of these principles, fight stealthily against their formal endorsement as they fear such "voluntary" concepts may someday be

(25) given the force of law. Few business leaders have forgotten the Sullivan Principles, in which a set of voluntary rules regarding business conduct with South Africa (giving benefits to workers and banning apartheid in the companies that worked with U.S. partners) became legislation.

6. Which of the following best states the central idea of the passage?

   (A) Politicians are quixotic in their assessment of the priorities of the State Department.

   (B) Multinational corporations have little if any influence on the domestic policies of their overseas partners.

   (C) Voluntary principles that are turned into law are unconstitutional.

   (D) Disagreement exists between the desires of human rights activists to improve the working conditions of overseas workers and the pragmatic approach taken by the corporations.

   (E) It is inappropriate to expect foreign corporations to adhere to American standards.

The main idea of the passage is usually stated in the first sentence or two. The first sentence of this passage discusses the difficulties that corporations have explaining their business ties to certain countries to politicians, human rights groups, and consumers. From this statement, you may infer that those groups disagree with the policies of the corporations. *Correct Answer:* D.

In choice A, do you know the word *quixotic?* It means idealistic or impractical (think of the fictional character Don Quixote tilting at windmills). Although the president in this passage may not be realistic in his assessment of State Department policies, his belief is not the main idea of the passage.

Just because a statement is (or may be) true does not necessarily mean it's the correct answer to a question. The answer choices to a main idea question in particular often are correct or at least look plausible.

To answer a main idea question, I like to pretend that a friend of mine just came up behind me and said, "Hey, what 'cha reading there?" My first response is the main idea: "Oh, I read this passage about how corporations are getting grief from politicians and other groups because they do business with certain countries." *Before* you look at the answer choices, predict in your own words what the main idea is. You'll be pleasantly surprised at how close your prediction is to the correct answer (and you won't be confused by all the other plausible-looking answer choices).

Choice E is a moral value, a judgment call. An answer that passes judgment, one that says something is morally right or morally wrong, is almost never the correct answer.

7. According to the passage, the president wants the voluntary principles to be initiated by businesses rather than by politicians or human rights activists because

   (A) businesses have empirical experience in the field and thus know what the conditions are and how they may/should be remedied.

   (B) businesses make profits from the labor of the workers and thus have a moral obligation to improve their employees' working conditions.

   (C) workers will not accept principles drawn up by politicians whom they distrust but may agree to principles created by the corporations that pay them.

   (D) foreign nations are distrustful of U.S. political intervention and are more likely to accept suggestions from multinational corporations.

   (E) political activist groups have concerns that are too dramatically different from those of the corporations for the groups to be able to work together.

When a question begins with the words "according to the passage," you need to go back to the passage and find the exact answer. In lines 21–22, you are told that ". . . businesses with experience in the field must initiate the process of developing such guidelines." Great — but what if you don't know the word *empirical*, which means based on experiment or experience rather than on theory? Keep reading. The rest of the sentence divulges the right answer. Don't tune out as soon as you encounter a difficult word.

Choices B, C, D, and E are all judgment calls. You are assuming facts not in evidence, as the lawyers say. Although you personally may believe the statements in these answer choices to be true, they don't answer the specific question. *Correct Answer:* A.

8. Which of the following best describes the reason the author mentions the boycott of a corporation's products by its customers?

   (A) to show the difficulties that arise when corporations attempt to become involved in politics

   (B) to predict the inevitability of failure of any plan that does not involve customer input

   (C) to disagree with the president's contention that big business is the best qualified to draw up the voluntary principles of workplace conduct

   (D) to indicate the pressures that are on the multinational corporations

   (E) to ridicule the consumers for believing that their small boycott would significantly affect the sales of a multinational corporation

This question is one of those mind-reading questions that I warned you about. You are expected to get into the author's mind and understand why he or she said what he or she did. The concept of the consumer boycott follows closely the main idea of the passage, which is that the corporations have difficulty trying to explain themselves and their actions to all sorts of groups, including their customers. From this, you may infer that the point of the statement is to indicate the pressures placed on the corporations.

The next line in the passage states that human rights organizations *also* are pressuring multinational corporations, leading you to infer that the consumers are applying pressure. Remember that one of your tips is to expand your horizons. Read until you find what you think is the right answer . . . and then read a little further.

Choices C and E begin with negative words, *disagree* and *ridicule*. Negative answer choices are rarely correct. Be careful, however, not to take this tip as a hard and fast rule. If you go back to the correct answer to Question 6, you can see that you may interpret that answer as negative.

Choice B seems logical; common sense tells you that a company that ignores its customers will probably fail. However, a strong, dramatic word like *inevitably* is rarely correct. Few things in life are inevitable, as I've said before: just death, taxes, and the GRE. *Correct Answer:* D.

9. Which of the following statements about the Sullivan Principles can best be inferred from the passage?

   (A) They had a detrimental effect on the profits of those corporations doing business with South Africa.

   (B) They represented an improper alliance between political and business groups.

   (C) They placed the needs of the foreign workers over those of the domestic workers whose jobs would therefore be in jeopardy.

   (D) They will be used as a model to create future voluntary business guidelines.

   (E) They will have a chilling effect on future adoption of voluntary guidelines.

Choice A is the major trap here. Perhaps you assumed that because the companies seem to dislike the Sullivan Principles, they hurt company profits. However, nothing was said in the passage about profits. Maybe the companies still made good profits but objected to the Sullivan Principles, well, on principle. The companies just may not have wanted such governmental intervention even if profits weren't decreased. If you chose A, you read too much into the question and probably didn't read the rest of the answer choices.

In choice E, the words *chilling effect* mean negative effect, discouraging effect. Think of something with a chilling effect as leaving you cold. If your friend asks you to taste some soup because the dog loved it when he lapped up a few swallows, the statement about canine cuisine can have a chilling effect on your desire to taste the soup. Because few corporations have forgotten the Sullivan Principles, you may infer that these principles may discourage the companies from agreeing to voluntary principles in the future. *Correct Answer:* E.

In order to get this question correct, you really need to understand the whole passage. If you didn't know what was going on here, you would be better off to just guess and go. An inference question usually means you have to read between the lines; you can't just go back to one specific portion of the passage and get the answer quickly.

Part III

Two Years of Math in 60 Pages: The Dreaded Math Review

In this part . . .

No, no, please don't go get your pillow and PJs. I promise that this math review won't put you to sleep. I'm not going to start at $1 + 1 = 2$ and take you through every math concept you've learned since kindergarten; I have more respect for you than that. This math review neither insults you nor wastes your time. Here, I keep the instruction down to what you really need for the GRE.

If you've been out of school for a while, don't despair. After you go through the math review, do as many of the math problems as you can. The answer explanations review the formulas and concepts again and again and again; some of them are bound to come back to you.

Chapter 11

More Figures Than a Beauty Pageant: Geometry Review

In This Chapter

▶ Angles
▶ Triangles
▶ Similar figures
▶ Area problems
▶ Quadrilaterals and other polygons
▶ Shaded area problems
▶ Circles

*Q*uestion: How can you learn geometry?

Answer: Do it by degrees!

You Gotta Have an Angle

Angles are a big part of the GRE geometry problems. Fortunately, understanding angles is easy after you memorize a few basic concepts. And keep in mind the best news: You don't have to do proofs. Finding an angle is usually a matter of simple addition or subtraction. These three rules generally apply to the GRE:

> ✔ There are *no negative angles.*
>
> ✔ There are *no zero angles.*
>
> ✔ It is extremely unlikely that you'll see any fractional angles. (For example, an angle won't measure 45½ degrees or 32¾ degrees.)

Angles are whole numbers. If you're plugging in a number for an angle, plug in a whole number, such as 30, 45, or 90.

1. **Angles greater than zero but less than 90 degrees are called *acute.*** Think of an acute angle as being a cute little angle.

45°
Acute

2. **Angles equal to 90 degrees are called *right angles*.** They are formed by perpendicular lines and are indicated by a box in the corner of the two intersecting lines.

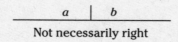

Right

A GRE trap is to have two lines appear to be perpendicular and look as if they form a right angle. Do not assume this to be true. An angle is a right angle *only* if (A) you're expressly told, "This is a right angle"; (B) you see the perpendicular symbol (⊥) indicating that the lines form a 90-degree angle; or (C) you see the box in the angle. Otherwise, you may be headed for a trap!

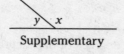

Not necessarily right

3. **Angles that sum up to 90 degrees are called *complementary angles*.**

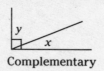

Complementary

Think of *C* for corner (the lines form a 90-degree corner angle) and *C* for complementary.

4. **An angle that is greater than 90 degrees but less than 180 degrees is called *obtuse*.** Think of obtuse as *obese;* an obese (or fat) angle is an obtuse angle.

Obtuse

5. **An angle that measures exactly 180 degrees is called a *straight angle*.**

180°

Straight

6. **Angles that sum up to 180 degrees are called *supplementary angles*.**

Supplementary

Think of *S* for straight angles and *S* for supplementary angles. Be careful not to confuse complementary angles (*C* for complementary; *C* for corner) with supplementary angles (*S* for supplementary; *S* for straight). If you're likely to get these confused, just think alphabetically. *C* comes before *S* in the alphabet; 90 comes before 180 when you count.

7. **An angle that is greater than 180 degrees but less than 360 degrees is called a *reflex angle*.**

320°

Reflex angle

Think of a reflex angle as the rest of the cake from which one slice (the acute angle) has been removed. It makes up the rest of the circle when there's an acute angle.

Reflex angles are rarely tested on the GRE.

8. Angles around a point total 360 degrees.

360 degrees

9. First define the point formed where lines cross. Then angles that are opposite each other have equal measures and are called *vertical angles*.

Note that vertical angles may actually be horizontal. Just remember that vertical angles are across the vertex from each other, whether they are up and down (vertical) or side by side (horizontal).

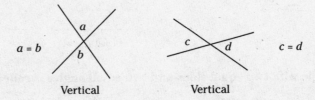

$a = b$ Vertical   Vertical $c = d$

10. Angles in the same position (corresponding angles) formed by two parallel lines and a *transversal* (a line that cuts through the two lines) have the same measures.

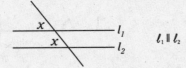

$\ell_1 \| \ell_2$

When you see two parallel lines and a transversal, number the angles. Start in the upper-right corner with 1 and go clockwise. For the second batch of angles, start in the upper-right corner with 5 and go clockwise:

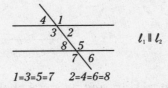

$\ell_1 \| \ell_2$

$1=3=5=7$ $2=4=6=8$

Note that all the odd-numbered angles are equal and all the even-numbered angles are equal.

Be careful not to zigzag back and forth when numbering, like this:

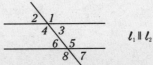

$\ell_1 \| \ell_2$

If you zig when you should have zagged, you can no longer use the tip that all even-numbered angles are equal to one another and all odd-numbered angles are equal to one another.

11. The exterior angles of any figure are supplementary to the interior angles and total 360 degrees.

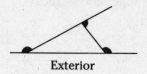

Exterior

Triangle Trauma

1. A triangle with three equal sides and three equal angles is called *equilateral* and *equiangular*.

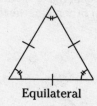

Equilateral

2. A triangle with two equal sides and two equal angles is called *isosceles*.

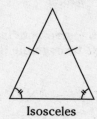

Isosceles

3. Angles opposite equal sides in an isosceles triangle are also equal.

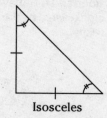

Isosceles

4. A triangle with no equal sides and no equal angles is called *scalene*.

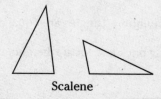

Scalene

5. In any triangle, the largest angle is opposite the longest side.

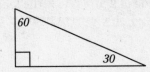

6. In any triangle, the sum of the lengths of two sides must be greater than the length of the third side. This is often written as $a + b > c$ where a, b, and c are the sides of the triangle.

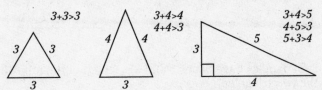

7. In any type of triangle, the sum of the interior angles is 180 degrees.

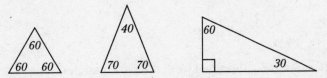

 Often a trap question wants you to assume that different-sized triangles have different angle measures. Wrong! A triangle can be seven stories high and have 180 degrees or be microscopic and have 180 degrees. The size of the triangle is irrelevant; every triangle's internal angles sum up to 180 degrees.

8. The measure of an exterior angle of a triangle is equal to the sum of the two remote interior angles.

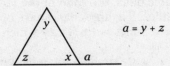

$$a = y + z$$

When you think about this rule logically, it makes sense. The sum of supplementary angles is 180. The sum of the angles in a triangle is 180. Therefore, angle $x = 180 - (y + z)$ or angle $x = 180 - a$. That must mean that $a = y + z$.

Similar figures

1. The sides of similar figures are in proportion. For example, if the heights of two similar triangles are in a ratio of 2:3, then the bases of those triangles are in a ratio of 2:3 as well.

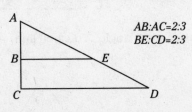

AB:AC=2:3
BE:CD=2:3

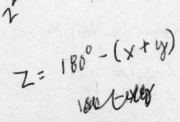

$$Z = 180° - (x + y)$$

2. **The ratio of the areas of similar figures is equal to the square of the ratio of their sides.** For example, if each side of figure A is ⅓ the length of each side of similar figure B, then the area of figure A is $\frac{1}{9}\left[(\frac{1}{3})^2\right]$ the area of figure B.

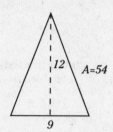

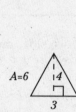

Two similar triangles have bases 5 and 25. Which of the following expresses the ratio of the areas of the two triangles?

(A) 1:5

(B) 1:15

(C) 1:25

(D) 2:15

(E) It cannot be determined from the information given.

The ratio of the sides is ⅕. The ratio of the areas is the square of the ratio of the sides: ⅕ × ⅕ = 1/25. Note that answer E is a trap for the unwary. You can't figure out the exact area of either figure because you don't know the height. (The area of a triangle is ½ *base* × *height*.) However, you aren't asked for an area, only for the ratio of the areas, which you can deduce from the formula discussed. *Correct Answer:* C.

Bonus: What do you suppose the ratio of the *volumes* of two similar figures is? Because volume is found in cubic units, **the ratio of the volumes of two similar figures is the cube of the ratio of their sides.** If figure A has a base of 5 and similar figure B has a base of 10, then the ratio of their volumes is 1:8 ($[1:2]^2$ which is ½ × ½ × ½ = ⅛).

Don't assume that figures are similar; you must be told that they are similar.

Area

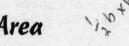

1. **The area of a triangle is ½ *base* × *height*.** The height is always a line perpendicular to the base. The height may be a side of the triangle, as in a right triangle.

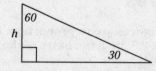

The height may be inside the triangle. A dashed line and a small 90-degree box often represent the height.

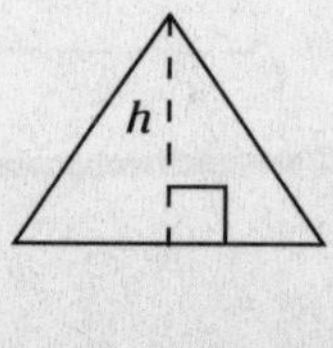

The height may be outside the triangle. This is very confusing and can be found in trick questions. You can always drop an altitude. That is, put your pencil on the tallest point of the triangle and draw a line straight from that point to the base or the extension of the base. The line can be outside the triangle.

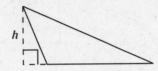

2. The perimeter of a triangle is the sum of the lengths of the sides.

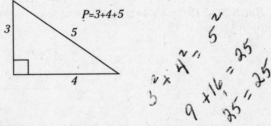

Pythagorean theorem

You have probably studied the Pythagorean theorem (known colloquially as PT). Keep in mind that it works only on *right* triangles. If a triangle doesn't have a right or 90-degree angle, you can't use any of the following information.

In any right triangle, you can find the lengths of the sides with the formula:

$$a^2 + b^2 = c^2$$

where a and b are the sides of the triangle and c is the hypotenuse. The *hypotenuse* is always opposite the 90-degree angle and is always the longest side of the triangle. Why? Because if one angle in a triangle is 90 degrees, no other angle can be more than 90 degrees. All the angles must total 180 degrees, and there are no negative or 0 angles. Because the longest side is opposite the largest angle, the hypotenuse is the longest side.

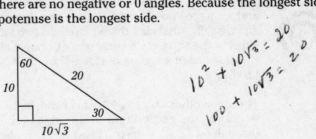

Pythagorean triples

It's a pain in the posterior to have to do the whole PT formula every time you want to find the length of a side. You'll find four very common PT ratios in triangles.

1. **Ratio 3:4:5:** In this ratio, if one side of the triangle is 3, the other side is 4, and the hypotenuse is 5.

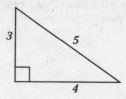

Because this is a ratio, the sides can be in any multiple of these numbers, such as 6:8:10 (twice 3:4:5), 9:12:15 (three times 3:4:5), or 27:36:45 (nine times 3:4:5).

2. **Ratio 5:12:13:** In this ratio, if one side of the triangle is 5, the other side is 12, and the hypotenuse is 13.

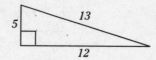

Because this is a ratio, the sides can be in any multiple of these numbers, such as 10:24:26 (twice 5:12:13), 15:36:39 (three times 5:12:13), or 50:120:130 (ten times 5:12:13).

3. **Ratio** $s:s:s\sqrt{2}$ where s stands for the side of the figure. Because two sides are the same, this formula applies to an isosceles right triangle — also known as a 45:45:90 triangle. If one side is 2, then the other side is also 2, and the hypotenuse is $2\sqrt{2}$.

This formula is great to know for squares. If a question tells you that the side of a square is 5 and wants to know the diagonal of the square, you know immediately that it is $5\sqrt{2}$. Why? A square's diagonal cuts the square into two isosceles right triangles (*isosceles* because all sides of the square are equal; *right* because all angles in a square are right angles). What is the diagonal of a square of side 64? $64\sqrt{2}$. What is the diagonal of a square of side 12,984? $12,984\sqrt{2}$.

There's another way to write this ratio. Instead of $s:s:s\sqrt{2}$, you can write it as $\frac{s}{\sqrt{2}}:\frac{s}{\sqrt{2}}:s$. Of course, the s still stands for the side of the triangle, but now you've divided everything through by $\sqrt{2}$. Why do you need this complicated formula? Suppose that you're told that the diagonal of a square is 5. What is the area of the square? What is the perimeter of the square? Chances are good that one of the trap answers is "It cannot be determined from the information given." Chances are even better that you may fall for that trap answer.

However, if you know this formula, $\frac{s}{\sqrt{2}}:\frac{s}{\sqrt{2}}:s$, you know that s stands for the hypotenuse of the triangle, which is the same as the diagonal of the square. If $s = 5$, then the side of the square is $\frac{5}{\sqrt{2}}$, and you can figure out the area or the perimeter. After you know the side of a square, you can figure out just about anything.

4. **Ratio** $s:s\sqrt{3}:2s$: This is a special formula for the sides of a 30:60:90 triangle.

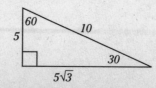

This type of triangle is a favorite of the test-makers. The important thing to keep in mind here is that the hypotenuse is twice the length of the side opposite the 30-degree angle. If you get a word problem saying, "Given a 30:60:90 triangle of hypotenuse 20, find the area," or "Given a 30:60:90 triangle of hypotenuse 100, find the perimeter," you can do so because you can find the lengths of the other sides.

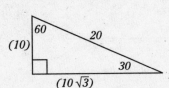 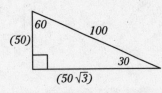 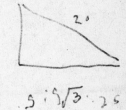

Thanks 4 Nothing: Quadrilaterals

1. Any four-sided figure is called a *quadrilateral*.

Quadrilateral

The interior angles of any quadrilateral total 360 degrees. Any quadrilateral can be cut into two 180-degree triangles.

2. A *square* is a quadrilateral with four equal sides and four right angles.

$A = S^2$
$A = \frac{1}{2} d^2$

Square

The area of a square is $side^2$ (also called $base \times height$), or $\frac{1}{2} diagonal^2$.

3. A *rhombus* is a quadrilateral with four equal sides and four angles that are not necessarily right angles.

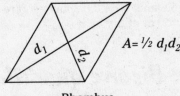

$A = \frac{1}{2} d_1 d_2$

Rhombus

A rhombus often looks like a drunken square, tipsy on its side and wobbly. The area of a rhombus is $\frac{1}{2}d_1d_2$ ($\frac{1}{2} diagonal_1 \times diagonal_2$).

Any square is a rhombus, but not all rhombuses are squares.

4. A *rectangle* is a quadrilateral with two opposite and equal pairs of sides. That is, the top and bottom sides are equal, and the right and left sides are equal. All angles in a rectangle are right angles (*rectangle* means right angle).

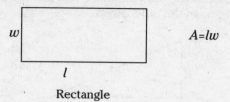

Rectangle

The area of a rectangle is *length* × *width* (which is the same as *base* × *height*).

5. A *parallelogram* is a quadrilateral with two opposite and equal pairs of sides. The top and bottom sides are equal, and the right and left sides are equal. Opposite angles are equal but not necessarily right (or 90 degrees).

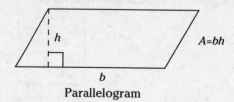

Parallelogram

The area of a parallelogram is *base* × *height*. Remember that the height always is a perpendicular line from the tallest point of the figure down to the base. Diagonals of a parallelogram bisect each other.

All rectangles are parallelograms, but not all parallelograms are rectangles.

6. A *trapezoid* is a quadrilateral with two parallel sides and two nonparallel sides.

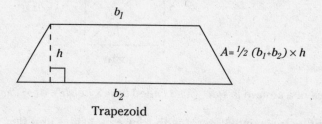

Trapezoid

The area of a trapezoid is ½ (*base₁* + *base₂*) × *height*. It makes no difference which base you label *base 1* and which you label *base 2* because you're adding them together anyway. Just be sure to add them *before* you multiply by ½.

Quaint quads: Bizarre quadrilaterals

Some quadrilaterals don't have nice, neat shapes or special names.

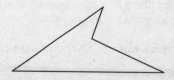

Don't immediately see a strange shape and say that you have no way to find the area of it. You may be able to divide the quadrilateral into two triangles and find the area of each triangle. You may also see a strange quadrilateral in a shaded-area problem; I tell you more about those in the next section.

Leftovers again: Shaded-area problems

Think of a shaded area as a *leftover*. It is "left over" after you subtract the unshaded area from the total area.

Shaded areas are often very unusual shapes. Your first reaction may be that you can't possibly find the area of that shape. Generally, you're right, but you don't have to find the area directly. Instead, be sly, devious, and sneaky; in other words, think the GRE way! Find the area of the total figure, find the area of the unshaded portion, and subtract.

1. $s = 8$

   Area of square = 64

2. $r = 4$

   Area of circle = 16π

3. Shaded area = $64 - 16\pi$

Missing Parrots and Other Polly-Gones: More Polygons

Triangles and quadrilaterals are probably the most common *polygons* (closed figures consisting of straight lines, such as squares, rectangles, decagons, and so on) tested on this exam. Here are a few other polygons you may see:

Number of Sides	Name
5	pentagon
6	hexagon (think of *x* in six and *x* in hex)
7	heptagon
8	octagon
9	nonagon
10	decagon

1. **A polygon with all equal sides and all equal angles is called *regular*.** For example, an equilateral triangle is a regular triangle, and a square is a regular quadrilateral.

   The GRE usually does not ask you to find the areas of any polygons with more than four sides. It may ask you to find the *perimeter*, which is just the sum of the lengths of all the sides. It may also ask you to find the exterior angle measure, which is always 360.

2. **The exterior angle measure of *any* polygon is 360.**

Total interior angle measure

You may also have to find the interior angle measure. Use this formula:

$(n - 2)\,180°$, where n stands for the number of sides

For example, the interior angles of the following polygons are

- ✓ **Triangle:** $(3 - 2)180 = 1 \times 180 = 180°$
- ✓ **Quadrilateral:** $(4 - 2)180 = 2 \times 180 = 360°$
- ✓ **Pentagon:** $(5 - 2)180 = 3 \times 180 = 540°$
- ✓ **Hexagon:** $(6 - 2)180 = 4 \times 180 = 720°$
- ✓ **Heptagon:** $(7 - 2)180 = 5 \times 180 = 900°$
- ✓ **Octagon:** $(8 - 2)180 = 6 \times 180 = 1{,}080°$
- ✓ **Nonagon:** $(9 - 2)180 = 7 \times 180 = 1{,}260°$
- ✓ **Decagon:** $(10 - 2)180 = 8 \times 180 = 1{,}440°$

Have you learned that proportional multiplication is a great timesaving trick? Numbers are in proportion, and you can fiddle with them to make multiplication easier. Suppose that you're going to multiply 5×180. Most people have to write down the problem and then work through it. But because the numbers are in proportion, you can double one and halve the other: Double 5 to make it 10. Halve 180 to make it 90. Now your problem is 10×90, which you can multiply to 900 in your head.

Try another one: $3 \times 180 = ?$ Double the first number: $3 \times 2 = 6$. Halve the second number: $^{180}\!/_2 = 90$. $6 \times 90 = 540$. You can do this shortcut multiplication in your head very quickly and impress your friends.

One interior angle

If you are asked to find the average measure of one angle in a figure, the formula is

$$\frac{(n - 2)\,180°}{n}$$

where *n* stands for the number of sides (which is the same as the number of angles).

Pentagon: $\dfrac{(5 - 2) \times 180}{5} = \dfrac{(3 \times 180)}{5} = \dfrac{540}{5} = 108°$

Because all angles are equal in a regular polygon, the same formula applies to one angle in a regular polygon.

TRAPS & TRICKS

If you are given a polygon and are *not* told that it's regular, you can't solve for just one angle.

What's the measure of angle *x?* It cannot be determined. You can't assume that it is

$$\frac{(7-2)\times 180}{7} = \frac{900}{7} = 128.57.$$

Be sure to divide through by *n*, the number of sides (angles), not by $(n-2)$. If you divide through by $(n-2)$, you always get 180 ($\frac{900}{5} = 180$). Knowing this, triple-check your work if you come up with 180 for an answer to this type of problem; you may have made this very typical but careless error.

Volume

1. **The volume of any polygon is (area of the base) × height.** If you remember this formula, you don't have to memorize any of the following more specific formulas.

2. **Volume of a cube:** e^3

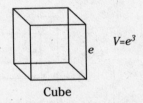

Cube

A cube is a three-dimensional square. Think of a die (one of a pair of dice). All of a cube's dimensions are the same; that is, *length = width = height*. In a cube, these dimensions are called *edges.* The volume of a cube is *edge × edge × edge = edge³ = e³*.

3. **Volume of a rectangular solid:** $l \times w \times h$

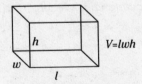

Rectangular solid

A rectangular solid is a box. The base of a box is a rectangle, which has an area of *length × width.* Multiply that by height to fit the original formula: *Volume = (area of base) × height,* or *V = l × w × h.*

4. **Volume of a cylinder:** (πr^2) height

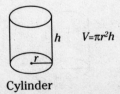

Cylinder

Think of a cylinder as a can of soup. The base of a cylinder is a circle. The area of a circle is πr^2. Multiply that by the height of the cylinder to get $(area\ of\ base) \times height = (\pi r^2) \times height$. Note that the top and bottom of a cylinder are identical circles. If you know the radius of either the top base or the bottom base, you can find the area of the circle.

Total surface area (TSA)

1. **The total surface area, logically enough, is the sum of the areas of all the surfaces of the figure.**

2. **TSA of a cube:** $6e^2$

Cube

A cube has six identical faces, and each face is a square. The area of a square is $side^2$. Here, that is called $edge^2$. If one face is $edge^2$, then the total surface area is $6 \times edge^2$, or $6e^2$.

3. **TSA of a rectangular solid:** $2(lw) + 2(hw) + 2(lh)$

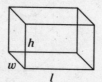

Rectangular solid

A rectangular solid is a box. You need to find the area of each of the six surfaces. The bottom and top have the area of $length \times width$. The area of the left side and right side is $width \times height$. The front side and the backside have the area of $height \times length$. Together, they total $2(lw) + 2(wh) + 2(hl)$ or $2(lw + wh + hl)$.

4. **TSA of a cylinder:** $(circumference \times height) + 2(\pi r^2)$

Cylinder

This is definitely the most difficult TSA to figure out. Think of it as pulling the label off the can, flattening it out, finding its area, and then adding that to the area of the top and bottom lids.

The label is a rectangle. Its length is the length of the circumference of the circle.

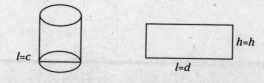

Its height is the height of the cylinder. Multiply *length* × *height* to find the area of the label.

You also need to find the area of the top and bottom of the cylinder. Because each is a circle, the TSA of the top and bottom is $2\left(\pi r^2\right)$. Add everything together.

I'm Too Much of a Klutz for Coordinate Geometry

The horizontal axis is the *x*-axis. The vertical axis is the *y*-axis. Points are labeled (*x,y*) with the first number in the parentheses indicating how far to the right or left of the vertical line the point is and the second number indicating how far above or below the horizontal line the point is.

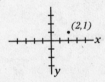

The intersection of the *x*- and *y*-axes is called the *point of origin,* and its coordinates are (0,0). A line connecting points whose *x*- and *y*-coordinates are the same forms a 45-degree angle with each axis.

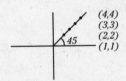

If you're asked to find the distance between two points, you can use the distance formula (which is based on the Pythagorean theorem):

$$\sqrt{\left(x_2 - x_1\right)^2 + \left(y_2 - y_1\right)^2}$$

Find the distance from (9,4) to (8,6).

$$9 = x_1$$
$$8 = x_2$$
$$4 = y_1$$
$$6 = y_2$$
$$(8-9)^2 = -1^2 = 1$$
$$(6-4)^2 = -2^2 = 4$$
$$1 + 4 = 5$$

$\sqrt{5}$ is the distance between the two points.

Running Around in Circles

Did you hear about the rube who pulled his son out of college, claiming that the school was filling his head with nonsense? As the rube said, "Joe Bob told me that he learned πr^2. But any fool knows that pie are round; *cornbread* are square!"

Circles are among the less-complicated geometry concepts. The most important things are to remember the vocabulary and to be able to distinguish an arc from a sector and an inscribed angle from an intercepted arc. Here's a quick review of the basics.

1. **A radius goes from the center of a circle to its circumference (perimeter).**

Radius

2. **A circle is named by its center.**

   circle M

Center

3. **A diameter connects two points on the circumference of the circle, going through the center, and *is equal to two radii*.**

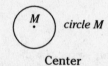

Diameter

4. **A chord connects any two points on a circle. The longest chord in a circle is the diameter.**

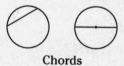

Chords

Here's a lovely question you may see on the test. Choose

A if the quantity in Column A is greater.

B if the quantity in Column B is greater.

C if the two quantities are equal.

D if the relationship cannot be determined from the information given.

 Column A   *Column B*

| Area of a circle of radius 6 | Area of a circle of longest chord 12 |

Many people choose D for this question. Although it's usually true that in QCs (Quantitative Comparisons, this type of problem) a geometry question with no figure is D because it depends on how you draw the picture, a circle is frequently an exception to this tip. A circle is a circle is a circle; it rarely depends on how you draw it. The key here is to know that the *longest chord* is a fancy-schmancy way of saying the *diameter*. Because the diameter is twice the radius, a circle of diameter (or longest chord) 12 has a radius of 6. Two circles with radii of 6 have the same area. (Don't waste even a nanosecond figuring out what that area actually is; it's irrelevant to comparing the quantities in the two columns.) *Correct Answer:* C.

Column A	_Column B_
Area of a circle of radius 10	Area of a circle of chord 20

If you chose C, you fell for the trap. A chord connects any two points on a circle. The *longest* chord is the diameter, but a chord can be any ol' thing. *Correct Answer:* D.

5. **The perimeter of a circle is called the *circumference*. The formula for the length of a circumference is $2\pi r$ or πd (logical, because $2\,radii = 1\,diameter$).**

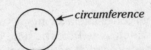
←circumference

Bonus: You may encounter a wheel question in which you're asked how much distance a wheel covers or how many times a wheel revolves. The key to solving this type of question is to know that one rotation of a wheel equals one circumference of that wheel.

A child's wagon has a wheel of radius 6 inches. If the wagon wheel travels 100 revolutions, approximately how many feet has the wagon rolled?

(A) 325

(B) 314

(C) 255

(D) 201

(E) It cannot be determined from the information given.

One revolution is equal to one circumference: $C = 2\pi = 2\pi6 = 12\pi = approximately$ 37.68 inches. Multiply that by 100 = 3,768 *inches* = 314 *feet*. Choice E is definitely the worst guess that you can make. If you have a radius, you can solve for nearly anything having to do with circles. Remember that there's a difference between "it cannot be determined" and "*I* cannot determine it." Just because you personally may not know what to do doesn't mean the problem is not "doable." If you're guessing, guess something else. *Correct Answer:* B.

6. **The area of a circle is $\pi\,radius^2$.**

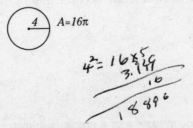

7. **A central angle has its endpoints on the circumference of the circle and its vertex at the center of the circle. The degree measure of a central angle is the same as the degree measure of its intercepted arc.**

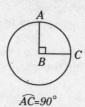

$\widehat{AC}=90°$

8. **An inscribed angle has both its endpoints and its vertex on the circumference of the circle. The degree measure of an inscribed angle is half the degree measure of its intercepted arc.**

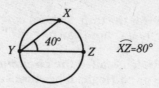

$\widehat{XZ}=80°$

You may see a figure that looks like a string picture you made at summer camp with all sorts of lines running every which way. Take the time to identify the endpoints of the angles and the vertex. You may be surprised at how easy the question suddenly becomes.

In this figure, find the sum of the degree measures of angles $a+b+c+d+e$.

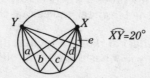

$\widehat{XY}=20°$

Note: Figure not drawn to scale

(A) 65

(B) 60

(C) 55

(D) 50

(E) 45

Each angle is an inscribed angle. That means the angle has half the degree measure of the central angle, or half the degree measure of its intercepted arc. If you look carefully at the endpoints of these angles, they're all the same: *XY*. Arc *XY* has a measure of 20°. Therefore, each angle is 10°, for a total of 50. *Correct Answer:* D.

9. **When a central angle and an inscribed angle have the same endpoints, the degree measure of the central angle is twice that of the inscribed angle.**

10. **The degree measure of a circle is 360.**

11. **An *arc* is a portion of the circumference of a circle. The degree measure of an arc is the same as its central angle and twice its inscribed angle.**

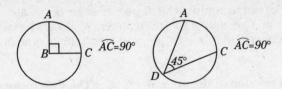

To find the length of an arc, follow these steps:

1. **Find the circumference of the entire circle.**

2. **Put the degree measure of the arc over 360 and then reduce the fraction.**

3. **Multiply the circumference by the fraction.**

Find the length of arc *AC*.

$18 \times 2 = 36$

$\cancel{360}^{\circ}$

(A) 36π

(B) 27π

(C) 18π

$^{60}/_{360} = \frac{1}{6}$

(D) 12π

$\frac{6\cancel{0}}{36\cancel{0}}$

(E) 6π

Take the steps one at a time. First, find the circumference of the entire circle. $C = 2\pi r = 36\pi$. Don't multiply π out; problems usually leave it in that form. Next, put the degree measure of the arc over 360. The degree measure of the arc is the same as its central angle, 60°, so $^{60}/_{360} = \frac{1}{6}$. The arc is ⅙ of the circumference of the circle. Multiply the circumference by the fraction: $36\pi \times \frac{1}{6} = 6\pi$. *Correct Answer:* E.

Try another one. After you get the hang of these, they're kinda fun.

$\frac{6^{0}}{360}$ $\cancel{1}/_{60}$

Angle *ROS* = 6°

Find the length of arc *RS* in this figure.

(A) ⅓π

(B) π

(C) 3π

(D) 4π

(E) 12

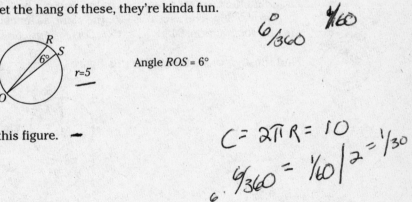

$C = 2\pi R = 10$

$^{6}/_{360} = \frac{1}{60}|2 = \frac{1}{30}$

First, find the circumference of the entire circle. $C = 2\pi r = 10\pi$. Second, put the degree measure of the arc over 360. Here, the inscribed angle is 6°. Because an inscribed angle is ½ of the central angle and ½ of its intercepted arc, the arc is 12°. $^{12}/_{360} = \frac{1}{30}$. The arc is ⅟30 of the circle. Finally, multiply the circumference by the fraction: $10\pi \times \frac{1}{30} = ^{10}/_{30}\pi = \frac{1}{3}\pi$. The length of the arc is ⅓π. *Correct Answer:* A.

Be very careful not to confuse the *degree measure* of the arc with the *length* of the arc. The length is always a portion of the circumference, always has a π in it, and always is in linear units. If you chose E in this example, you found the degree measure of the arc rather than its length.

12. A *sector* is a portion of the area of a circle. The degree measure of a sector is the same as its central angle and twice its inscribed angle.

To find the area of a sector, do the following:

1. **Find the area of the entire circle.**

2. **Put the degree measure of the sector over 360 and then reduce the fraction.**

3. **Multiply the area by the fraction.**

Finding the area of a sector is very similar to finding the length of an arc. The only difference is in the first step. Whereas an arc is a part of the *circumference* of a circle, a sector is a part of the *area* of a circle. Try a few examples for sectors.

Find the area of sector *ABC*.

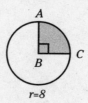

(A) 64π

(B) 36π

(C) 16π

(D) 12π

(E) 6π

First, find the area of the entire circle. $A = \pi r^2 = 64\pi$. Second, put the degree measure of the sector over 360. The sector is 90°, the same as its central angle: $^{90}/_{360} = ^{1}/_{4}$. Third, multiply the area by the fraction: $64\pi \times ^{1}/_{4} = 16\pi$. *Correct Answer:* C.

Find the area of sector *XYZ* in this figure.

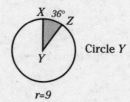

(A) 9.7π

(B) 8.1π

(C) 7.2π

(D) 6.3π

(E) 6π

First, find the area of the entire circle. $A = \pi r^2 = 81\pi$. Second, put the degree measure of the sector over 360. A sector has the same degree measure as its intercepted arc, in this case 36°: $^{36}/_{360} = ^{1}/_{10}$. Third, multiply the area by the fraction: $81\pi \times ^{1}/_{10} = 8.1\pi$. *Correct Answer:* B.

Chapter 12

Gotta Catch Some (Xs, Ys, and) Zs: Algebra and Other Sleeping Aids

- -

In This Chapter

▶ Bases and exponents

▶ Ratios

▶ Symbolism

▶ Algebra basics and the FOIL method

▶ Roots and radicals

▶ Probability

- -

Trivia Question: Where was algebra supposedly invented?

Answer: Algebra was invented in Zabid, Yemen, by Muslim scholars. See — you can't blame the Greeks for everything!

The Powers That Be: Bases and Exponents

Many GRE questions require you to know how to work with bases and exponents. The following sections explain some of the most important concepts.

1. **The *base* is the big number (or letter) on the bottom. The *exponent* is the little number (or letter) in the upper-right corner.**

    In x^5, x is the base; 5 is the exponent.

    In 3^y, 3 is the base; y is the exponent.

2. **A base to the zero power equals one.**

    $x^0 = 1$

    $5^0 = 1$

    $129^0 = 1$

There is a long, *soporific* (sleep-causing) explanation as to why a number to the zero power equals one, but you don't really care, do you? For now, just memorize the rule.

3. A base to the second power is *base* $\times$ *base*.

This is pretty familiar stuff, right?

$$x^2 = x \times x$$
$$5^2 = 5 \times 5$$
$$129^2 = 129 \times 129$$

The same is true for bigger exponents. The exponent tells you how many times the number is repeated. For example, 5^6 means that you write down six 5s and then multiply them all together.

$$3^9 = 3 \times 3 \times 3 \times 3 \times 3 \times 3 \times 3 \times 3 \times 3$$

4. A base to a negative exponent is the reciprocal of something.

This one is a little more confusing. A reciprocal is the upside-down version of something. (Here's a *conundrum* [riddle]: Is the North Pole the reciprocal of the South Pole?) When you have a negative exponent, just put the base and exponent under a 1 and make the exponent positive again.

$$x^{-4} = 1/_{(x^4)}$$

$$5^{-3} = 1/_{(5^3)}$$

$$129^{-1} = 1/_{(129^1)}$$

The *number* is not negative. When you flip it, you get the reciprocal, and the negative just sort of fades away. *Don't* fall for the trap of saying that $5^{-3} = (1/5)^3$ or $-1/125$.

When you take a base of 10 to some power, the number of the power equals the number of zeros in the number.

$$10^1 = 10 \text{ (one zero)}$$
$$10^4 = 10,000 \text{ (four zeros)}$$
$$10^0 = 1 \text{ (zero zeros)}$$

5. To multiply like bases, add the exponents.

You can multiply two bases that are the same; just add the exponents.

$$x^3 \times x^2 = x^{(3+2)} = x^5$$
$$5^4 \times 5^9 = 5^{(4+9)} = 5^{13}$$
$$129^3 \times 129^0 = 129^{(3+0)} = 129^3$$

You cannot multiply *unlike* bases. Think of it as trying to make dogs multiply with cats — it doesn't work. All you end up with is a miffed meower and a damaged dog.

$$x^2 \times y^3 = x^2 \times y^3 \text{ (no shortcuts)}$$
$$5^2 \times 129^3 = 5^2 \times 129^3 \text{ (you actually have to work it out)}$$

6. To divide like bases, subtract the exponents.

You can divide two bases that are the same by subtracting the exponents.

$$x^5 \div x^2 = x^{(5-2)} = x^3$$

$$5^9 \div 5^3 = 5^{(9-3)} = 5^6$$

$$129^4 \div 129^0 = 129^{(4-0)} = 129^4$$

(Did I getcha on that last one? It should make sense. Any base to the zero power is 1. Any number divided by 1 is itself.)

Did you look at the second example, $5^9 \div 5^3$, and think that it was 5^3? It's easy to fall into the trap of dividing instead of subtracting, especially when you see numbers that just beg to be divided, like 9 and 3. Keep your guard up.

7. Multiply the exponents of a base inside and outside the parentheses.

That's quite a mouthful. Here's what it means:

$$\left(x^2\right)^3 = x^{(2 \times 3)} = x^6$$

$$\left(5^3\right)^3 = 5^{(3 \times 3)} = 5^9$$

$$\left(129^0\right)^3 = 129^{(0 \times 3)} = 129^0$$

Try a few QC questions testing this concept.

The answer choices are

A if the quantity in Column A is greater.

B if the quantity in Column B is greater.

C if the two quantities are equal.

D if the relationship cannot be determined from the information given.

Column A	_Column B_

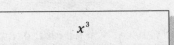   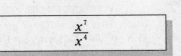

$x^{(7-4)} = x^3$, no matter what the value of x is. *Correct Answer:* C.

Column A	_Column B_

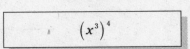

No matter what value x has, the two columns are the same: $x^{12} = x^{12}$. *Correct Answer:* C.

Column A	Column B
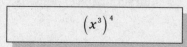 $\left(x^3\right)^4$	12

Everything *depends* on the value of *x*. Boy, this trap is really easy to fall for. You are so busy thinking of $3 \times 4 = 12$ that you may be tempted to choose C. But the automatic shut down valve in the back of your brain should alert you to the fact that *when two columns appear to be equal, it is usually a trap*. (See Chapter 14 for more information on this QC trick.) *Correct Answer:* D.

8. **To add or subtract like bases to like powers, add or subtract the numerical coefficient of the bases.**

   The *numerical coefficient* (a great name for a rock band, don't you think?) is simply the number *in front of* the base. Notice that it is not the little exponent in the right-hand corner but the full-sized number to the left of the base.

   In $31x^3$, 31 is the numerical coefficient.

   In $-8y^2$, -8 is the numerical coefficient.

   In x^3, the numerical coefficient is 1, because any number is itself times 1; the 1 is not always written out. Good trap.

   In $37x^3 + 10x^3 = 47x^3$, just add the numerical coefficients: $37 + 10 = 47$.

   In $15y^2 - 10y^2 = 5y^2$, just subtract the numerical coefficients: $15 - 10 = 5$.

You cannot add or subtract like bases with *different exponents*.

   $13x^3 - 9x^2$ is *not* equal to $4x^3$ or $4x^2$ or $4x$. All it is equal to is $13x^3 - 9x^2$. The bases *and* exponents must be the same for you to add or subtract the terms.

Column A	Column B
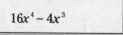 $16x^4 - 4x^3$	$12x$

The answer depends on the value of *x*. If you chose C, you fell for the trap I just discussed. *Correct Answer:* D.

9. **You cannot simply add or subtract the numerical coefficients of unlike bases.**

   Again, this is like working with cats and dogs. They don't mingle.

   $16x^2 - 4y^2 = 16x^2 - 4y^2$

   It is *not* $12x^2$ or $12y^2$ or $12xy^2$.

Column A	Column B
$10x^3 - 2y^3$	$8xy$

It depends on the values of *x* and *y*. C is the trap answer. *Correct Answer:* D.

Keep It in Proportion: Ratios

After you know the tricks, ratios are some of the easiest problems to answer quickly. I call them "heartbeat" problems because you can solve them in a heartbeat. Of course, if someone drop-dead gorgeous sits next to you and makes your heart beat faster, it may take you two heartbeats to solve a ratio problem. So sue me.

1. **A ratio is written as $\frac{of}{to}$ or of:to.**

   The ratio *of* sunflowers *to* roses = sunflowers:roses

   The ratio *of* umbrellas *to* heads = $\frac{\text{umbrellas}}{\text{heads}}$.

2. **A possible total is a multiple of the sum of the numbers in the ratio.**

   You may be given a problem like this: At a party, the ratio of blondes to redheads is ⅘. Which of the following can be the total number of blondes and redheads at the party?

   Mega-easy. Add the numbers in the ratio: $4 + 5 = 9$. The total must be a multiple of 9: 9, 18, 27, 36, and so on. If this "multiple of" stuff is confusing, think of it another way: The sum must divide evenly into the total. That is, the total must be divisible by 9. Can the total, for example, be 54? Yes, 9 goes evenly into 54. Can it be 64? No, 9 does not go evenly into 64.

After a rough hockey game, Bernie checks his body and finds that he has three bruises for every five cuts. Which of the following can be the total number of bruises and cuts on poor ol' Bernie's body?

   (A) 53

   (B) 45

   (C) 35

   (D) 33

   (E) 32

Add the numbers in the ratio: $3 + 5 = 8$. The total must be a multiple of 8 (or, looking at it another way, the total must be evenly divisible by 8). Only E is a multiple of 8 ($8 \times 4 = 32$). *Correct Answer:* E.

Did you notice the trap answers? 53 is a good trap because it features both 5 and 3, the numbers in the ratio. 45 is a trap. If you multiply $3 \times 5 = 15$, you may think that the total has to be a multiple of 15. No, the total is a multiple of the *sum*, not of the product. *Add* the numbers in the ratio; don't multiply them. 35 again has both terms of the ratio. 33 is a multiple of 3. Only 32 is a multiple of the *sum* of the terms in the ratio.

One more, because you should always get this type of problem correct.

Trying to get Willie to turn down his stereo, his downstairs neighbor pounds on the ceiling and shouts up to his bedroom. If she pounds 7 times for every 5 times she shouts, which of the following can be the total number of poundings and shouts?

   (A) 75

   (B) 57

   (C) 48

   (D) 35

   (E) 30

Add the numbers in the ratio: 7 + 5 = 12. The total must be a multiple of 12 (it must be evenly divisible by 12). Here, only 48 is evenly divisible by 12. Of course, 75 and 57 try to trick you by using the numbers 7 and 5 from the ratio. Choice D is the product of 7 × 5. *Correct Answer:* C.

Notice how carefully I have been asking which can be the possible total. The total can be any multiple of the sum. If a question asks you which of the following is the total, you have to answer, "It cannot be determined." You know only which answer can be true.

Column A	*Column B*

Ratio of CDs to tapes = 2:9

Total of CDs and tapes	11

You know the total must be a multiple of 11, but it can be an infinite number of terms: 11, 22, 33, 44, 55, and so on. This trap has destroyed a lot of overly confident students over the years. *Correct Answer:* D.

When given a ratio and a total and asked to find a specific term, do the following in order:

1. **Add the numbers in the ratio.**

2. **Divide that sum into the total.**

3. **Multiply that quotient by each term in the ratio.**

4. **Add the answers to double-check that they sum up to the total.**

Pretty confusing stuff. Take it one step at a time.

Yelling at the members of his team, which had just lost 21–0, the irate coach pointed his finger at each member of the squad, calling everyone either a wimp or a slacker. If there were 3 wimps for every 4 slackers and every member of the 28-man squad was either a wimp or a slacker, how many wimps were there?

1. **Add the numbers in the ratio:** 3 + 4 = 7.

2. **Divide that sum into the total:** $^{28}/_7 = 4$.

3. **Multiply that quotient by each term in the ratio:** 4 × 3 = 12; 4 × 4 = 16.

4. **Add to double-check that the numbers sum up to the total:** 12 + 16 = 28.

Now you have all the information you need to answer a variety of questions: How many wimps were there? Twelve. How many slackers were there? Sixteen. How many more slackers than wimps were there? Four. How many slackers would have to be kicked off the team for the number of wimps and slackers to be equal? Four. The math-mogul test creators can ask all sorts of things, but if you've got this information, you're ready for anything they throw at you.

Be sure that you actually do Step 4, adding the terms to double-check that they sum up to the total again — you can catch any careless mistakes you may have made. For example, suppose you divided 7 into 28 and got 3 instead of 4. Then you said that there were 3 × 3, or 9, wimps and 3 × 4, or 12, slackers. That means that the total was 9 + 12 = 21 — *ooooops!* You know that the total has to be 28, so you can go back and try again. You'll also catch a careless mistake in your multiplication. Suppose that you correctly divide 7 into 28 and get 4. But when you multiply 4 × 3, you get 43 instead of 12. (Hey, when the adrenaline's flowing during the exam, you'd be surprised at the kinds of mistakes you can make.) When you add the numbers, you get 43 + 16 = 59 instead of the 28 that you know is the total.

It takes longer to talk through these steps than it does to do them. After you learn this technique, it makes a lot of sense. Think of ratios as cliques. If there are 3 boys for every 5 girls, there are 8 kids in one clique. If there are 48 kids at a party, there must be 6 cliques (8 divided into 48 = 6). If there are 6 cliques at 3 girls per clique, there are $6 \times 3 = 18$ girls. If there are 6 cliques at 5 boys each, there are $6 \times 5 = 30$ boys.

Things Aren't What They Seem: Symbolism

You may encounter two basic types of symbolism problems. If so, do one of the following:

✔ Substitute the number given for the variable in the explanation.

✔ Talk through the explanation to see which constraint fits and then do the indicated operations.

1. Substitute for the variable in the explanation.

You see a problem with a strange symbol. It may be a variable inside a circle, a triangle, a star, or a tic-tac-toe sign. That symbol has no connection to the real world at all. Don't panic, thinking that your teachers forgot to teach you something. Symbols are made up for each problem.

The symbol is included in a short explanation. It may look like this:

$$a\#b\#c = \frac{(a+b)^c}{(b+c)}$$

$$x*y*z = \frac{z}{x} + \left(\frac{y}{z}\right)^x$$

$$m@n@o = mn + no - om$$

Again, the symbols don't have any meaning in the outside world; they mean only what the problem tells you they mean, and that meaning holds true only for this problem.

Below the explanation is the question itself:

$$3\#2\#1 =$$

$$\frac{3+2\cdot5^1}{2+1} = 5/3$$

$$4*6*8 =$$

$$2@5@10 =$$

Your job is one of substitution. Plug in a number for the variable in the equation. Which number do you plug in? The one that's in the same position as that variable. For example:

$$a\#b\#c = \frac{(a+b)^c}{(b+c)}$$

$$3\#2\#1 = \frac{(3+2)^1}{(2+1)} = \frac{5}{3}$$

Because *a* was in the first position and 3 was in the first position, substitute a 3 for an *a* throughout the equation. Because *b* was in the second position and 2 was in the second position, substitute a 2 for a *b* throughout the equation. Because *c* was in the third position and 1 was in the third position, substitute a 1 for a *c* throughout the equation.

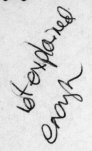

Do the same for the other problems.

$$x * y * z = \frac{z}{x} + \left(\frac{y}{z}\right)^x$$

$$4 * 6 * 8 = \left(\frac{8}{4}\right) + \left(\frac{6}{8}\right)^4 = 2 + \left(\frac{6}{8}\right)^4 = 2 + .316 = 2.316$$

$$m@n@o = mn + no - om$$

$$2@5@10 = (2 \times 5) + (5 \times 10) - (10 \times 2) = 10 + 50 - 20 = 40$$

This is the simpler of the two types of symbolism problems. Just substitute the number for the variable and work through the equation.

2. Talk through the explanation and do the operations.

This type of symbolism problem may seem more confusing until you've done a few. Then it becomes so easy that you wonder why you didn't see it before. Here are two possibilities.

> $\boxed{x} = 3x$ if x is odd.
>
> $\boxed{x} = \frac{x}{2}$ if x is even.

Solve for $\boxed{5} + \boxed{8}$.

First, talk through the explanation. You have something in a circle. If that something in the circle is odd, you multiply it by 3. If that something in the circle is even, you divide it by 2.

In the question, there's a 5 in the circle. Because 5 is odd, you multiply it by 3 to get $5 \times 3 = 15$. In the second half of the question, there's an 8 in a circle. Because 8 is even, you divide it by 2. $\frac{8}{2} = 4$. Now add: $15 + 4 = 19$.

Don't keep going. Do *not* say, "Well, 19 is odd, so I have to multiply it by 3, getting 57." You can bet that 57 is one of the trap multiple-choice answers.

You may still think of this second type of problem as a plug-in or substitution problem because you are plugging the number into the equation for x and working it through. However, you first have to figure out which equation to plug it into. That requires talking things through. You have to understand what you're doing in this type of problem. Try another:

> $\triangle{x} = 3x + \frac{1}{3}x$ if x is prime.
>
> $\triangle{x} = x^2 + \sqrt{x}$ if x is composite.

$$\triangle{16} + \triangle{3} =$$

Aha! Now you have to know some math vocabulary. *Prime numbers* are numbers greater than 1, and cannot be divided other than by 1 and themselves. Examples are 2, 3, 5, 7, 11, and 13. *Composite numbers* are numbers that *can* be divided other than by just 1 and themselves, like 4, 6, 8, 9, 10, and 12. First, decide whether the term in the triangle is a composite number or a prime number.

In $\triangle{16}$, because 16 is a composite number, use the second equation. Square 16: $16 \times 16 = 256$. Take the square root of 16: $\sqrt{16} = 4$. Add them together: $256 + 4 = 260$.

In $\triangle{3}$, because 3 is a prime number, use the first equation. $3^2 + \frac{1}{3}(3) = 9 + 1 = 10$.

Add the two solutions: $260 + 10 = 270$.

Sometimes, the solutions have symbols in them as well. Here's an example:

$$\boxed{\begin{array}{l} \textcircled{x} = 1/2x \text{ if } x \text{ is composite.} \\ \textcircled{x} = 2x \text{ if } x \text{ is prime.} \end{array}}$$

Solve for $\textcircled{5} \times \textcircled{10}$.

(A) $\textcircled{15}$

(B) $\textcircled{25}$

(C) $\textcircled{50}$

(D) $\textcircled{100}$

(E) It cannot be determined from the information given.

First, you know to eliminate answer E. This is the sucker's answer, the one for people who have no idea what the cute little circle means and are clueless as to where to begin. You know by now that you *can* solve a symbolism problem — and pretty quickly, too.

Because 5 is prime, you multiply it by 2: $5 \times 2 = 10$.

Because 10 is composite, you multiply it by $\frac{1}{2}$: $10 \times \frac{1}{2} = 5$

Multiply: $10 \times 5 = 50$.

Noooo! Don't choose answer C; that's the trap answer. Choice C doesn't say 50; it says $\textcircled{50}$. That means that you have to solve the answer choice to see what it really is. Think of it as a choice in disguise with a false beard and glasses. Because 50 is even, you take half of it: $50 \div 2 = 25$. That's not the answer you want. Now go through the rest of the choices:

$\textcircled{15}$: Because 15 is composite, multiply it by $\frac{1}{2}$: $15 \times \frac{1}{2} = 7.5$.

$\textcircled{25}$: Because 25 is composite, multiply it by $\frac{1}{2}$: $25 \times \frac{1}{2} = 12.5$.

$\textcircled{100}$: Because 100 is composite, multiply it by $\frac{1}{2}$: $100 \times \frac{1}{2} = 50$. You have a winner!

Whenever you see a symbol, get to work. That symbol may be in the question or in the answer choices. You still follow the explanation. But remember the trap I already discussed: Be super careful not to keep on going. That is, when you come up with 50 as your answer, don't say, "Well, 50 is composite, so I have to multiply it by ½ getting 25." Stop when there are no more symbols. *Correct Answer:* D.

Have you studied functions? Maybe not in school, but if you've read the preceding material on symbolism, you have just studied functions. A function is very much like the symbolism you've just read about. You may see a problem like this:

$f(x) = (2x)^3$. Solve for $f(2)$.

The *f* stands for function. You do the same thing you did before: Talk through the problem. You say, "I have something in parentheses. My job is to multiply that something by two and then cube the whole disgusting mess." In other words, just plug in the 2 where you see an *x* in the explanation.

$f(2) = (2 \times 2)^3 = 4^3 = 64$

Try another one.

$f(x) = x + x^2 + x^3$, Solve for $f(10)$.

Just plug the 10 in for the x: $f(10) = 10 + 10^2 + 10^3 = 10 + 100 + 1,000 = 1,110$.

Now that you've acquired this skill, you can call yourself "fully functional."

Abracadabra: Algebra

You must be able to do three basic algebra concepts for the GRE.

✔ Solve for x in an equation.

✔ Use the FOIL method (first, outer, inner, last — the order in which you multiply the variables in parentheses).

✔ Factor down a quadratic equation and take an algebraic expression from its final form back to its original form of two sets of parentheses.

Solving for x

To solve for x, follow these steps:

1. **Isolate the variable, which means getting all the x's on one side and all the non-x's on the other side.**

2. **Add all the x's on one side; add all the non-x's on the other side.**

3. **Divide both sides of the equation by the number in front of the x.**

Now you try it: $3x + 7 = 9x - 5$

1. **Isolate the variable. Move the $3x$ to the right, *changing the sign* to make it $-3x$.**

   Forgetting to change the sign is one of the most common, careless mistakes students make. The test makers realize that and often include trap answer choices to catch this mistake.

2. **Move the -5 to the left, *changing the sign* to make it $+5$. You now have $7 + 5 = 9x - 3x$.**

3. **Add the x's on one side; add the non-x's on the other side.**

   $12 = 6x$

4. **Divide both sides through by what is next to the x.**
   $$\frac{12}{6} = \frac{6x}{6}$$
   $$2 = x$$

If you're weak on algebra or know that you often make careless mistakes, plug the 2 back into the equation to make sure that it works.

$3(2) + 7 = 9(2) - 5$

$6 + 7 = 18 - 5$

$13 = 13$

If you absolutely hate algebra, see whether you can simply plug in the answer choices. If this were a Problem Solving question with multiple-choice answers, you could plug 'n' chug.

$3x + 7 = 9x - 5$. Solve for x.

(A) 5

(B) 3½

(C) 2

(D) 0

(E) −2

Don't ask for trouble. Keep life simple by starting with the simple answers first. That is, try plugging in 5. When it doesn't work, don't bother plugging in 3½. That's too much work. Go right down to 2. If all the easy answers don't work, then you can go back to the hard answer of 3½, but why fuss with it unless you absolutely have to? *Correct Answer:* C.

Curses! FOlLed again

The second thing you need to know to do algebra is how to use the FOIL method. FOIL stands for *First, Outer, Inner, Last* and refers to the order in which you multiply the variables in parentheses. With the equation $(a + b)(a - b) =$

1. **Multiply the *First* variables:** $a \times a = a^2$.

2. **Multiply the *Outer* variables:** $a \times (-b) = -ab$.

3. **Multiply the *Inner* variables:** $b \times a = ba$ **(which is the same as *ab*).**

4. **Multiply the *Last* variables:** $b \times (-b) = -b^2$.

Add like terms: $-ab + ab = 0ab$. (Remember that you can multiply numbers forward or backward, such that $ab = ba$.) The positive and negative ab cancel each other out. You're left with only $a^2 - b^2$.

Try another one: $(3a + b)(a - 2b)$.

1. **Multiply the *First* terms:** $3a \times a = 3a^2$.

2. **Multiply the *Outer* terms:** $3a \times (-2b) = -6ab$.

3. **Multiply the *Inner* terms:** $b \times a = ba$ **(which is the same as *ab*).**

4. **Multiply the *Last* terms:** $b \times (-2b) = 2b^2$.

5. **Combine like terms:** $-6ab + ab = -5ab$. **The final answer:** $3a^2 - 5ab - 2b^2$.

You should memorize the following three FOIL problems. Don't bother to work them out every time; know them by heart.

1. $(a + b)^2 = a^2 + 2ab + b^2$

You can prove this equation by using FOIL: $(a + b)(a + b)$.

a. **Multiply the *First* terms:** $a \times a = a^2$.

b. **Multiply the *Outer* terms:** $a \times b = ab$.

c. **Multiply the *Inner* terms:** $b \times a = ba$ **(which is the same as *ab*).**

d. **Multiply the *Last* terms:** $b \times b = b^2$.

e. **Combine like terms:** $ab + ab = 2ab$.

Final solution: $a^2 + 2ab + b^2$.

2. $(a-b)^2 = a^2 - 2ab + b^2$

You can prove this equation by using FOIL: $(a-b)(a-b)$.

    a. Multiply the *First* terms: $a \times a = a^2$.

    b. Multiply the *Outer* terms: $a \times (-b) = -ab$.

    c. Multiply the *Inner* terms: $-b \times a = -ba$ **(which is the same as** *–ba***).**

    d. Multiply the *Last* terms: $-b \times (-b) = +b^2$.

    e. Combine like terms: $-ab + (-ab) = -2ab$.

 Final solution: $a^2 - 2ab + b^2$.

Be careful to note that the b^2 at the end is *positive,* not negative, because multiplying a negative times a negative gives a positive.

3. $(a-b)(a+b) = a^2 - b^2$

You can prove this equation by using FOIL: $(a-b)(a+b)$.

    a. Multiply the *First* terms: $a \times a = a^2$.

    b. Multiply the *Outer* terms: $a \times b = ab$.

    c. Multiply the *Inner* terms: $-b \times a = -ba$ **(which is the same as** *–ab***).**

    d. Multiply the *Last* terms: $-b \times b = -b^2$.

    e. Combine like terms: $ab + (-ab) = 0ab$.

Final solution: $a^2 - b^2$. Note that the middle term drops out because $+ab$ cancels out $-ab$.

Memorize these three equations. Doing so saves you time, careless mistakes, and acute misery on the actual exam.

Fact or fiction: Factoring

Now you know how to do algebra forward; are you ready to do it backward? The third thing you need to know is how to factor down a quadratic equation and take an algebraic expression from its final form back to its original form of two sets of parentheses.

Given $x^2 + 13x + 42 = 0$, solve for x. Take this problem one step at a time.

1. Draw two sets of parentheses.

    $(\ \ )(\ \ ) = 0$

2. To get x^2, the *First* terms have to be x and x. Fill those in.

    $(x)(x) = 0$

3. Look now at the *Outer* terms.

You need two numbers that multiply together to be $+42$. Well, there are several possibilities: 42×1, 21×2, or 6×7. You can even have two negative numbers: -42×-1, -21×-2, or -6×-7. You aren't sure which one to choose yet. Go on to the next step.

4. Look at the *Inner* terms.

You have to add two values to get $+13$. Now you know that you need *two positive* values to get the $+13$. What's the first thing that springs to mind? $6 + 7$, probably. Hey, that's one of the possibilities in the preceding step! Plug it in and try it.

    $(x+6)(x+7) = x^2 + 7x + 6x + 42 = x^2 + 13x + 42$

Great, but you're not finished yet. If the whole equation equals zero, then either $(x + 6) = 0$ or $(x + 7) = 0$ because the only way to make a product zero is to make one of the factors zero. Therefore, x can equal -6 or -7.

Again, if you have a multiple-choice problem, you can simply try the answer choices. Never start doing a lot of work until you absolutely have to.

Too Hip to Be Square: Roots and Radicals

To simplify working with square roots (or cube roots or any radicals), think of them as variables. You work the same way with $\sqrt{7}$ as you do with x, y, or z.

Addition and subtraction

1. **To add or subtract *like* radicals, add or subtract the number in front of the radical (your old friend, the numerical coefficient).**

   $2\sqrt{7} + 5\sqrt{7} = 7\sqrt{7}$ $2x + 5x = 7x$

   $9\sqrt{13} - 4\sqrt{13} = 5\sqrt{13}$ $9x - 4x = 5x$

2. **You *cannot* add or subtract unlike radicals (just as you cannot add or subtract unlike variables).**

   $6\sqrt{5} + 4\sqrt{3} = 6\sqrt{5} + 4\sqrt{3}$ (You cannot add the two and get $10\sqrt{8}$.)

   $6x + 4y = 6x + 4y$ (You cannot add the two and get 10xy.)

Don't glance at a problem, see that the radicals are not the same, and immediately assume that you cannot add the two terms. You may be able to simplify one radical to make it match the radical in the other term.

   $\sqrt{52} + \sqrt{13} = 2\sqrt{13} + \sqrt{13} = 3\sqrt{13}$

   To simplify: Take out a perfect square from the term. $\sqrt{52} = \sqrt{4} \times \sqrt{13}$. Because $\sqrt{4} = 2$, $\sqrt{52} = 2\sqrt{13}$.

   $\sqrt{20} + \sqrt{45} = (\sqrt{4} \times \sqrt{5}) + (\sqrt{9} \times \sqrt{5}) = 2\sqrt{5} + 3\sqrt{5} = 5\sqrt{5}$

Beware! You must simplify *first*. You can't say that $\sqrt{20} + \sqrt{45} = \sqrt{65} = 8.06$. When you work out the correct answer, $5\sqrt{5}$, you see that it's not 8.06, but 11.18.

Multiplication and division

1. **When you multiply or divide radicals, you just multiply or divide the numbers and then pop the radical sign back onto the finished product.**

   $\sqrt{5} \times \sqrt{6} = \sqrt{30}$

   $\sqrt{15} \div \sqrt{5} = \sqrt{3}$

2. **If you have a number in front of the radical, multiply it as well. Let everyone in on the fun.**

$$6\sqrt{3} \times 4\sqrt{2} =$$

$$6 \times 4 = 24$$

$$\sqrt{3} \times \sqrt{2} = \sqrt{6}$$

$$24\sqrt{6}$$

Try this example: $37\sqrt{5} \times 3\sqrt{6} =$

(A) $40\sqrt{11}$

(B) $40\sqrt{30}$

(C) $111\sqrt{11}$

(D) $111\sqrt{30}$

(E) $1,221$

$37 \times 3 = 111$ and $\sqrt{5} \times \sqrt{6} = \sqrt{30}$, so $111\sqrt{30}$. Straightforward multiplication. *Correct Answer:* D.

Inside out

When there is an operation under the radical, do it first and then take the square root.

$$\sqrt{\frac{x^2}{40} + \frac{x^2}{9}}$$

First, solve for $\frac{x^2}{40} + \frac{x^2}{9}$. You get the common denominator of $360\,(40 \times 9)$ and then find the numerators: $9x^2$ and $40x^2$ which make $\frac{49x^2}{360}$. *Now* take the square roots: $49x^2 = 7x$ (because $7x \times 7x = 49x^2$). $\sqrt{360} = 18.97$. Gotcha, I bet! Did you say that $\sqrt{360} = 6$? Wrong! $\sqrt{36} = 6$, but $\sqrt{360}$ = approximately 18.97. Beware of assuming too much; you can be led down the path to temptation.

Your final answer is $\frac{7x}{18.97}$. Of course, you can bet that the answer choices will include $\frac{7x}{6}$.

Probably Probability

Probability questions are usually word problems. They may look intimidating with a lot of words that make you lose sight of where to begin. Two simple rules can solve nearly every probability problem tossed at you.

1. **Create a fraction.**

To find a probability, use this formula:

$$P = \frac{\text{Number of possible desired outcomes}}{\text{Number of total possible outcomes}}$$

Make a probability into a fraction. The denominator is the easier of the two parts to begin with. The denominator is the total possible number of outcomes. For example, when you're flipping a coin, there are two possible outcomes, giving you a denominator of 2. When you're tossing a die (one of a pair of dice), there are six possible outcomes, giving you a denominator of 6. When you're pulling a card out of a deck of cards, there are 52 possible outcomes (52 cards in a deck), giving you a denominator of 52. When 25 marbles are in a jar and you're going to pull out one of them, there are 25 possibilities, giving you a denominator of 25. Very simply, the *denominator* is the whole shebang — everything possible.

The *numerator* is the total possible number of the things you want. If you want to get a head when you toss a coin, there is exactly one head, giving you a numerator of 1. The chances of tossing a head, therefore, are ½, one possible head, two possible outcomes altogether. If you want to get a 5 when you toss a die, there is exactly one 5 on the die, giving you a numerator of 1. Notice that your numerator is *not* 5. The number you want happens to be a 5, but there is only *one* 5 on the die. The probability of tossing a 5 is ⅙. One 5 and six possible outcomes exist altogether.

If you want to draw a jack in a deck of cards, there are four jacks: hearts, diamonds, clubs, and spades. Therefore, the numerator is 4. The probability of drawing a jack out of a deck of cards is ⁴⁄₅₂ (which reduces to ¹⁄₁₃). If you want to draw a jack of hearts, the probability is ¹⁄₅₂ because there is only one jack of hearts.

A jar of marbles has 8 yellow marbles, 6 black marbles, and 12 white marbles. What is the probability of drawing out a black marble?

Use the formula. Begin with the denominator, which is all the possible outcomes: 8 + 6 + 12 = 26. The numerator is how many there are of what you want: 6 black marbles. The probability is ⁶⁄₂₆, which can be reduced or (as is more customary) changed to a percentage. What's the probability of drawing out a yellow marble? ⁸⁄₂₆. A white marble? ¹²⁄₂₆. *Correct Answer:* ⁶⁄₂₆ or ³⁄₁₃ or 23%.

A drawer has 5 pairs of white socks, 8 pairs of black socks, and 12 pairs of brown socks. In a hurry to get to school, Austin pulls out a pair at a time and tosses them on the floor if they are not the color he wants. Looking for a brown pair, Austin pulls out and discards a white pair, a black pair, a black pair, and a white pair. What is the probability that on his next reach into the drawer he will pull out a brown pair of socks?

This problem is slightly more complicated than the preceding one, although it uses the same formula. You began with 25 pairs of socks. However, Austin, that slob, has thrown 4 pairs on the floor. That means that there are only 21 pairs left. The probability of his pulling out a brown pair is ¹²⁄₂₁, or ⁴⁄₇, or about 57%. *Correct Answer:* 57%.

A cookie jar has chocolate, vanilla, and strawberry wafer cookies. There are 30 of each type. Bess reaches in, pulls out a chocolate, and eats it and then in quick succession pulls out and eats a vanilla, chocolate, strawberry, strawberry, chocolate, and vanilla. Assuming that she doesn't get sick or get caught, what is the probability that the next cookie she pulls out will be a chocolate one?

Originally, there were 90 cookies. Bess has scarfed down 7 of them, leaving 83. Careful! If you're about to put ³⁰⁄₈₃, you're headed for a trap. There are no longer 30 chocolate cookies; there are only 27 because Bess has eaten 3. The probability is now ²⁷⁄₈₃, or about 33%. *Correct Answer:* 33%.

Probability must always be between zero and one. You cannot have a negative probability and you cannot have a probability greater than 1, or 100%.

2. Multiply consecutive probabilities.

What is the probability that you'll get two heads when you toss a coin twice? You find each probability separately and then *multiply* the two. The chance of tossing a coin the first time and getting a head is ½. The chance of tossing a coin the second time and getting a head is ½. Multiply those consecutive probabilities: ½ × ½ = ¼. The chances of getting two heads are one out of four.

What is the probability of tossing a die twice and getting a 5 on the first toss and a 6 on the second toss? Treat each toss separately. The probability of getting a 5 is ⅙. The probability of getting a 6 is ⅙. Multiply consecutive probabilities: ⅙ × ⅙ = ¹⁄₃₆.

Here's a good trick question.

Column A	*Column B*

A fair die is tossed twice.

Chances of getting a 5 on the first toss and a 2 on the second toss	Chances of getting a 6 on both tosses

If you chose A, you fell for the trap. You may think that it's harder to roll the same number twice, but the probability is the same as rolling two different numbers. Treat each roll separately. The probability of rolling a 5 is $\frac{1}{6}$. The probability of rolling a 2 is $\frac{1}{6}$. Multiply consecutive probabilities: $\frac{1}{6} \times \frac{1}{6} = \frac{1}{36}$. For Column B, treat each toss separately. The probability of rolling a 6 is $\frac{1}{6}$. The probability of rolling a second 6 is $\frac{1}{6}$. Multiply consecutive probabilities: $\frac{1}{6} \times \frac{1}{6} = \frac{1}{36}$. *Correct Answer:* C.

If you've had a course in statistics, you may have learned about independent events, mutually exclusive events, and interdependent events. Forget about them; they're not on the GRE. The material you just learned is about as complicated as probability gets.

Chapter 13

Miscellaneous Math You Probably Already Know

· ·

In This Chapter

▶ Time, rate, and distance problems

▶ Averages

▶ Percentages

▶ Number sets and prime and composite numbers

▶ Mixture, interest, and work problems

▶ Absolute value

▶ Order of operations

▶ Units of measurement

▶ Decimals and fractions

▶ Statistics

▶ Graphs

· ·

You probably already know the material in this chapter, but a quick review can't hurt you. (The humor — now that's another story!)

DIRTy Math: Distance, Rate, and Time

D.I.R.T. Distance Is Rate × Time. *D = RT.* When you have a time, rate, and distance problem, use this formula. Make a chart with the formula across the top and fill in the spaces on the chart.

Jennifer drives 40 miles an hour for two and a half hours. Her friend Ashley goes the same distance but drives at one and a half times Jennifer's speed. How many *minutes* longer does Jennifer drive than Ashley?

Do *not* start making big, hairy formulas with *x*'s and *y*'s. Jennifer has no desire to be known as Madame *x*; Ashley refuses to know *y*. Make the DIRT chart.

| **Distance** | **=** | **Rate** | **×** | **Time** |

When you fill in the 40 mph and 2½ hours for Jennifer, you can calculate that she went 100 miles. Think of it this simple way: If she goes 40 mph for one hour, that's 40 miles. For a second hour, she goes another 40 miles. In a half-hour, she goes ½ of 40, or 20 miles. (See? You don't have to write down 40 × 2½ and do all that pencil pushing; use your brain, not your yellow #2.) Add them together: 40 + 40 + 20 = 100. Jennifer has gone 100 miles.

Distance	=	Rate	×	Time
100 (Jennifer)		40 mph		2½ hours

Because Ashley drives the same distance, fill in 100 under distance for her. She goes one and a half times as fast. Uh-uh, put down that pencil. Use your brain! 1×40 is 40; $\frac{1}{2} \times 40$ is 20. Add $40 + 20 = 60$. Ashley drives 60 mph. Now this gets really easy. If she drives at 60 mph, she drives one mile a minute. (60 minutes in an hour, 60 miles in an hour. You figure it out, Einstein.) Therefore, to go 100 miles takes her 100 minutes. Because the question asks for your final in minutes, don't bother converting this to hours; leave it the way it is.

Distance	=	Rate	×	Time
100 (Ashley)		60 mph		100 minutes

Last step. Jennifer drives 2½ hours. How many minutes is that? Do it the easy way, in your brain. One hour is 60 minutes. A second hour is another 60 minutes. A half hour is 30 minutes. Add them together: $60 + 60 + 30 = 150$ minutes. If Jennifer drives for 150 minutes and Ashley drives for 100 minutes, Jennifer drives 50 minutes more than Ashley. However, Ashley gets a speeding ticket, has her driving privileges taken away by an irate father, and doesn't get to go to this weekend's party. Jennifer goes and gets her pick of the hunks, ending up with Tyrone's ring and frat pin. The moral of the story: Slow . . . but steady!

Distance	=	Rate	×	Time
100 (Jennifer)		40 mph		150 minutes
100 (Ashley)		60 mph		100 minutes

Be careful to note whether the people are traveling in the *same* direction or *opposite* directions. Suppose that you're asked how far apart drivers are at the end of their trip. If you are told that Jordan travels 40 mph east for 2 hours and Connor travels 60 mph west for 3 hours, they are going in opposite directions. If they start from the same point at the same time, Jordan has gone 80 miles one way, and Connor has gone 180 miles the opposite way. They are 260 miles apart. The trap answer is 100, because careless people (not *you!*) simply subtract: $180 - 80$.

It All Averages Out: Averages

You can always do averages the way Ms. Jones taught you when you were in third grade: Add all the terms, and then divide by the number of terms.

$$5 + 11 + 17 + 23 + 29 = 85$$

$$\frac{85}{5} = 17$$

Or you can save wear-and-tear on the brain cells and know the following rule:

1. The average of evenly spaced terms is the middle term.

First, check that the terms are evenly spaced. If the terms are evenly spaced, an equal number of units are between each pair of terms. In this case, the terms are six apart. Second, circle the middle term, which is 17 here. Third, go home, make popcorn, and watch the late-night movie with all the time you've saved.

Try another one. Find the average of these numbers:

32, 41, 50, 59, 68, 77, 86, 95, 104

Don't reach for your pencil. You look and see that the terms are all nine units apart. Because they are evenly spaced, the middle term is the average: 68.

This is an easy trick to love, but don't march down the aisle with it yet. The tip works only for *evenly spaced* terms. If you have just any old batch of numbers, such as 4, 21, 97, 98, 199, you can't look at the middle term for the average. You have to find the average of those numbers the old-fashioned way.

Find the average of these numbers:

3, 10, 17, 24, 31, 38, 45, 52

First, double-check that they are evenly spaced. Here, the numbers are spaced by sevens. Next you look for the middle number . . . and there isn't one. You can, of course, find the two central terms, 24 and 31, and find the middle between them. That's a pain, but suppose that you have 38 numbers. It's very easy to make a mistake as to which terms are the central ones. If you're off just a little bit, you miss the question. Instead, use rule number two:

2. **The average of evenly spaced terms is** $^{(first + last)}/_2$.

Just add the first and the last terms, which are obvious at a glance, and divide that sum by 2. Here, 3 + 52 = 55. $^{55}/_2$ = 27.5.

Note: Double-check using your common sense. Suppose that you made a silly mistake and got 45 for your answer. A glance at the numbers tells you that 45 is not in the middle and therefore cannot be the average.

This tip works for *all* evenly spaced terms. It doesn't matter whether there is a middle number, as in the first example, or no middle number, as in the second example. Go back to the first example.

32, 41, 50, 59, 68, 77, 86, 95, 104

Instead of finding the middle term, add the first and last terms and divide by 2, like this: 32 + 104 = 136. $^{136}/_2$ = 68. Either way works.

Missing term average problem

You are likely to find a problem like this:

A student takes seven exams. Her scores on the first six are 91, 89, 85, 92, 90, and 88. If her average on all *seven* exams is 90, what did she get on the seventh exam?

This is called a *missing term average problem* because you are given an average and asked to find a missing term. Duh.

1. **You can do this the basic algebraic way.**

$$Average = \frac{Sum}{Number\ of\ terms}$$

$$90 = \frac{Sum}{7}$$

Because you don't know the seventh term, call it x. Add the first six terms (and get 535) and x.

$$90 = \frac{(535 + x)}{7} \quad \text{Cross-multiply: } 90 \times 7 = 535 + x$$

$$630 = 535 + x$$

$$95 = x$$

The seventh exam score was 95.

2. **You can do these problems the commonsense way.**

There is another quick way to do this problem. You've probably done it this way all your life without realizing what a genius you are.

Suppose that your dad tells you that if you average a 90 for the semester in advanced physics, he'll let you take that summer trip through Europe with your buddies that the two of you have been arguing about for months. (He figures he's safe because there's no way you're going to get such a high grade in that incredibly difficult class.) You take him at his word and begin working hard.

On the first exam, you get 91 and you're +1 point. That is, you're one point above the ultimate score you want, a 90. On the second exam, you get 89 and you're –1. On that test, you're one point below the ultimate score you want, a 90. On the third exam, you get an 85, which is –5. You're five points below the ultimate score you want, a 90.

Are you getting the hang of this? Here's how it looks.

> 91 = +1
>
> 89 = –1
>
> 85 = –5
>
> 92 = +2
>
> 90 = 0
>
> 88 = –2

The +1 and –1 cancel each other out, and the +2 and –2 cancel each other out. You're left with –5, meaning you're five points in the hole. You have to make up those five points on the last exam or get five points *above* what you want for your ultimate score. Because you want a 90, you need a 95 on the last test.

Try another, using the no-brainer method. A student takes seven exams. She gets an 88 average on all of them. Her first six scores are 89, 98, 90, 82, 88, and 87. What does she get on the seventh exam?

> Average = 88
>
> 89 = +1
>
> 98 = +10
>
> 90 = +2
>
> 82 = –6
>
> 88 = 0
>
> 87 = –1

The +1 and –1 cancel. Then you have $(10 + 2) = +12$ and –6, for a total of +6. You are six points *above* what you need for the ultimate outcome. You can afford to lose six points on the final exam or to be six points *below* the average. That gives you an 82.

You may be given only five out of seven scores and asked for *the average of the missing two* terms. Do the same thing and then divide by 2.

Algebraic way:

> *Average* of seven exams: 85
>
> *Scores* of the first five exams: 86, 79, 82, 85, 84
>
> *Find:* The average score of each of the remaining exams
>
> $$85 = \frac{(86 + 79 + 82 + 85 + 84) + x + x}{7}$$
>
> Cross-multiply: $595 = 416 + 2x$
>
> $595 - 416 = 2x$
>
> $179 = 2x$
>
> $89.5 = x$

Commonsense way:

> Average = 85
>
> 86 = +1
>
> 79 = –6
>
> 82 = –3
>
> 85 = 0
>
> 84 = –1

The +1 and –1 cancel each other out. You are left with –9 for *two* exams or –4.5 per exam. If you are *down* four and a half points, you must *gain* those four and a half points on each of the two exams:

> $85 + 4.5 = 89.5$

 The shortcut, commonsense way is quick and easy, but don't forget to make the change at the end. That is, if you decide that you are *minus nine* points going into the final exam, you need to be *plus nine* points on that last exam to come out even. If you subtract nine points from the average rather than add them, you'll probably come up with one of the trap answers.

Weighted averages

In a *weighted average,* some scores count more than others.

Number of Students	Score
12	80
13	75
10	70

If you are asked to find the average score for the students in this class, you know that you can't simply add 80, 75, and 70 and divide by three because the scores weren't evenly distributed among the students. Because 12 students got an 80, multiply $12 \times 80 = 960$. Do the same with the other scores:

$13 \times 75 = 975$

$10 \times 70 = 700$

$960 + 975 + 700 = 2,635$

Divide *not by three* but by the total number of students: $35\,(12 + 13 + 10)$

$\dfrac{2635}{35} = 75.29$

You can often answer a Quantitative Comparison question on weighted averages without doing all the work, as demonstrated in the following example. (See Chapter 14 for more information about QC questions and how to answer them.)

The answer choices are

A if the quantity in Column A is greater.

B if the quantity in Column B is greater.

C if the two quantities are equal.

D if the relationship cannot be determined from the information given.

Column A		Column B

Clothing	Quantity	Cost per Item
Black T-shirts	5	$20
Denim shirts	8	$25
Blue jeans	20	$30

Average cost per item of clothing	$25

You can work this whole problem out, finding the cost of all the T-shirts, denim shirts, and jeans and then dividing that cost by the number of items of clothing. When you do all that work, you get 27.27 (and a headache and a sore pencil-pushing finger). Or you can use your brain and common sense: 13 items are $25 or less, and 20 items are $30. Therefore, there are more items at above $25 than below $25. The average must be more than $25. Remember, because this is a QC problem, you don't need to solve it through for the final, precise solution; you need only enough information to compare the quantities in the two columns. *Correct Answer:* A.

Percentage Panic

The mere mention of the word *percent* may strike terror in your heart. There's no reason to panic over percentages; there are ways of getting around them.

Ignorance is bliss

Whoever imagined that ignoring percentage marks can help you figure percentages. A couple of ways this works include:

1. **Ignore the percentage's very existence. You can express a percentage as a decimal, which is a lot less intimidating. You do so by putting a decimal point two places to the left of the percentage and dropping the % sign.**

   35% = .35   83% = .83   50% = .50   33.3% = .333   66.6% = .666

   If you have a choice of working with decimals or percentages, it's better to choose decimals.

2. **Another way to ignore a percentage is to convert it to a fraction. The word percent means per cent, or per hundred. Every percentage is that number over 100.**

   $50\% = {}^{50}/_{100}$ $33\% = {}^{33}/_{100}$ $75\% = {}^{75}/_{100}$

   If you can't ignore the percentage, remember that a percent is

   $$\frac{\text{Part}}{\text{Whole}} \times 100, \text{ or } \frac{is}{of} \times 100$$

   What percent *is* 45 *of* 90? Put the part, 45, over the whole, 90. Or put the *is*, 45, over the *of*, 90:

   $${}^{45}/_{90} = \frac{1}{2} \times 100 = {}^{100}/_{2} = 50\%$$

   42 *is* what percent *of* 126? Put the part, 42, over the whole, 126. Or put the *is*, 42, over the *of*, 126.

   $${}^{42}/_{126} = \frac{1}{3} \times 100 = {}^{100}/_{3} = 33\frac{1}{3}\%$$

   Want one that's a little harder? What is 40% of 80? You may be tempted to put the *is*, 40, over the *of*, 80, and get ${}^{40}/_{80} = \frac{1}{2} \times 100 = {}^{100}/_{2} = 50\%$. However, when the problem is worded this way, you don't know the *is*. Your equation must be ${}^{x}/_{80} = {}^{40}/_{100}$. Cross-multiply: $3200 = 100x$. $x = 32$. There's an easier way to do it: *of* means *times*, or multiply. Because 40% = .40, multiply $.40 \times 80 = 32$.

Life has its ups and downs: Percent increase/decrease

You may see a problem asking you what percent increase or decrease occurred in the number of games a team won or the amount of commission a person earned. To find a percent increase or decrease, use this formula:

$$\text{percent increase or decrease} = \frac{\text{number increase or decrease}}{\text{original whole}}$$

In basic English, to find the percent by which something has increased or decreased, you take two simple steps:

1. **Find the *number* (amount) by which the thing has increased or decreased.** For example, if a team won 25 games last year and 30 games this year, the number increase was 5. If a salesperson earned $10,000 last year and $8,000 this year, the number decrease was 2,000. Make that the numerator of the fraction.

2. **Find the *original whole.*** This figure is what you started out with before you increased or decreased. If a team won 25 games last year and won 30 games this year, the original number was 25. If the salesperson earned $10,000 last year and $8,000 this year, the original number was 10,000. Make that the denominator.

You now have a fraction. Make it a decimal, and multiply by 100 to make it a percentage.

In 1992, Coach Jarchow won 30 prizes at the county fair by tossing a basketball into a bushel basket. In 1993, he won 35 prizes. What was his percent increase?

(A) 100

(B) 30

(C) 16⅔

(D) 14.28

(E) .1$\overline{66}$

The number by which his prizes increased, from 30 to 35, is 5. That is the numerator. The original whole, or what he began with, is 30. That is the denominator. *Correct Answer:* C.

$$\text{⁵/₃₀} = \text{⅙} = 16\text{⅔}\%$$

If you chose E, I fooled you. The question asks what *percent* increase there was. If you say E, you're saying that there was a .1$\overline{66}$ percent increase. Not so. The .1$\overline{66}$ increase *as a percentage* is 16⅔%. If you chose D, you fell for another trap. You put the 5 increase over the 35 instead of over the 30.

Two years ago, Haylie scored 22 goals while playing soccer. This year, she scored 16 goals. What was her approximate percentage decrease?

(A) 72

(B) 37.5

(C) 27

(D) 16

(E) .$\overline{27}$

Find the number of the decrease: 22 − 16 = 6. That is the numerator. Find the original whole from which she is decreasing: 22. That is the denominator. ⁶/₂₂ ≈ .$\overline{27}$, or approximately 27 percent. *Correct Answer:* C.

If you chose A, you put 16 over 22 instead of putting the decrease over the original whole. If you chose E, again you forgot the difference between .27 and .27 *percent.* If you chose B, you put the decrease of 6 over the new amount, 16, rather than over the original whole. Note how easy these traps are to fall for. My suggestion: Write down the actual formula and then plug in the numbers. Writing down the formula may be boring, but doing so takes only a few seconds and may save you points.

Here's a tricky question that many people do in their heads (instead of writing down the formula and plugging in numbers) and blow big time.

Carissa has three quarters. Her father gives her three more. Carissa's wealth has increased by what percent?

(A) 50

(B) 100

(C) 200

(D) 300

(E) 500

Did you fall for the trap answer, C? Her wealth has doubled, to be sure, but the percent increase is only 100. You can prove that with the formula: The number increase is .75 (she has three more quarters, or 75 cents). Her original whole was .75. $^{75}/_{75} = 1 = 100\%$. *Correct Answer:* B.

When you double something, you increase by 100 percent because you have to subtract the original "one" you began with. When you triple something, you increase by 200 percent because you have to subtract the original you began with. For example, if you had three dollars and you now have nine dollars, you have tripled your money but increased by only 200 percent. Do the formula: number increase = 6 dollars. Original whole = 3 dollars. $^{6}/_{3} = 2 = 200$ percent. Take a wild guess at what percent you increase when you quadruple your money? That's right, 300 percent. Just subtract the original 100 percent.

Ready, Sets, Go: Number Sets

There's no escaping vocabulary. Even on the math portion of the test, you need to know certain terms. How can you solve a problem that asks you to "state your answer in integral values only" if you don't know what integral values are? Here are the number sets with which you'll be working.

- **Counting numbers:** 1, 2, 3 . . . Note that 0 is *not* a counting number.

- **Whole numbers:** 0, 1, 2, 3 . . . Note that 0 *is* a whole number.

- **Integers:** . . . –3, –2, –1, 0, 1, 2, 3 . . . When a question asks for *integral values,* it wants the answer in integers only. For example, you can't give an answer like 4.3 because that's not an integer. You need to round down to 4.

- **Rational numbers:** Rational numbers can be expressed as $^{a}/_{b}$, where *a* and *b* are integers.

  Examples: 1 (because 1 = $^{1}/_{1}$ and 1 is an integer), $^{1}/_{2}$ (because 1 and 2 are integers), $^{9}/_{2}$ (because 9 and 2 are integers), and $^{-4}/_{2}$ (because –4 and 2 are integers).

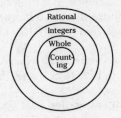

Notice that every number set so far has included the previous number sets. Whole numbers include counting numbers, integers include counting numbers and whole numbers, and rationals include counting numbers, whole numbers, and integers.

- **Irrational numbers:** The highly technical definition here is *anything not rational.* That is, an irrational number cannot be written as $^{a}/_{b}$, where *a* and *b* are integers. Numbers whose decimals do not terminate and do not repeat can't be written as a fraction and therefore are irrational.

  Examples: π cannot be written *exactly* as 3.14; it is nonterminating and nonrepeating. $\sqrt{2}$ is approximately 1.4142 but is nonterminating and nonrepeating.

  Irrational numbers *do not* include the previous number sets. That is, irrational numbers don't include counting numbers, whole numbers, integers, or rational numbers.

✔ **Real numbers:** Briefly put, all of the preceding. Real numbers include counting numbers, whole numbers, integers, rationals, and irrationals. For all practical purposes, real numbers are everything you think of as numbers. When a question tells you to "express your answer in real numbers," don't sweat it. That's almost no constraint at all because nearly everything you see is a real number.

There are such critters as *imaginary* numbers, which are *not* on the GRE. (Most of you probably stopped reading right there, figuring that you don't even want to hear about them if they're not going to be tested. I don't blame you.) Imaginary numbers are expressed with a lowercase *i* and are studied in upper-division math classes. I won't go into them here because, once again, *they are not tested on the GRE.* All numbers on the GRE are real numbers.

Prime Time: Prime and Composite Numbers

Prime numbers are positive integers that have exactly two positive integer factors; they cannot be divided by numbers other than 1 and themselves. Examples include 2, 3, 5, 7, and 11.

There are a few lovely tricks to prime numbers:

✔ Zero is *not* a prime number (by definition). Why? Because it is divisible by more than two factors. Zero can be divided by 1, 2, 3, and on to infinity. Although division by zero is undefined (and isn't tested on the GRE), you can divide zero by other numbers; the answer of course is always zero. $0 \div 1 = 0$; $1 \div 2 = 0$; $1 \div 412 = 0$.

✔ One is *not* a prime number (by definition). There are not two factors of 1. It cannot be divided only by 1 *and* itself. Confused? Don't worry about it. Just memorize the fact that 1 is not a prime number.

✔ Two is the *only* even prime. People tend to think that all prime numbers are odd. Well, almost. Two is prime because it has only two factors; it can be divided only by 1 and itself.

✔ Not all odd numbers are prime. Think of 9 or 15; those numbers are odd but not prime because they have more than two factors and can be divided by more than just 1 and themselves. $9 = (1 \times 9)$ *and* (3×3). $15 = (1 \times 15)$ *and* (3×5).

Composite numbers have more than two factors and can be divided by more than just 1 and themselves. Examples: 4, 6, 8, 9, 12, 14, and 15.

Note that composite numbers (called that because they are *composed* of more than two factors) can be even or odd.

Don't confuse *prime* and *composite* and *even* and *odd* with *positive* and *negative.* That's an easy mistake to make in the confusion of the exam. If a problem that you know should be easy is flustering you, stop and ask yourself whether you're making this common mistake.

I said that 0 and 1 are not prime. They are also not composite. What are they? Neither. You express this as, "Zero and one are neither prime nor composite." It's rather like wondering whether zero is positive or negative. You say, "Zero is neither positive nor negative." Why should you know this? Here's an example when the information can win you ten points (the approximate value of one correct math question).

The answer choices are

A if the quantity in Column A is greater.

B if the quantity in Column B is greater.

C if the two quantities are equal.

D if the relationship cannot be determined from the information given.

Column A	_Column B_
The number of prime numbers from 0 to 10 inclusive	The number of prime numbers from 11 to 20 inclusive

The prime numbers from 0 to 10 inclusive are 2, 3, 5, and 7. Note that 0 and 1 are *not* prime. If you count either or both as prime, you miss an otherwise very easy question. In Column B, the prime numbers from 11 to 20 inclusive are 11, 13, 17, and 19. Both columns have four prime numbers. *Correct Answer:* C.

I'm All Mixed Up: Mixture Problems

A mixture problem is a word problem that looks much more confusing than it actually is. There are two types of mixtures: problems in which the items remain separate (when you mix peanuts and raisins, you still have peanuts and raisins, not pearains or raispeans) and problems in which the two elements blend (these are usually chemicals, like water and alcohol). Check out the separate mixture first.

Marshall wants to mix 40 pounds of beads selling for 30 cents a pound with a quantity of sequins selling for 80 cents a pound. He wants to pay 40 cents per pound for the final mix. How many pounds of sequins should he use?

The hardest part for most students is knowing where to begin. Make a chart.

	Pounds	_Price_	_Total_
Beads	40	$.30	$12.00
Sequins	x	$.80	.80x
Mixture	40 + x	$.40	.40(40 + x)

Reason it out. In pennies, the cost of the beads (1200) plus the cost of the sequins (80x) must equal the cost of the mixture (1600 + 40x). Note that you dump the decimal point (officially, you multiply by 100 to get rid of the decimal point, but really, you dump it). Now you have a workable equation:

$$1200 + 80x = 1600 + 40x$$

$$80x - 40x = 1600 - 1200$$

$$40x = 400$$

$$x = 10$$

Careful! Keep in mind what x stands for. It represents the number of pounds of sequins, what the question asks for.

Go back and double-check by plugging this value into the equation. You already know that Marshall spent $12 on beads. If he buys 10 pounds of sequins for 80 cents, he spends $8, for a total of $20. He spends that $20 on 50 pounds: 2000 ÷ 50 = 40. How about that, it works!

Greed Is Great: Interest Problems

This is a pretty problem: PRTI, to be exact. *P* = Principal, the amount of money you begin with, or the amount you invest. *R* = Rate, the interest rate you're earning on the money. *T* = Time, the amount of time you leave the money in the interest-bearing account. *I* = Interest, the amount of interest you earn on the investment. A problem usually asks you how much interest someone earned on his or her investment.

The formula is $PRT = I.$ Principal × Rate × Time = Interest.

Janet invested $1,000 at 5 percent annual interest for one year. How much interest did she earn?

This is the simplest type of problem. Plug the numbers into the formula.

$$PRT = I$$

$1000 \times .05 \times 1 = 50.$ She earned $50 interest.

The answer choices may try to trap you with variations on a decimal place, making the answers 5, 50, 500, and so on. You know that 5% = $\frac{5}{100}$ = .05; be careful how you multiply.

These problems are not intentionally vicious (unlike 99 percent of the rest of the GRE, right?). You won't see something that gets crazy on interest rates, like "5 percent annual interest compounded quarterly for 3 months and 6 percent quarterly interest compounded daily," blah, blah, blah.

(Useless but fascinating trivia: In Bulgarian, the word for *thank you* is pronounced *blah-go-dah-ree-uh*. But a shortened form, like *thanks*, is simply *blah*. If your mother takes you to task for being a smart aleck and going "blah, blah, blah" when she talks, you can innocently claim that you're practicing your Bulgarian and are just thanking her for her wisdom.)

All Work and No Play: Work Problems

The formula most commonly used in a work problem is

$$\text{Work} = \frac{\text{Time put in}}{\text{Capacity (time to do the whole job)}}$$

Find each person's contribution. The denominator is the easy part; it represents how many hours (minutes, days, weeks, and so on) it would take the person to do the whole job, working alone. The numerator is how long the person has already worked. For example, if Janie can paint a house in four days and has been working for one day, she has done ¼ of the work. If Evelyn can paint a house in nine days and has been working for five, she has done 5/9 of the project.

So far, so good. The problem comes when more than one person works at the task. What happens when Janie and Evelyn work together?

Janie working alone can paint a house in six days. Evelyn working alone can paint it in eight days. Working together, how long will it take them to paint the house?

Find Janie's work: ⅚. Find Evelyn's work: ⅞. Together, the two fractions must add up to 1, the entire job.

⅚ + ⅞ = 1

Multiply by the common denominator, 48, to eliminate the fractions.

$^{48}x/_6 + ^{48}x/_8 = 8$

$8x + 6x = 48$

$14x = 48$

x = approximately 3.43

It would take the two women working together about 3.43 days to paint the house.

Double-check by using your common sense. If you get an answer of 10, for example, you know that you must have made a mistake because the two women working together should be able to do the job *more quickly* than either one working alone.

Reading Between the Lines: Absolute Value

The absolute value is the magnitude of a number. So much for the official definition. The *For Dummies* definition (that is, the easy way to think about it) of *absolute value* is the positive form of a number. Absolute value is indicated by two vertical parallel lines (like this: | |).

Any number within those lines is read as "The absolute value of that number." For example, |3| = 3 is read as "The absolute value of three equals three." That seems straightforward enough, but what if the number inside the straight lines is negative? Its absolute value is still positive: |−3| = 3. Here's a tricky problem you're likely to see on the exam.

$-|-3| = -3$

The answer may seem contrary to common sense. Isn't a negative times a negative a positive? True, but you have to work from the inside out. The absolute value of negative three is three. Then you multiply three by the negative to get negative three. *Correct Answer: −3.* Here's another example that's even a little harder.

$-|-|-5|| =$

Here's the official way to work the problem (**Hint:** The word *official* is a clue that in a minute I'm going to give you an unofficial, much easier way to solve this.) Work from the inside out. Say it to yourself as you go along: "The absolute value of negative five is 5. Then the negative of that is negative 5. But the absolute value of negative 5 is 5. And finally, the negative of that is −5." *Correct Answer: −5.*

Do you see the super-shortcut for the above example? You actually don't have to work the problem out at all! Anything and everything inside the absolute value signs is going to be positive. Then the one negative sign outside changes the whole problem to negative. You don't, in other words, have to go through the intermediate steps. With an absolute value, look to see whether a negative sign is outside the first absolute value symbol. If it is, the number is negative. If it's not, the number is positive. Simple as that.

Smooth Operator: Order of Operations

When you have several operations (addition, subtraction, multiplication, division, squaring, and so on) in one problem, there is a definite order in which you must perform the operations:

1. **Parentheses.** Do what's inside the parentheses first.

2. **Power.** Do the squaring or the cubing, whatever the exponent is.

3. **Multiply or divide.** Do these left to right. If multiplication is to the left of division, multiply first. If division is to the left of multiplication, divide first.

4. **Add or subtract.** Do these left to right. If addition is to the left of subtraction, add first. If subtraction is to the left of addition, subtract first.

An easy *mnemonic* (memory) device for remembering these is *Please Praise My Daughter And Son* (PPMDAS): Parentheses, Power, Multiply, Divide, Add, Subtract.

$$10\,(3-5)^2 + (^{30}\!/_5)^0 =$$

First, do what's inside the parentheses: $3 - 5 = -2$. $^{30}\!/_5 = 6$. Next, do the power: $-2^2 = 4$. $6^0 = 1$. (Did you remember that any number to the zero power equals one?) Next, multiply: $10 \times 4 = 40$. Finally, add: $40 + 1 = 41$. *Correct Answer:* 41. Try another.

$$3 + (9-6)^2 - 5(^8\!/_2)^{-2} =$$

First, do what's inside the parentheses: $9 - 6 = 3$. $^8\!/_2 = 4$. Second, do the powers: $3^2 = 9$. $4^{-2} = ^1\!/_{(4^2)} = ^1\!/_{16}$. Multiply: $5 \times ^1\!/_{16} = ^5\!/_{16}$. Finally, add and subtract left to right. $3 + 9 = 12$. Then $12 - ^5\!/_{16} = 11^{11}\!/_{16}$. *Correct Answer:* $11^{11}\!/_{16}$.

Measuring Up: Units of Measurement

Occasionally, you may be expected to know a unit of measurement that the test makers deem obvious but which you have forgotten. Take a few minutes to review this brief list.

International students, in particular, need to memorize these because you may not have grown up using some of the same units of measurement as those used in the United States (and on the GRE).

1. **Quantities**

    16 ounces = 1 pound

    2,000 pounds = 1 ton

    2 cups = 1 pint

    2 pints = 1 quart

    4 quarts = 1 gallon

You can calculate that a gallon has 16 cups, or eight pints. To help you remember, think of borrowing a cup of sugar. Sugar is sweet, and you have a Sweet 16 birthday party: 16 sweet cups of sugar in a gallon. It may be silly, but the best memory aids usually are.

2. **Length**

    12 inches = 1 foot

    3 feet (36 inches) = 1 yard

    5,280 feet (1,760 yards) = 1 mile

Everyone knows that there are 12 inches in a foot. How many square inches are there in a square foot? If you say 12, you've fallen for the trap. $12 \times 12 = 144$ square inches are in a square foot.

Here's how you may fall for that trap in an otherwise easy problem.

The answer choices are

A if the quantity in Column A is greater.

B if the quantity in Column B is greater.

C if the two quantities are equal.

D if the relationship cannot be determined from the information given.

Column A	_Column B_
Number of square inches in 3 square feet	36

Your first reaction is to think that the columns are equal because there are 12 inches to a foot and $12 \times 3 = 36$. However, a square foot is $12 \times 12 = 144$ inches. Because 144×3 is definitely greater than 36 (don't waste any time doing the math), the answer is A. _Correct Answer:_ A.

Bonus: How many cubic inches are there in a cubic foot? Not 12, and not even 144. A cubic foot is $12 \times 12 \times 12 = 1,728$ cubic inches.

3. Time

> 60 seconds = 1 minute
>
> 60 minutes = 1 hour
>
> 24 hours = 1 day
>
> 7 days = 1 week
>
> 52 weeks = 1 year
>
> 365 days = 1 year
>
> 366 days = 1 leap year

Leap year is an interesting concept in terms of math problems. It comes around every four years. The extra day, February 29, makes 366 days in the year. Why do you need to know this? Suppose that you see this problem:

Mr. Pellaton's neon sign flashes four hours a day, every day all year, for four years. If it costs him three cents a day for electricity, how much will he owe for electricity at the end of the fourth year?

You may be tempted to say that this problem is super easy — multiply 365×4 to find the number of days and then multiply that number by .03. Wrong-o! You forgot that extra day for leap year, and your answer is off by three cents. You _know_ that the test makers will have that wrong answer lurking among the answer choices just to trap you. Whenever there is a four-year period, look out for the leap year with an extra day.

What's the Point: Decimals

Here's where a calculator would be very helpful. But until the test makers join the twenty-first century and let you use a calculator, you'll have to rely on brainpower, not battery power. (By the way, did you know that students taking the SAT and ACT are now allowed to use a calculator? Things are changing.)

Adding and subtracting decimals

Line up the decimal points vertically and add or subtract the numbers.

```
    3.09
    4.72
   31.9
  121.046
  160.756
```

If you're rushed for time and don't want to do the whole problem, go to extremes. The extremes are the far-left and far-right columns. Often, calculating them alone gives you enough information to choose the right answer to a multiple-choice problem. In this case, you can look at the far right, which is the thousands column, and know that it has to end in a 6. Suppose that the answer choices are

(A) 160.999

(B) 160.852

(C) 160.756

(D) 159.831

(E) 159.444

You know immediately that C has to be the correct choice.

Maybe more than one of the answer choices uses the correct digit for the far-right column. Okay, you're flexible; head for the far-left column, which here is the hundreds place. You know in this problem it has to be a 1. The answer choices are

(A) 160.756

(B) 201.706

(C) 209.045

(D) 210.006

(E) 301.786

Only choice A has the correct far-left number.

Multiplying decimals

The biggest trap is keeping the number of decimal places correct. The number of decimal places in the product (the number you get when you multiply the terms together) must be the same as the sum of the number of decimal places in all the terms.

$5.06 \times 3.9 =$

$$\begin{array}{r} 5.06 \\ \times 3.9 \\ \hline 19.734 \end{array}$$

There are two decimal places in the first term and one in the second, for a total of three. Therefore, the final answer must have three decimal places.

The shortcut you learned for addition and subtraction works here as well. Go to extremes. Look at the far-right and far-left terms. You know that $6 \times 9 = 54$, so the last digit in the answer has to be a 4. You can eliminate wrong answers by using that information. You know that $5 \times 3 = 15$, but you may have to carry over some other numbers to make the far-left value greater than 15 (as it turns out here). At least you know that the far-left digits must be 15 *or more*. An answer choice starting with 14, 13, or anything less than 15 can be eliminated.

Dividing decimals

Turn the decimals into integers by moving the decimal point to the right the appropriate number of places for both terms, the one you are dividing and the one you are dividing by (called the *divisor,* should you happen to care).

$$4.44 \div .06 = {}^{444}\!/_{6} = 74$$

I won't spend much time on decimals because you almost certainly won't spend much time on them yourself. Just remember two things:

- ✔ Keep a wary eye on the decimal point; its placement is often a trap for the careless.

- ✔ Go to extremes: Determine the far-left or far-right digit and use that information to eliminate incorrect answer choices.

Broken Hearts, Broken Numbers: Fractions

Fractions strike fear into the hearts of most mere mortals. Fortunately, the number of fraction problems on the GRE is small and getting smaller all the time.

Adding or subtracting fractions

1. **You can add or subtract fractions only when they have the same denominator.**

$$\frac{1}{3} + \frac{4}{3} = \frac{5}{3}$$

$$\frac{3}{8} - \frac{2}{8} = \frac{1}{8}$$

2. **When fractions have the same denominator, add or subtract the numerators only.**

3. **When fractions don't have the same denominator, you have to find a common denominator.**

You can, of course, multiply all the denominators, but that often doesn't give you the *lowest* common denominator. You end up with some humongous, overwhelming number that you'd rather not work with. Instead, use this little trick:

4. **To find the lowest common denominator, identify the highest denominator and count by it.**

Find the lowest common denominator of 15 and 6. Sure, you can multiply $15 \times 6 = 90$, but that's not the *lowest* common denominator. Instead, count by 15's because it's the larger of the two. 15? No, 6 doesn't go into that. 30? Yes, both 15 and 6 go into 30. That's the *lowest* common denominator.

Try another one: Find the lowest common denominator for 2, 4, and 5. Count by 5's: 5? No, 2 and 4 don't go into it. 10? No, 4 doesn't go into it. 15? No, 2 and 4 don't go into it. 20? Yes, all the numbers divide evenly into 20. That number is much smaller than the one you get when you multiply $2 \times 4 \times 5 = 40$.

5. **In many problems, you don't even have to find the lowest common denominator. You can find any common denominator by multiplying the denominators.**

$$\frac{4}{15} + \frac{1}{6} =$$

The common denominator is $15 \times 6 = 90$. Cross-multiply: $4 \times 6 = 24$. The first fraction becomes $^{24}\!/_{90}$. Cross-multiply: $1 \times 15 = 15$. The second fraction becomes $^{15}\!/_{90}$. Now add the numerators: $24 + 15 = 39$. Put the sum over the common denominator: $^{39}\!/_{90}$. Can you reduce? Yes, by 3: $^{13}\!/_{30}$.

Do the same thing when working with variables instead of numbers.

$$\frac{a}{b} + \frac{c}{d} =$$

Find the common denominator by multiplying the two denominators: $b \times d = bd$. Cross-multiply: $a \times d = ad$. Cross-multiply: $c \times b = cb$. Put the difference of the results of the cross-multiplication over the common denominator: $\frac{(ad - cb)}{bd}$.

Multiplying fractions

This is the easy one. Just do it. Multiply horizontally, multiplying the numerators and then multiplying the denominators.

$$\frac{3}{4} \times \frac{2}{5} = \frac{(3 \times 2)}{(4 \times 5)} = \frac{6}{20} = \frac{3}{10}$$

Always check whether you can cancel before you begin working to avoid having to deal with big, awkward numbers and to avoid having to reduce at the end. In the preceding example, you can cancel the 4 and the 2, leaving you with

$$\frac{3}{\underset{2}{4}} \times \frac{\overset{1}{2}}{5} = \frac{(3 \times 1)}{(2 \times 5)} = \frac{3}{10}$$

You get to the right solution either way; canceling in advance just makes the numbers smaller and easier to work with.

Dividing fractions

To divide by a fraction, invert it (turn it upside down) and multiply.

$$\frac{1}{3} \div \frac{2}{5} = \frac{1}{3} \times \frac{5}{2} = \frac{5}{6}$$

Mixed numbers

A mixed number is a whole number with a fraction tagging along behind it, like $2\frac{1}{3}$, $4\frac{2}{5}$, or $9\frac{1}{2}$. Multiply the whole number by the denominator and add that to the numerator. Put the sum over the denominator.

$$2\,\frac{1}{3} = (2 \times 3) + 1 = 7 \rightarrow \frac{7}{3}$$
$$4\,\frac{2}{5} = (4 \times 3) + 2 = 22 \rightarrow \frac{22}{5}$$
$$9\,\frac{1}{2} = (9 \times 2) + 1 = 19 \rightarrow \frac{19}{5}$$

The Stats Don't Lie: Statistics

Don't panic; statistics are tested on the GRE only in the most rudimentary way. If you can master three basic concepts, you can do any statistics on this exam. Those concepts are median, mode, and range.

Median

Simply put, the *median* is the middle number when all the terms are arranged in order. Think of the median strip, which is the middle of the road. Median = middle. Be sure you arrange the numbers in order (increasing or decreasing, it makes no difference) before you find the median.

Find the median of –3, 18, –4, ½, 11.

(A) –3

(B) 18

(C) –4

(D) ½

(E) 11

Put the numbers in order: –4, –3, ½, 11, 18. The one in the middle, ½, is the median. It's as simple as that. *Correct Answer:* D.

Do not confuse median (middle) with mean. A mean is simply the average.

Mode

The *mode* is the most frequent number. I suggest you put the numbers in order again. Then look for the one that shows up the most often. It's the mode.

Find the mode of 11, 18, 29, 17, 18, –4, 0, 19, 0, 11, 18.

(A) 11

(B) 17

(C) 18

(D) 19

(E) 29

There are three 18s but no more than two of any other number. *Correct Answer:* C.

Range

The *range* is the distance from the greatest to the smallest. In other words, you take the biggest term and subtract the smallest term and that's the range.

Find the range of the numbers 11, 18, 29, 17, 18, –4, 0, 19, 0, 11, 18.

(A) 33

(B) 29

(C) 19

(D) 0

(E) –4

Ah, did this one getcha? True, 33 is not one of the numbers in the set. But to find the range, subtract the smallest from the largest number: $29 - -4 = 29 + 4 = 33$. *Correct Answer:* A.

The only trap you are likely to see in the statistics questions is in the answer choices. The questions themselves are quite straightforward, but the answer choices may assume that some people don't know one term from another. For example, one answer choice to a median question may be the mean (the average). One answer choice to a range question may be the mode. Mentally note the word in the question that tells you what you are looking for to keep from falling for this trap.

A Picture Is Worth a Thousand Words: Graphs

You may have one or two graphs. When you have a graph, all the questions following it are kept together. In other words, you won't have a graph with a question, then a question on something else, then a second graph question. Even the GRE isn't that vicious! Four basic types of graphs show up frequently:

> ✔ **Circle or pie graph:** The circle represents 100 percent. The key to this graph is noting of what total the percentages are part of. Below the graph you may be told that in 1994, 5,000 students graduated with Ph.D.s. If a 25-percent segment on the circle graph is labeled "Ph.D.s in history," you know to say that the number of history Ph.D.s is 25 percent of 5,000, or 1,250.

✔ **Two axes line graph:** A typical line graph has a bottom and a side axis. You plot a point or read a point from the two axes. This is probably the simplest type of graph you will encounter.

✔ **Three axes line graph:** This type of graph is rare. It has a left side axis, a bottom axis, and a right side axis. The left axis, for example, may represent the number of crates of a product while the right side axis represents the percentage that those crates are of the whole shipment. You read the points on the graph the same way as you read them on a two axes graph, simply paying special attention that you answer what the question is asking you. If the question asks you for the number of crates, read the left side. If the question asks you for the percentage of crates, read the right side.

✔ **Bar graph:** A bar graph has vertical or horizontal bars. The bars may represent actual numbers or percentages. If the bar goes all the way from one side of the graph to the other, it represents 100 percent.

Some questions use two graphs in one problem. The following is such an example.

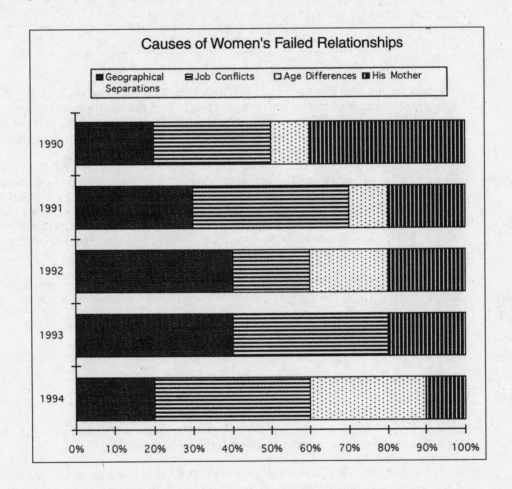

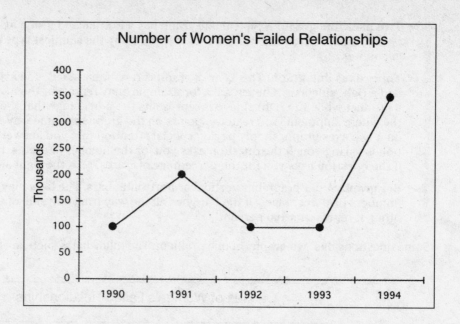

The two graphs here must be read in conjunction. The first graph is a bar graph going from 0 to 100 percent. Read the graph by *subtracting* to find the appropriate percentage. For example, in 1990, job conflict begins at 20 and goes to 50, a difference of 30 percent. If you say that job conflicts were 50 percent, you're falling for a trap. In 1993, His Mother (as a cause of failed relationships) goes from 80 to 100, or 20 percent.

The second graph gives you the actual number of failed relationships in thousands. Be sure to look at the labels of the axes. For example, in 1990, there were not 100 failed relationships but 100,000. Use the graphs together to find out the number of relationships caused to fail by a particular event or situation. For example, in 1991, there were 200,000 failed relationships. Also in 1991, age differences (from 70 to 80, or 10 percent) made up 10 percent of these relationships. Multiply 10 percent or .10 × 200,000 = 20,000 relationships.

Ready to try some practice questions? Usually, there are three to five questions below a graph. Answer the following two questions based on the two practice graphs.

How many relationships did women have from 1990 to 1994 inclusive?

(A) 850

(B) 8,500

(C) 85,000

(D) 850,000

(E) It cannot be determined from the information given.

Did I getcha? The title of the graph says it all: The Causes of Women's *Failed* Relationships. You have no way to determine how many relationships worked. *Correct Answer:* E.

The number of women's relationships in 1994 that failed due to job conflicts was what percent greater than the number of women's relationships in 1992 that failed due to age differences?

(A) 700

(B) 600

(C) 500

(D) 120

(E) 7

In 1994, job conflicts accounted for 40 percent of women's failed relationships (from 20 to 60). Because there were 350,000 failed relationships in 1994, multiply .40 × 350,000 = 140,000. In 1992, age differences accounted for 20 percent of women's failed relationships (60 to 80). In 1992, there were 100,000 failed relationships. Multiply .20 × 100,000 = 20,000. *Correct Answer:* B.

If you chose answer D, you simply subtracted the two amounts: 140,000 − 20,000 = 120,000.

If you chose choice E, 7, or choice A, 700, you fell for the trap. Take the job conflicts number, 140,000, and put it over the age differences number — 20,000. 140,000 ÷ 20,000 = 7. The 7 translates to 700 percent. If you're confused why 7 is 700 percent, not 7 percent, or why 7 times is 600 percent greater than 1, go back to the percentages section of the math review.

Part IV
Your Number's Up: Math Questions

The 5th Wave   By Rich Tennant

"For the next month, instead of practicing on a baseball diamond, we'll be practicing on a baseball trapezoid. At least until everyone passes the geometry section of the GRE test."

In this part . . .

There are two types of people in the world: those who never met an equation they didn't like . . . and those who wish they had never met an equation at all. The following math chapters and practice questions can be a lot of fun.

In these chapters, you learn all sorts of good tricks. Sure, I also sneak in some Real Math (stuff like formulas and rules), but I really focus on the tricks and traps you're likely to see on the GRE, including tips for sidestepping them. But please note: GRE math has no relation to the Real World. Just review it, ace the math sections, and be done with it.

The math section features two types of problems: Quantitative Comparisons and Problem Solving questions. You get the unexpected pleasure of using your brain, your whole brain, and nothing but your brain to solve these problems. In other words, you can't use a calculator. You may not bring in your own calculator, and the computer you use won't have any calculator functions available to you. The proctor will provide you with scratch paper (you may not bring in your own) that you can use to jot down calculations — or to gnaw on and rip up if you get totally frustrated!

Note: The computer intersperses the two types of math questions. For example, you may see one Quantitative Comparisons question, then two Problem Solving questions, then another Quantitative Comparisons question, and so on. The directions for each type of question are available to you on the screen at any time. In this book, I group all the questions of one type together so that you don't have to keep flipping back and forth to the directions.

Chapter 14

The Incomparable Quantitative Comparisons

A riddle for you: What do quicksand and quantitative comparisons have in common?

Answer: They both can suck you in and pull you down before you realize what's happening.

Quantitative Comparisons (QCs) consist of 14 or so questions, but a zillion or more traps. The QCs rarely require power math; they require paranoia (to recognize the traps) and finesse (to avoid the traps). Hmmm, "Paranoia & Finesse." Sounds like a firm of attorneys, doesn't it?

Where Did All the Answers Go? The QC Format

A QC question lists a quantity in Column A and another quantity in Column B. The quantities can be numbers, variables, equations, words, figures, compromising photos of you at the last fraternity party — anything. Your job is to compare the quantity in Column A to the quantity in Column B. (Hence the title, "Quantitative Comparisons." I bet some rocket scientist got big bucks for thinking this one up!)

No answer choices are given below the quantities in QC questions. You are to compare the quantities and

▶ Choose A if the quantity in Column A is greater than the quantity in Column B.

▶ Choose B if the quantity in Column B is greater than the quantity in Column A.

▶ Choose C if the quantity in Column A is equal to the quantity in Column B.

▶ Choose D if not enough information is provided for you to determine the relationship between the quantities.

Got all that? Just choose A if A is bigger, B if B is bigger, C if they're the same (with C standing for *Same* if you spell as badly as I do), and D if you can't tell (as in D for *duuuuuh!*).

As Easy as π: Approaching QC Questions

The hardest part of a QC question is knowing where to begin. You can save considerable time — and frustration — if you develop good habits now that carry over to the exam later. Follow this simple, three-step approach:

1. **Solve for the quantity in Column A.** You may solve an equation, talk through a word problem, or do nothing but look at what's given. Here are some examples of what you may see in Column A.

Column A

$$x^2$$

40% of 340

The number of miles hiked by Ken, who hikes at 3 mph for 6½ hours

2. **Solve for the quantity in Column B.** Again, this can mean solving an equation, talking through a word problem, or just looking at the column. Here are some examples:

Column B

$$x^3$$

340% of 40

18

3. **Compare the two columns.**

Sounds simple enough, right? Wait until you see some of the traps that they can build into the QCs.

Gotchas and Other Groaners: Tips, Traps, and Tricks

QCs have so many tricks and traps that I give you a separate section for each one, with a few examples to illustrate how easily you can fall for the traps.

As unbalanced as the rest of us

If the columns look equal, it's a trap. If two columns appear at first glance to be equal, a trap is almost always involved. Suppose that you see this question:

Column A	*Column B*
π	3.14

Your gut reaction may be to choose C because they are equal. At school, you've had 3.14 drilled into your head as π. (If you've been out of school for quite a while, you may be very pleased with yourself for remembering that. Put the self-congratulations on hold; you've just fallen for a trap.) But π is only *approximately* 3.14; it is actually larger. The correct answer to this problem is A. For convenience, π is rounded to two decimal places: 3.14. Actually, however, π continues as a nonrepeating, nonterminating decimal: 3.141592. . . . *Correct Answer:* A.

Column A	*Column B*
.0062 × 3600	6200 × .3600

Again, you probably checked that the number of digits and decimal places is the same and chose C. But the answer is B. When you multiply them out, Column A equals 22.32 and Column B equals 2,232. *Big* difference. The moral of the story: If your first reaction is that the problem is a no-brainer — that the answer is obviously, clearly, undoubtedly C — slap yourself upside the head and work through the problem. *Correct Answer:* B.

No scale, no sale

If a figure is not drawn to scale, the answer is often choice D. A problem may show a figure. Underneath the picture may appear the words: "*Note:* Figure not drawn to scale." This message should be a warning buzzer alerting you to the presence of a built-in trap. If a figure is not drawn to scale, you can't rely on it. Because you can't just eyeball it to figure things out, you need solid information such as the lengths of lines or the measures of angles. If that information is not provided, you often can't determine the relationship between the columns and must choose D.

Column A	*Column B*

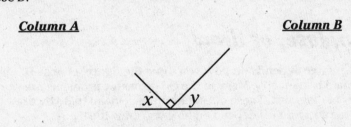

Note: Figure not drawn to scale.

Column A	*Column B*
x	*y*

Sure, x and y each appear to be 45 degrees. Go ahead and choose C. You'll blow the GRE, never get into grad school, and end up walking some rich woman's poodles for a living, lamenting, "If only I had noticed that the figure was not drawn to scale!"

Because the figure is not drawn to scale, you can't use it to estimate. You can't look at the figure and deduce that x and y are equal. Yes, x and y add up to 90 degrees. That's because angles along a straight line add up to 180 degrees, and you already have a right angle: $180 - 90 = 90$. But you *don't* know how much of the 90 is x and how much is y. Are they 45 and 45? 60 and 30? 89 and 1? The figure is not to scale, so any of those values may be correct. Because you don't have enough information to compare the quantities, choice D is the right answer. *Correct Answer:* D.

Column A	*Column B*

Note: Figure not drawn to scale.

2x	y

If you fell for this one, you can kiss your 800 goodbye. This is a classic D. Yes, yes — the figure appears to be an isosceles right triangle. You know that the two x's are equal and that the angles in a triangle add up to 180 degrees. But no one said that angle y is 90 degrees. What's that you say? It *looks* like 90 degrees? Tooooo bad. You can't look at the figure if it's not drawn to scale. As far as you know, angle y may be 89 degrees or 91 degrees or all sorts of other possibilities. Maybe $x = 40$, so $2x = 80$ and $y = 100$. Maybe $y = 60$, so $2x = 120$ and $y = 60$. What? That can't be, because it's obvious that this is not an equilateral triangle with all angles equal? Nothing is obvious; you can't use the figure if it's not drawn to scale. Because anything is possible, choose D. *Correct Answer:* D.

"Not drawn to scale" problems have fallen out of favor with the GRE lately. In my opinion, these problems were just too easy for students to get right, so the GRE naturally took them off the test. Don't be surprised if you don't see a "not drawn to scale" problem — but be prepared just in case you do. (You will definitely see some on the practice exams. I want you to be prepared for every possibility.)

Win, lose, or draw

If the answer depends on how you draw the figure, choose D. Approximately one third of GRE math is geometry. Many of the QC geometry problems are word problems that give no figures or diagrams. These questions often demand that you draw the figure yourself. In that case, the answer may depend on how you draw the figure.

Column A	*Column B*
Area of a decagon	Area of a pentagon

The trap answer is A. True, a decagon has ten sides and a pentagon has five sides, and true, 10 > 5, even in new math. The correct answer, however, depends on how you draw the figures: and how long each side is. For example, I can draw the shapes three different ways:

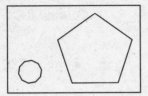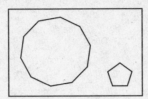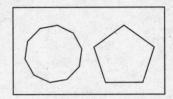

If everything *deeeeee*-pends on the *deeeeee*-rawing, choose D. *Correct Answer:* D.

Column A	**Column B**

A skating rink is 5 miles from a yogurt shop
and 6 miles from a restaurant.

Distance from the yogurt shop to the restaurant	1 mile

Did you fall for the trap answer, C? Two tips come into play here:

- ✔ **If the columns look equal, it's a trap.**
- ✔ **If the answer depends on how you draw the figure, choose D.**

Here are a couple ways of drawing the figure:

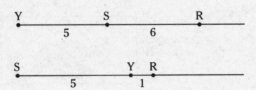

Picture perfect

If a picture is drawn, the answer is rarely D. This is the flip side of the preceding tip. The GRE is rather wishy-washy about figures. The directions say something like this: "Questions have figures that are drawn as accurately as possible, but you should use mathematics, not estimation or measurement based on the figure, to answer the questions." Huh? What does all that mean? It means that the figures really are pretty much drawn to scale, but that the GRE doesn't want you just looking at a figure to get the answer; the GRE wants you to calculate and do things the hard, "official" way. My advice is this: Don't worry about scale. As far as you're concerned, the figures are to scale unless a note specifically says otherwise. Your measurements would have to be incredibly precise for the lack of exact scale to mess you up. The answer, therefore, is rarely D when a figure is given.

Keep in mind that these are just tips, not rules. That means that they work most of the time, but not always. (I have seen, for example, some questions with figures that were unsolvable, requiring a D answer.) Never shut off your own brain in favor of a tip. The purpose of a tip is just to make you think twice before falling for a trap.

<u>*Column A*</u>   <u>*Column B*</u>

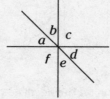

$a + b$	$d + e$

Angle *a* is a vertical angle to angle *d,* meaning that they are opposite and of equal measure. Angle *b* is a vertical angle to angle *e,* meaning that they are opposite and of equal measure. Because each part of Column A is equal to its counterpart in Column B, both columns are equal. *Correct Answer:* C.

At first glance, you may be tempted to choose D for this problem because no numbers are given. It's true that you cannot solve for the exact measure of *a + b* or the exact measure of *d + e,* but the question doesn't expect you to do so. This section is not about problem solving; it's quantitative comparisons — all you need to do is compare the quantities. You can compare them here (and see that they are equal), so D is wrong.

<u>*Column A*</u>   <u>*Column B*</u>

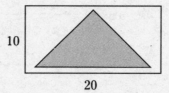

Number of square units in the area of the triangle	100

Fight the temptation to choose D automatically just because you don't have numbers for the lengths of the sides of the triangle. You know that the figure is drawn to scale; you can probably compare the quantities.

The formula for the area of a triangle is ½ *base* × *height*. What is the base? You don't know, but you *do* know that it is less than the base of the rectangle because the sides of the triangle don't extend all the way to the sides of the rectangle. Just call it *less than 20.* How much is the height? You don't know, but you do know that it is less than 10 because the top and bottom of the triangle don't touch the top and bottom of the rectangle. Call it *less than 10.* *Less than 10 × less than 20 = less than 200.* Half of *less than 200* is *less than 100.* Because *less than 100* is smaller than 100, choose B. *Correct Answer:* B.

Been there, done that

Cancel quantities that are identical in both columns. Think of it as clearing the decks or simplifying the picture. A QC problem is like a scale — a balance. If something is the same on one side as on the other, it doesn't affect the balance — you can ignore it. Be careful that you cancel only *identical* things; −5 does not cancel 5, for example.

Column A	**Column B**
$x^2 - 21$	$x^2 - 35$

Cancel the x^2 in both columns. Copy the problem on your scratch paper, just so you can have the joy of scratching out the identical quantities. That leaves you with −21 and −35. Caution! Remember that a *negative* 21 is greater than a *negative* 35. *Correct Answer:* A.

Column A	**Column B**
	$a > b > c > 2$
$(a+b)^2$	$(a-b)^2$

You can't cancel out the a and b on both sides and say that the columns are equal. $(a+b)^2$ is *not* the same as $(a-b)^2$. You should memorize these two expressions (they are discussed in detail in Chapters 11–13):

$$(a+b)^2 = a^2 + 2ab + b^2 \qquad (a-b)^2 = a^2 - 2ab + b^2$$

Now you can cancel identical terms: slash off the a^2 and the b^2 from both columns. You are left with $+2ab$ in Column A and $-2ab$ in Column B. Because both a and b are greater than 2, you don't need to worry about negatives or fractions. Correct *Answer:* A.

In the preceding problem, you don't need to do any pencil pushing if you reason the answer out. Because a is greater than b and both a and b are positive numbers (greater than 2), you know that the sum $(a+b)$ must be greater than the sum $(a-b)$. Squaring a larger (positive) number gives you more than squaring a smaller number. You can deduce that Column A is bigger without doing any paperwork.

Six of one, a half dozen of the other

Compare each part of Column A to its counterpart in Column B. Again, think of QCs as a scale. If both parts of Column A are greater, or "heavier," than both parts of Column B, A is greater.

Column A	**Column B**
$\dfrac{17}{21} + \dfrac{47}{80}$	$\dfrac{19}{81} + \dfrac{23}{97}$

Don't even *think* about reaching for your pencil to work this problem through. Compare each part of Column A to its counterpart in Column B. Which is greater: $^{17}/_{21}$ or $^{19}/_{81}$? Reason that 17 is more than half of 21, whereas 19 is much less than half of 81. The same is true for the second pair of numbers. You know that 47 is more than half of 80; 23 is less than half of 97. Because both parts of Column A are greater than both parts of Column B, A is the answer. No muss, no fuss. *Correct Answer:* A.

Of course, some spoilsport always wants to know what happens if one part of Column A is greater than its counterpart in Column B, but the other part of Column A is less than its counterpart in Column B. Doesn't happen. Why? It ruins the trick that the test makers want you to recognize and use — you'd miss the entire point of the question. The question would reach back to a basic arithmetic, pull-out-your-pencil problem. If lightning strikes and that problem does arise, well, you have no choice but to lift a finger. *Which* finger you lift is up to you.

Keep plugging away

When plugging in numbers, use 1, 2, 0, –1, –2, ½ — in that order. This is the best tip you're likely to get outside a racetrack. Whenever you have variables, *plug in numbers*. Instead of randomly choosing any old numbers, plug in these Sacred Six: 1, 2, 0, –1, –2, ½. You should memorize these numbers and throw them into a problem whenever possible. These numbers cover most of the contingencies: positive, negative, zero, odd, even, fraction, and 1, which has special properties.

Column A	*Column B*
x^2	x^4

The trap answer is B. Everyone says that, *of course,* something to the fourth power is greater than the same number squared. (A variable must have the same value in Column A as in Column B *within any one problem.* That is, if x is 5 in Column A, it is also 5 in Column B. Always. No exceptions. A rose is a rose is a rose.)

Ah, but whenever you hear yourself saying *"of course,"* you know that you're headed for a trap. Play the *what if* game: What if $x = 1$? Then the two columns are alike, and answer C prevails. What if $x = 2$? Then Column $A = 4$ and Column $B = 16$, and the answer is B. Therefore, the answer can be A or it can be B, depending on what you plug in. If an answer *de*pends on what you plug in, choose D. *Correct Answer:* D.

Notice that you didn't have to go through all the Sacred Six numbers. As soon as you find that you get two different answers, you can stop. If plugging in 1 and 2 gives you the same answer, you should go on to 0, –1, –2, and ½, plugging in as many as necessary. You'll be pleasantly surprised, however, to find out how often 1 and 2 alone get the job done.

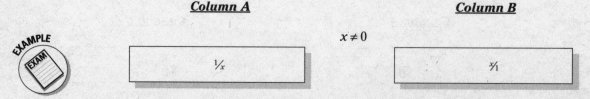

Column A	$x \neq 0$	*Column B*
$^1/x$		$^x/_1$

The *trap* answer is B. Most people think that Column A comes out to be a fraction of less than 1. It may . . . or it may not. And who's to say that x is more than 1 in the first place? Play the *what if* game again.

What if $x = 1$? Then the columns are equal, and choice C is correct. What if $x = 2$? Then Column B is greater. It depends on what you plug in, so choose D. *Correct Answer:* D.

On the real exam, you would stop here, but for now, plug in a few more numbers to see what else can happen. You can't plug in 0 because the problem tells you that x is not equal to 0 (division by 0 is undefined). What if $x = -1$? Then Column A is −1 and Column B is −1; they're equal. What if $x = -2$? Then Column A $= -\frac{1}{2}$ and Column B $= -2$; now A is bigger. You've seen all the possibilities at this point: A can be bigger, B can be bigger, or the two columns can be the same. I haven't even gotten into fractions yet. And if it's all the same to you, I won't.

Looking like a hundred bucks

Plug in 100 for dollars and percentages. This is an exception to plugging in the Sacred Six $(1, 2, 0, -1, -2, \frac{1}{2})$. If a question deals with dollars or percentages, plug in 100 to make it a nice round number. I'm all for an easy life here.

Column A	*Column B*

A book bag costs x dollars.

Cost of the book bag on sale at 60% off	$.6x

If you make the book bag cost $100, you can easily determine that 60 percent of 100 is 60; subtract 100 − 60, and you get 40. In Column B, .6 (100) = 60. The answer is B. This type of problem is easy to miss because of carelessness. Many people choose C automatically. Of course, you know by now that *if the columns look equal, it's probably a trap.* You should slow down, plug in 100, and work out the problem. *Correct Answer:* B.

Column A	*Column B*

One year's interest on x dollars at 6% annual interest	$12

Gotcha! I threw this one in to remind you once again that these are *tips*, not rules, and that you should never sacrifice common sense in favor of tips. Sure, if you plug in 100 for x dollars, you know that the interest is $6 and B is the answer. But what if $x = \$1,000,000$? Then Column A is significantly larger. Here, the correct answer *de*pends on which value you plug in for x. Although 100 often works, it is not infallible. Think! *Correct Answer:* D.

Get outta that rut

Plug in consecutive terms first and then nonconsecutive terms. If you need to plug in numbers for two or three variables, first plug in the numbers all in a row: 1, 2, and 3. Then try it again, plugging in numbers that are not in a row: 1, 5, and 7. Sometimes the spacing between the numbers makes a difference.

When pigs fly . . .

Question: Can you ever plug in all the Sacred Six and still fall for the trap?

Answer: Yeah, you can (although it's unlikely). Here's an example:

Column A   **Column B**

$$x \neq 0$$

$\frac{1}{x}$ 3

Now you play the *what if* game. What if $x = 1$? Then Column B is larger. What if $x = 2$? Then Column B is larger. Because x is not equal to 0 (division by 0 is undefined), you skip to the next number in the Sacred Six. What if $x = -1$? Column B is still larger. What if $x = -2$?

Yes, yes, Column B is still larger. Finally, what if $x = \frac{1}{2}$? Then Column A = 2 (to divide by a fraction, invert and multiply) and Column B is still larger. Now, 99 percent of the Thinking World would choose B at this point and feel very confident. And 99 percent of the Thinking World would go straight down the tubes. The answer, in fact, is D. What if $x = \frac{1}{3}$? Then Column A = 3, and the two columns are equal — choice C. If the answer could be B and could also be C, the answer *de*pends and therefore is choice D.

A problem in which the Sacred Six don't do the job for you is incredibly rare, but it could happen. Sorry about that. This is a *tip*, not a rule. It's not perfect. Close, though. . . .

Column A   **Column B**

$$a < b < c$$

$\frac{a + c}{2}$ b

The normal response is to plug in consecutive numbers: 1, 2, and 3. If you do that, Column A is 1 + 3, or 4, divided by 2 = 2. In Column B, b is 2. The columns are equal. *Uh-oh!* You know by now that *if the columns look equal, it's often a trap* and you should double-check your work.

Plug in some nonconsecutive numbers: 1, 5, and 7. Now Column A is 1 + 7 = 8, divided by 2 = 4. In Column B, b is 5. Now the answer is B. If the answer *de*pends on which values you plug in for the variables, choose D. *Correct Answer:* D.

Column A   **Column B**

$$x > y > z$$

$y + z$ x

The *trap* answer is C. The right answer is D because the answer depends on which numbers you plug in. If you plug in 3, 2, and 1, $y + z = 2 + 1 = 3$. Because $x = 3$, the columns are equal. But plug in nonconsecutive numbers: 100, 2, and 1. Now $y + z = 2 + 1 = 3$. But $x = 100$; Column B is larger. The answer can be C or B — it depends on what you plug in. Choose D. *Correct Answer:* D.

Familiarity Breeds Content (ment): A Review

Before going on to the sample questions in the following chapter, review the approach and the tricks described here.

Approach

1. Solve for the quantity in Column A.

2. Solve for the quantity in Column B.

3. Compare the two quantities.

4. Choose A if the quantity in Column A is greater than the quantity in Column B.

   Choose B if the quantity in Column B is greater than the quantity in Column A.

   Choose C if the quantity in Column A is equal to the quantity in Column B.

   Choose D if you don't have enough information to determine the relationship between the quantities.

Tricks

- If the columns look equal, the question is usually a trap.

- If a figure is not drawn to scale, the answer is often choice D.

- If the answer depends on how you draw the figure, choose D.

- If a picture is drawn to scale, the answer rarely is D.

- Cancel quantities that are identical in both columns.

- Compare each part of Column A to its counterpart in Column B.

- When plugging in numbers, use 1, 2, 0, –1, –2, and ½ in that order.

- Plug in 100 for dollars and percentages.

- Plug in consecutive terms first and then nonconsecutive terms.

Chapter 15

Putting It All Together: QC Practice Questions

• •

1 f you're waiting until someone makes a movie about this stuff, forget it. You're outta luck. The information on quantitative comparisons in the preceding chapter is all she wrote (so to speak). If you didn't read it carefully, please go back and do so now — before you humiliate yourself on this practice exam.

All done? Good. Now, check your ego at the door or it may get trashed on this exam. I've written a dozen problems that incorporate the meanest, the cruelest, the stupidest traps you're likely to see on the real GRE. How many are you going to fall for?

The answer choices are

A if the quantity in Column A is greater.

B if the quantity in Column B is greater.

C if the two quantities are equal.

D if the relationship cannot be determined from the information given.

<u>Column A</u>	<u>Column B</u>
1.	
$10\left[(4\times3)^2+5^0\right]$	1440

This question tests two concepts: order of operations and the zero exponent. Always do what is inside of the parentheses first: $4\times3=12$. $12^2=144$. Next, do what's inside the brackets. $5^0=1$. Any number to the zero power equals one. Add: $144+1=145$. Then multiply by what's outside the brackets: $10\times145=1,450$. *Correct Answer:* A.

If you chose C, you thought that 5^0 was zero, giving you $144+0=144$; $144\times10=1,440$. Look out for the zero exponent; it is often in tricky questions. Also, double-check all your C answers. I've found more traps in which people choose C than all the other traps combined.

<u>Column A</u>	<u>Column B</u>
A cubic box has a total surface area of 600 square units.	
2.	
Number of cubic units in the volume of the box	1,000

The total surface area of a cube is the sum of the areas of all surfaces. A cube has six surfaces: $600\div6=100$. Each surface of the cube, which is a square, has an area of 100. That means each edge is 10 because the area of a square is *side × side*. The volume of a cube is $edge^3$. $10\times10\times10=1,000$. *Correct Answer:* C.

Many of the geometry problems ask you to go forwards and backwards. You're given a volume and asked to find a total surface area, or vice versa. You may be given a circumference and asked to find a sector, or vice versa. Be comfortable enough with the geometry formulas to work problems inside out, upside down, and any which way. If you don't know how to find a volume and a total surface area, return to the thrilling pages of Chapter 11.

Column A	**_Column B_**

3.

$$\sqrt{66+85}$$

12

First, add the numbers under the square root sign. $66 + 85 = 151$. Then take the square root of that. Stop! Don't have a panic attack right here. No, you are not allowed to use a calculator. That's the bad news. The good news is that you don't have to. You don't have to get an exact answer for a QC problem; you just have to compare the quantities in the columns. Look for a perfect square close to 151. How about 144, which is 12^2, or 169, which is 13^2. Because 151 is between 144 and 169, the square of it must be between 12 and 13. You couldn't care less exactly how much it is. (Do not bother finding the exact square root!) As long as it's more than 12, Column A is larger. *Correct Answer:* A.

Column A	**_Column B_**

4.

$$.10 \times 10 \times 100$$

1

You needn't have withdrawal pains from your calculator. This problem is much easier than it looks. Multiply $.10 \times 10$ to get 1. You know that $1 \times 100 = 100$, which is certainly greater than 1. That's all you have to do. If you chose C, you got careless and were swayed by the hypnotic power of the columns. Don't let the C's *mesmerize* (hypnotize) you; double-check C-type answers any time you encounter them. *Correct Answer:* A.

Column A	**_Column B_**

On a road trip, Kimberly drove 600 miles and used 45 gallons of gas.
Her friend Whitney drove half as far and used 30 gallons of gas.

5.

Miles per gallon of Kimberly's car	Miles per gallon of Whitney's car

This is a basic arithmetic problem. To find the mileage, divide the number of miles driven by the gallons used. $600 \div 45$ compared to $300 \div 30$. *Correct Answer:* A.

Before you begin making the pencil scratches, look at both columns. You'll be surprised how often you don't have to work through the actual arithmetic. You know that $300 \div 30$ is 10; you can do that in your head. Is $600 \div 45$ more than 10, equal to 10, or less than 10? It's more than 10, because $600 \div 60$ would be 10. Stop right there. You don't have to work the problem through to the bitter end; just compare the quantities. I want you to be able not only to get all the QC questions correct, but also to get them correct quickly.

Column A	**_Column B_**

6.

$$18y + 18x$$

$$18y - 18x$$

You didn't fall for the cheesy and *egregious* (heinous, truly terrible) trap built into this very simple question, did you? If so, please consider yourself totally humiliated. One tip you learned in the lecture in Chapter 14 was to cross off quantities that are identical in both columns. Cancel the 18y. You are now left with 18x compared to −18x. Common sense tells you that 18x is greater. Common sense should take a flying leap. There's nothing common about the QC questions. Play the *what-if* game: What if $x = 1$? Then A is greater. What if $x = 2$? Then A is still greater. Ah, but what if $x = 0$? Then the columns are equal. If the answer *de*pends on what you plug in, choose D. *Correct Answer:* D.

The more variables you have, the greater the likelihood that the answer is D because those variables could, well, vary. Whenever you plug in, use the Sacred Six I cover in Chapter 14. (If you skipped Chapter 14 and went right to the practice problems, you missed some good stuff. Here's your second chance.) Plug in 1, 2, 0, −1, −2, and ½, in that order. You won't usually have to plug them *all* in. As soon as you get two different possibilities, you know the answer *de*pends on what you plug in, and you choose D.

Column A	**_Column B_**
	$ab = -40$

7.

$(a+b)^2$	$(a-b)^2$

Did you memorize the expanded form of these two expressions $(a+b)^2 = a^2 + 2ab + b^2$? (If you don't know how I got that, go back to the discussion of FOIL methods in Chapter 12.) $(a-b)^2 = a^2 - 2ab + b^2$. Now use another trick from Chapter 12: Cancel quantities that are identical in both columns. Slash off a^2 and b^2. You're left with $+2ab$, which would be -80, compared to $-2ab$, which would be $+80$ (because a negative times a negative is a positive). *Correct Answer:* B.

If you chose A, you got careless with your negative. Keeping the signs straight is one of the most important things you can do in any algebra problem. Write the problem on your scratch paper just to be sure of avoiding this type of careless mistake (easy to make when you're working a problem through in your mind).

Column A	**_Column B_**

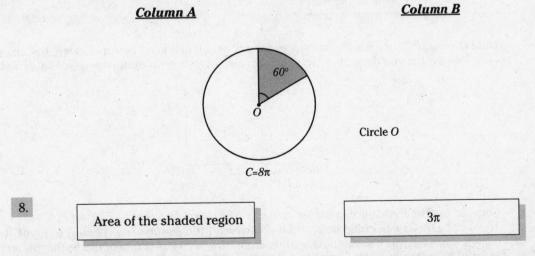

Circle O

$C = 8\pi$

8.

Area of the shaded region	3π

A shaded portion of a circle is called a sector. Its area is a fraction of the area of the circle. To find the area of a sector, first find the area of the circle. The formula for the area of a circle is $\pi \times radius^2$. You have to work backwards from the circumference to find the radius. The circumference of a circle is $2\pi \times radius$. Therefore, $C = 8\pi$, so $2\pi r = 8\pi$, or $r = 4$. $Area = \pi r^2$ or 16π.

Next, you know that the degrees in a circle total 360. The shaded portion has a 60-degree angle, making it $\frac{1}{6}$ ($\frac{60}{360}$) of the circle. Multiply the fraction by the area: $\frac{1}{6} \times 16\pi = \frac{16}{6}\pi$ or $\frac{8}{3}\pi$, which is less than 3π. *Correct Answer:* B.

The geometry review section (Chapter 11) has a good discussion of everything to do with circles, including sectors. Circles, in my not-so-humble opinion, are among the easiest of the geometry problems to get correct. Consider these "gimmes."

<u>**Column A**</u>	<u>**Column B**</u>
9. $\frac{47}{299} + \frac{18}{101}$	$\frac{17}{31} + \frac{7}{13}$

Did you see the shortcut? Surely you know by now that you are not expected to do common denominators and go through all the garbage math. If it's a QC problem, there's usually a trick. Use my tip: *Compare each element of Column A to its counterpart in Column B.* That is, compare $\frac{47}{299}$ to $\frac{17}{31}$. Because 47 out of 299 is less than half, and 17 out of 31 is more than half, Column B is larger. Next, compare the remaining two quantities. Because 18 out of 101 is less than half and 7 out of 13 is more than half, Column B is larger here as well. Both parts of Column B are greater than both parts of Column A; B is greater. *Correct Answer:* B.

And for you people who insist on creating drama: No, the test makers will not, repeat, will *not* give you a problem of this sort in which one quantity is larger in Column A but the other quantity is larger in Column B. Doing so would defeat the point that this question is asking. Believe it or not, the test makers don't get a fiendish glee out of watching you do a lot of pencil pushing. They're trying to see whether you're smart enough to *avoid* doing the work.

<u>**Column A**</u>	<u>**Column B**</u>

Michelle and Mike begin walking and go 5 miles due north.
Their friend Devrae begins at the same point and goes 12 miles due west.

10. Shortest distance from Michelle to Devrae	13 miles

Did I trick you? True, usually when a geometry problem has no picture drawn, the answer is D. However, if you draw this picture, you see that you get a right triangle of sides 5 and 12.

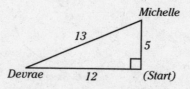

You can use the Pythagorean theorem of $a^2 + b^2 = c^2$ and find that $5^2 + 12^2 = (25 + 144) = 169$; $169 = c^2$; $c = 13$. Or you could be grateful you weren't too *parsimonious* (cheap) to plunk the dough down for this book and remember from Chapter 11 that one of the Pythagorean triples is 5:12:13. That is, in a right triangle (which is true if one person goes due north and the other person goes due west), if one side is 5, and the other side is 12, the hypotenuse must be 13. You don't have to do the work at all. *Correct Answer:* C.

Did you have trouble figuring out the square root of 169? You should have memorized certain square roots and perfect squares as given in Chapter 11. If you didn't do so, you could, of course, always work backwards from the Column B quantity: $13 \times 13 =$ (son of a gun!) 169. Once again I say unto you: Don't panic, especially over square roots. In my experience, I've never seen a GRE question that depended on your being able to find an exact square root. I have seen a *plethora* (an abundance), indeed a *superfluity* (an excessive number) of problems that can be answered by knowing the basic Pythagorean triples, which just happen to be given and explained in Chapter 11.

Column A	*Column B*
11. The greatest prime factor of 1,210	The greatest prime factor of 12,100

A prime factor is a prime number, a number that can be divided only by itself and 1. The prime numbers are 2, 3, 5, 7, 11, and so on. (Notice that 0 and 1 are not prime numbers.) To factor down a number ending in 0, divide by 10. For Column A, that gives you 121×10. You should have memorized your perfect squares and know that $121 = 11 \times 11$. For Column B, dividing by 10 gives you $1,210 \times 10$. Divide by 10 again to get $121 \times 10 \times 10$. Because 10 factors down into 2 and 5, the greatest prime factor of both columns is 11. *Correct Answer:* C.

Column A	*Column B*

$$9x^2 - 4x = 69; 3x^2 - 10x = -3$$

12. $x^2 + x$	15

This is a straightforward algebra problem. Traps are rarely found in algebra problems; usually they are pretty basic. For this example, write the two expressions vertically and either add or subtract to make the numerical coefficients (the numbers before the x^2 and the x) the same.

$$9x^2 - 4x = 69$$
$$3x^2 - 10x = -3$$

If you add the two equations, you get $12x^2 - 14x = 66$, not the same numerical coefficient. Because the numerical coefficients are not the same, no variable "drops out" or can be canceled. On to plan B. If adding the equations doesn't work, subtract the second equation, which means changing the signs on all the numbers.

$$9x^2 - 4x = 69$$
$$-3x^2 + 10x = 3$$

You get $6x^2 + 6x = 72$. Divide both sides through by 6 to get $x^2 + x = 12$. *Correct Answer:* B.

Chapter 16

Real Math at Last: Problem Solving

In This Chapter
▶ Developing a plan of attack for Problem Solving questions
▶ Separating the boring from the bewildering
▶ Side stepping snares and avoiding built-in traps

*P*roblem Solving is a rather ritzy name for "regular" math problems. A Problem Solving question, amazingly enough, actually expects you to solve a problem. This is different from the Quantitative Comparison questions (covered in Chapter 14), in which you often don't need to solve the problem through to the bitter end — you just compare the quantities. (Who thinks of these catchy names anyway? How much do they get paid, and where can I apply for the job?)

Strategic Planning: The Attack Strategy

Are you an Algebra Ace? Mathematics Master? Geometry Guru? Me neither. Isn't it lucky that you don't have to be one of these enlightened individuals to do well on the Problem Solving questions? To improve your chances of acing the material, try to understand and apply the strategies I discuss in this chapter.

I realize that some of you who are reading this book haven't taken math classes in a long, long time. Maybe you are a senior in college, and because you tested out of your math while you were still in high school, you never took any math at all in college. Maybe you're returning to school after spending several years working or having a family or traveling or pursuing the idle and decadent lifestyle of the independently wealthy. Whatever the cause, you may be so rusty in math that your pencil creaks when you pick it up. I realize that you are not going to get every single math question correct; you should realize that you don't have to. The following suggestions help you maximize your points with a minimum of time and bother.

1. **Read the problem through carefully and jot down on your scratch paper what the question is asking for.**

   People who are really math-phobic often miss this crucial point. It's easy to "predict" or "anticipate" what the question is asking for and not take note of what it really wants. Your goal is to give 'em what they want. If the question asks for a circumference, circle or jot down the word *circumference* and don't solve for an area. If the question wants you to find the number of hours already worked rather than the total number of hours a job would take, be sure that you supply the correct figure.

   Of course, of course, *of course*, the answer choices feature trap answers; this goes without saying on the GRE. If the question asks for the perimeter, you can bet your bottom dollar that the area will also be one of the answers — it's a trap for those of you who don't read the question carefully. Just because the answer you got is staring you in the face does not mean that it is the correct answer. It might be . . . or it might be a trap. Before you press the CONFIRM button on your computer, go back and look at the information: Are you answering the right question?

2. **Preview the answer choices; look to see how precise your answer has to be and how careful you have to be on the decimal points.**

   If the answer choices are 4, 5, 6, 7, and 8, you probably have to solve the problem to the bitter end, calculating rather than estimating. This type of problem may take a long time. However, if the answer choices are .05, .5, 5, 50, and 500, you know that the digit is definitely going to be a 5 and that you have to keep your decimal point straight. You may be able to use common sense on this type of problem and estimate the answer without working it out.

3. **Solve the problem forwards and backwards.**

   Work out the problem and get an answer; then plug that answer back into the problem to make sure that it makes sense. If you found the average of 4, 6, 7, 9, and 10 to be 36, you can look at the answer and reason that you made a mistake somewhere because the average can't be bigger than the biggest number. (Did you see the mistake? If you got 36, you found the sum of the terms but forgot to divide by the number of terms. "Interim" answers of this sort are common trap answer choices on the GRE.)

Three Commonsense Suggestions

The Problem Solving questions are much more straightforward than the Quantitative Comparison (QC) problems I cover in Chapter 14. There aren't as many tricks or traps, but you can learn a few good, fairly commonsense techniques that can speed up your work or help you avoid careless mistakes.

Eliminate illogical (stupid) answer choices

You know how some teachers always reassure students by saying, "Oh, there's no such thing as a stupid question or answer; just try!" Wrong. There *are* such things as stupid answers. If you're asked for the temperature of a liquid and one of the answer choices is −200° Fahrenheit, it's unlikely that a liquid would be that cold; it would freeze and no longer be a liquid! If you're asked for the age of a person and one answer is 217, I'd like to know what kind of vitamins that person has been taking! When you preview the answers, dump the ones that seem to make no sense.

Don't choose a "close enough" answer

Suppose that you do a ton of calculations and get the answer 36. One of the answer choices is 38. Don't shrug and say, "Ahh, close enough; I must have made a mistake somewhere." You sure did, and you're about to make a second mistake by being lazy and choosing an answer that's close.

Close counts only in horseshoes (which you may want to bring to the exam for luck, come to think of it) and hand grenades (which may be what you feel has hit you when you see some of these math questions!).

Don't let me scare you *too* much about the math. The GRE does not, repeat does *not*, test trigonometry or calculus. It tests basic arithmetic, algebra, and geometry. Even if you haven't had those subjects in years, you can cover enough ground in a quick math review to do well. As a private tutor, I recently worked with a student in her 60s who wanted to go back to graduate school after her husband passed away. She had never taken geometry in her life because the subject wasn't required when she applied to college 40 years ago. She memorized formulas, went through some sample problems, kept an eye open for tricks, and did just as well as anyone else.

Give your pencil a workout

During the GRE, you are given scratch paper — you can't use your own; the proctor supplies it and will give you as much as you want, a few sheets at a time — and you can scribble to your heart's content. As you'll see when you go through the sample questions and practice exam, writing down formulas and plugging numbers into them or drawing pictures and putting numbers on the pictures is an excellent means of avoiding careless errors and clarifying and organizing thoughts. Don't think you're wasting time by using your pencil; you may actually be saving time by avoiding confusion.

I'm Sure I Know You from Somewhere: A Quick Review

Before you go on to the sample questions, review the approach and the tricks.

Approach

Although a Problem Solving question is a basic multiple-choice math question similar to what you've done on exams all your life, using these commonsense suggestions can help you answer the questions more quickly and with fewer errors.

1. **Read the problem through carefully and circle or jot down what the question is asking for.**
2. **Preview the answer choices.**
3. **Solve the problem forwards and backwards (plugging in the multiple-choice answers).**

Tricks

The test-makers know all the traps students can fall for and delight in building those traps into the questions. Just because the answer you got is one of the answer choices in front of you does not mean that your answer is correct. Keep the following tricks in mind as you go through the Problem Solving questions:

- ✔ Eliminate illogical (dumb) answer choices.
- ✔ Don't choose a "close enough" answer.
- ✔ Plug in numbers, write down formulas, and draw pictures. Give your pencil a workout.

Chapter 17

A Chance to Show Off: Problem Solving Practice Questions

S o you think that you understand everything from the lecture? Prove it! I'm calling your bluff. Let's see you ace these practice questions.

1. At a park, the ratio of softball players to volleyball players is 3:4. If the total number of softball and volleyball players is 63, how many more volleyball players than softball players are in the park?

   (A) 3

   (B) 4

   (C) 6

   (D) 9

   (E) 12

   The total of a ratio is a multiple of the sum of the numbers in that ratio. In simple English that means you add the numbers in the ratio: 3 + 4 = 7. Think of 7 as the number of athletes in one clique or one batch. In 63, there are 9 cliques or batches, because $^{63}/_7$ = 9. If there are 9 batches of 3 softball players, that's 27. If there are 9 batches of 4 volleyball players, that's 36. 36 − 27 = 9. *Correct Answer:* D.

   Ratios should be among the easiest of questions to answer correctly. The math review in Chapter 12 has a very easy explanation of how to get through these problems without even lifting your pencil.

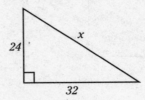

2. What is the length of side *x* in the figure above?

   (A) 48

   (B) 40

   (C) 35

   (D) 32

   (E) 30

   Because the longest side of any right triangle is always the hypotenuse (the side opposite the right or 90-degree angle), you know that answers less than or equal to 32 are wrong. Eliminate choices D and E.

You could do this problem the long and boring way, using the Pythagorean theorem to find that $a^2 + b^2 = c^2$. That means you have to square 24, square 32, and then find the square root of whatever humongous number results. (Don't ask me what it is; I'm not about to do all that hard work.) At this stage, you should be reminding yourself that there should be an easier way. And there is.

Right triangles have their sides in specific proportions or ratios, called the Pythagorean triples. If you haven't learned these yet, go back to Chapter 11 and do so right now. You'll save yourself a lot of work (and points) if you memorize some special triples. The one that works here is the most common triple used on the test: 3:4:5. Each side is a multiple of those terms. The first side is 3×8, or 24. The next side is 4×8, or 32. That means the last side must be 5×8, or 40. Brain overload avoided. *Correct Answer: B.*

3. Given a regular hexagon of side 5, what is the sum of the interior angles?

   (A) 900

   (B) 720

   (C) 540

   (D) 360

   (E) 180

The term *regular* just means that all sides and all angles are equal. For example, an equilateral triangle and a square are regular figures. The interior angles of a figure are found with the formula $(n - 2)\,180$ degrees, where n stands for the number of sides of the figure. Because a hexagon has six sides (think of the x in *six* and the x in *hex* to help you to remember this), your formula is $(6 - 2)\,180 = (4 \times 180) = 720$. *Correct Answer: B.*

If you chose C, you fell for the trap. You let the 5, which is the *length* of the side, be the number of sides. The two numbers are totally different: six sides, each measuring 5 units. Only the number of sides is important here.

Chapter 11 provides a very good analysis of how to find the interior (and exterior) angles of any figure. Because geometry problems are the easiest to get right after you've learned formulas, I suggest that you spend the majority of your study time working on geometry if you have only a limited time to work on this material.

4.

> $\left(\!x\!\right) = x^2$ if x is prime.
>
> $\left(\!x\!\right) = (x + 1)^2$ if x is composite.

Solve for $\left(\!3\!\right) + \left(\!4\!\right)$.

   (A) 41

   (B) 34

   (C) 25

   (D) 23

   (E) 7

This is a symbolism problem. Talk your way through it, substituting the number in the circle for the x in the directions. First, you have $\left(\!3\!\right)$. Because 3 is a prime number (a prime number has no positive integer factors other than one and itself), you use the first line of the directions. Square 3 to get 9. Next you have a ④. Because 4 is composite (it has factors other than just one and itself), you use the second line of directions. Add 1 to the 4 first and then square the sum. $1 + 4 = 5; 5^2 = 25$. Now add the two answers: $9 + 25 = 34$. *Correct Answer:* B.

Did you fall for one of the trap answers? If you added 1 to both terms and squared them, you got choice A. If you didn't add 1 to either term but squared them alone, you got choice C. I want you to avoid a false sense of security. The mere fact that the answer you got is among the answer choices doesn't mean it's the correct answer (although if it's not there, it's definitely the wrong answer).

5. Given that $a \neq 0$, solve for $\dfrac{a^2 aa^3}{a^4}$.

   (A) $a^{3/2}$

   (B) a^1

   (C) a^2

   (D) a^3

   (E) a^9

This is a relatively simple problem, after you know how to work with bases and exponents. When you multiply like bases, you add the exponents. Keeping in mind that a by itself is a^1, you get $a^{(2+1+3)} = a^6$. When dividing like bases, subtract the exponents like this $a^{(6-4)} = a^2$. The answer is not $a^{3/2}$; even the GRE wouldn't put an answer that nasty on the exam. Well, let me *renege* (take back) that statement. It would put an answer that nasty on the test; the answer just wouldn't be correct. *Correct Answer:* C.

If you chose B, you forgot that a is the same as a^1. You thought it was a^0 and added $a^{(2+0+3)} = a^5$. But any number to the zero power is 1, not that number itself.

Yes, you guessed it: There's an explanation in the math review (Chapter 12 if you want the specifics) of working with bases and exponents. It's to your advantage to go back and study it now.

6. $a - 3b + c = 15; 6a - 2b + 6c = 23$. $b =$

   (A) $^{11}/_{15}$

   (B) 1

   (C) $^{15}/_{11}$

   (D) $^{-60}/_{11}$

   (E) $^{-67}/_{16}$

To find b, you have to make the a and c variables "drop out." That means you need to subtract one equation from the other until you are left only with b. Multiply the first equation by 6 so that you have $6a - 18b + 6c = 90$. Then subtract the second equation from that. It looks like this:

$$6a - 18b + 6c = 90$$
$$-(6a - 2b + 6c = 23)$$

When you subtract, you change the signs on the second term. That means you have $6a - 6a$; the a's drop out. You have $-18b + 2b = -16b$. You have $6c - 6c$; the c's drop out. All you have now is $-16b = 67$. Divide both sides through by the -16: $b = ^{-67}/_{16}$. *Correct Answer:* E.

Part V
Getting into Analysis: Analytical Writing

The 5th Wave By Rich Tennant

THOUGH HIS "CALL" TO THE SCHOOL NEVER WENT THROUGH, GARY WAS PLEASED TO LATER FIND THAT AN ANALYTICAL ABILITY SCORE WASN'T REQUIRED AS PART OF THEIR ADMISSION REQUIREMENTS.

Hmm—still no dial tone.

In this part . . .

The GRE features two essay questions. One, Present Your Perspective on an Issue, is 45 minutes; the second, Analyze an Argument, is 30 minutes. Your creativity and erudition can shine on the perspective essay because the test-makers want to know what you think, what your take on the issue is. The second essay, alas, is not as kind to your free-spirited side. With the Analyze an Argument essay, the GRE essay gurus give you an issue and an argument and simply expect you to determine how well or poorly the topic is argued — they don't want you to provide your opinion on the issue at hand.

Chapter 18

Analytical Writing

In This Chapter

▶ Putting in your two cents

▶ Sitting in the critic's seat

▶ Watching the numbers

The GRE features two essays: a 45-minute essay called Present Your Perspective on an Issue and a 30-minute essay called Analyze an Argument.

Different schools evaluate your performance on the Analytical Writing section differently. Some schools place little importance on this section; some consider it critical. Before you pull your hair out over this portion of the GRE, find out the policies of the schools to which you are applying.

The computer program used for the essay portion of the GRE is specially written just for this test. It has NO spell checker or grammar checker; you're responsible for your own mistakes. The program, thank goodness, does have a cut-and-paste function, so if you need to, you can swap parts of your essay around.

Your Opinion Counts: Present Your Perspective on an Issue

In the Present Your Perspective on an Issue portion, the GRE test-makers give you an issue and ask you to introduce and then explain your views on that issue. The format goes a little something like this:

Directions: Present your perspective on the issue below using relevant reasons and examples to support your views.

   "Criticism is the weakest tool an educator can use; praise is the strongest tool."

How do you get started? If your writer's block looks as big as an Egyptian pyramid, you're welcome to use the following organized plan of attack. (*Note:* A much more detailed discussion of the steps to take when writing the essays comes later in this chapter. The following material is just an overview to get you going.)

✔ Begin by considering the issue or opinion: What exactly is the *point* that the statement makes? (In the preceding example, the point is that praise is a better teaching tool than criticism.)

✔ Specifically state your point of view on the opinion or issue: Do you agree or disagree; do you think that the author has gone too far or not far enough?

✔ Support your point of view with examples from personal or professional experiences, readings, or other general background knowledge that you possess: What have you seen, done, or heard about that formed your opinion?

Full of Sound and Fury: Analyze an Argument

The second essay topic is called Analyze an Argument and consists of a paragraph with a specific conclusion or argument. Your job is to analyze that argument.

Directions: Discuss how well reasoned you find this argument.

> "Many considerations point to the conclusion that Flint's restaurant should be changed from a youth-oriented, family-style restaurant to a Western-style saloon serving alcoholic beverages and featuring country bands. First, few families live in the area surrounding the restaurant; most have gone farther out into the suburbs. Second, Flint owns and operates two other saloons that have liquor licenses, making him experienced in the field. And finally, alcohol has a higher profit margin than food."

Discuss how compelling you find this argument. Analyze the reasoning presented in the argument, paying special attention to the evidence that supports the argument. Explain your analysis of the argument, addressing details that would make the argument more convincing or evidence that, in fact, weakens the conclusion.

Your opinion on the issue counts for zilch here; no one cares. Don't confuse the two writing samples. With the Analyze an Argument essay, you're not asked to express a personal preference (as in should Flint's change from a family restaurant to a saloon?). The fine men and women responsible for the GRE want you to analyze the author's argument. The only opinion you should give is whether you find the author's arguments valid and sound. Proceed by doing the following:

✔ Begin by stating the assumptions the author of the statement makes and analyzing whether you consider those assumptions sound or unsound.

✔ Identify evidence in the author's argument that strengthens or weakens his or her position.

✔ Provide outside counterexamples or supporting information to strengthen or weaken your analysis of the author's argument.

Half a Dozen Is Better than None: Scoring

For each essay, the GRE graders give you a score from zero to six. The final score on your score report represents an average of two scores from separate graders. Zero is the lowest possible score. Almost the only way to receive a score that low is not to write on the assigned topic. (I know someone who wrote, "While pollution was important, our generation has that under control. What is really of concern to us is the economy, which I will address." Guess what her score was?) A score of 6 is considered outstanding. It demonstrates your grasp of writing with focus, developing a position on an issue, and identifying strengths and weaknesses of an argument.

Hunting for the next Hemingway: What do evaluators look for?

Apart from offering the evaluators huge bribes to score big (If you're a GRE evaluator and you're reading this book, I was just kidding . . . unless, of course — no forget it. Really.), you need to take care of business by paying attention to the following advice:

- ✔ **Be obvious.** Make it clear to the evaluator what your opinion is on the issue or whether you think the argument is sound or unsound.

  The evaluators hate nothing more than not knowing where you stand. Although good writers address both sides of an argument and anticipate objections and counter-examples, the evaluator must clearly know what you think. Students often fall for a common trap by being so PC (politically correct) or fair minded that they fail to take and support a position. For the issue essay, it's okay to express an opinion that's different from that of the mainstream (as long as you can write a strong essay explaining yourself). For the analysis of an argument essay, if you think that the argument is weak and unsubstantiated, don't hesitate to say so.

- ✔ **Make sure that your content is logical.** The evaluators want to be certain that your supporting statements are reasonable and feasible. For example, if you state that capital punishment is useless as a deterrent against crime, you need to cite instances in which many people were executed and then explain that crime rates went up anyway. Do not give a wholly emotional argument such as, "Too many people are upset when there is an execution, and the other prisoners don't like it." Also, don't attack a person rather than an argument. Saying something like "The proponent of this plan of action is most likely a racist; he is certainly narrow-minded and not open to new situations" is not a proper analysis. Go after the logic and reasoning of the argument itself, not the person making the argument.

- ✔ **Clearly organize your essay.** Ding! Ding! Ding! You've hit upon probably the most important feature of an essay. The points must flow logically from one to another. As you're writing, stop every few minutes to reread what you've written. Your computer will have a cut-and-paste or edit function; make use of it.

- ✔ **Use proper diction, grammar, usage, and spelling.** The GRE analytical writing section is *not* a test of grammar, spelling, and so on. Assessing your thinking and analytical skills — your critical reasoning — is the point of all this. But the graders are only human. (Interesting tidbit: The GMAT features two very similar essays. Those essays are actually graded by a computer, not by humans! However, your GRE essays will be graded by two humans, at least for the time being.) Evaluators note and probably can't help being influenced by (at least subconsciously) any mistakes you make. Even the best analysis is hurt by numerous misspellings and grammar mistakes.

Grading: A foreign language with subtitles

Graders, readers, evaluators: They're known by many different names, and they, themselves, have different names for the essays. Here are the titles they will bestow on your works (with the corresponding point totals in parentheses).

- ✔ Outstanding (6)
- ✔ Strong (5)
- ✔ Adequate (4)
- ✔ Limited (3)
- ✔ Seriously Flawed (2)
- ✔ Fundamentally Deficient (1)
- ✔ No Essay (0)

Pointless information: What drives the evaluators crazy

A pointless paper is one that gets zero points. So far, the only ways to get a zero have been not to write an essay at all or to write an essay that is totally off subject (addressing the economy, for example, when the topic is pollution). But you can do several things to end up with next to nothing.

🗸 **Avoid taking a stand.** Although it is good to argue both sides of an issue or discuss strengths and weaknesses, you must — I repeat *must* — make your opinion or conclusion clear. Remember that there is no right or wrong answer. You can be against moms, apple pies, and puppies and still receive an outstanding score. Taking a stand and supporting your stand are the important factors.

🗸 **Peregrinate and meander.** Sounds like spices found in hot sauce, doesn't it? Well, your stomach will feel like you just drank some hot sauce when you get your essay scores if you let your thoughts wander around the page as you write. I have three words for you: Organization, organization, organization! Think of this suggestion as the GRE version of the real estate axiom: location, location, location! Put your thoughts in logical order. The writers' philosophy, "Tell 'em what you're going to tell 'em, tell 'em, and then tell 'em what you told 'em," works well here. Do not put your conclusion in the middle paragraph and then remember a few more points to add at the end. Follow your (mental) outline.

🗸 **Improperly use sesquipedalianism.** (*Sesqui* means one and a half; for example, a sesqui-centennial celebration is a 150-year anniversary. *Ped* means foot. *Sesquipedalianism* is using foot and a half long words ... in other words, putting your foot in your mouth.) You are not paid by the word; you are not credited by the syllable. Don't outsmart yourself by using big words. You may misuse a word or simply look idiotic and pompous and pretentious, not the impression you want to give to the evaluator.

🗸 **Use off-color language, slang, or inappropriate humor.** You say you're the Seinfeld of your crowd? Well, there's no accounting for taste. The joke that absolutely cracked up your friends at the coffee shop will not necessarily appeal to the evaluators. Scatological humor (anything dealing with bodily functions and bathrooms) is definitely out. Even if a joke is pure and wholesome, it may drop like a lead balloon and annoy the evaluators. Play it safe: Be as dull and boring as the exam itself.

Presenting Your Perspective in a Well-Wrapped Package

Had enough of my generalities? Okay, I'll get down to specifics. The following sections present a boilerplate or standard format you can use to practice writing a good Present Your Perspective on an Issue essay.

Paragraph one

Use your first sentence to address the issue specifically. For example, if the point is whether capital punishment does or does not serve as a deterrent to crime, your topic sentence may be, "Capital punishment fails in its stated purpose of deterring crime." In your topic sentence, make your perspective on the issue obvious.

The most egregious mistake you can make is to fail to present your perspective on the issue. It's right there in the title of the essay. So do it.

In your second sentence, show that you recognize the presence of two sides to the issue and that you will, in fact, anticipate and address objections to your point of view while crushing them under the weight of your brilliant logic and reasoning. Here's a good second sentence: "Although capital punishment may have, in specific instances, deterred people who otherwise would have committed crimes, I argue that these instances are infrequent and insignificant." The rest of your first paragraph fleshes out these first lines. You may want to discuss how you came to this opinion using personal examples: Did you work in a prison or do volunteer work with troubled youth? Have you taken classes in social welfare or law enforcement? Have you known someone who took a wrong turn in life and became a criminal?

 One of the major, major, MAJOR points the evaluators consider is organization. A paragraph, by definition, is centered around one point — you should state and then support one point per paragraph. Don't take a scattered approach, introducing one point after another after another but not backing-up any one of them. (To see an example of this flawed approach, look at the essay that scored a 2/1 in Chapter 19.)

 First impressions count. A super-strong first sentence can cover a multitude of weaknesses later in the paper. If the evaluator is impressed by your opening gambit, he or she is probably going to score your paper higher than if you start off slowly and warm up. Ever hear of the halo effect in psychology? Roughly stated, it means that the person who thinks highly of you in one area transfers that high opinion of you over to other areas; your halo surrounds everything you do. Take the time to write a great first sentence or two.

Paragraph two

Your second paragraph introduces a specific point that supports your argument. For example, the first sentence of your second paragraph may be, "In states such as Texas that have carried out the death penalty, violent crime has dropped significantly." See how I used a specific state in my argument? Good writing is specific, not vague like, "States with no death penalties have higher violent crime rates than states with death penalties." Oh yeah, sez who?

 You do not need to be 100 percent correct in your statements. You can fudge a little bit as long as what you are saying sounds feasible. The evaluator is not going to head to the newspaper archives to find out exactly how many executions took place in each state last year.

The next sentences in the second paragraph support the topic sentence. Give more information on how the violent-crime rate has dropped in Texas: Are murders down? Are rapes down? Are armed robberies down? Define your terms: What do you mean by violent crime? On what do you base your statements? Did you read this information, learn it in a class, or discover it in the course of doing your job? Again, remember that all the information in this paragraph should be on the same topic; don't introduce something new in the middle of the paragraph. Ideas should be grouped or clustered.

 International students, here's your chance to shine. The evaluators, who are understandably bored by reading a thousand similar essays from American students, will be intrigued if you discuss a problem from a foreign perspective. Talk, for instance, of how capital punishment has or has not worked in your own country.

 Using strong transitions can greatly contribute to the organization and coherence of your essay. Don't just jump abruptly from one topic to another. Use transitioning statements. You may want to have a list of handy phrases in mind that you can draw upon as needed while writing your essay. Here are a few gems you can include on your list:

- Closely related to this idea is. . . .
- Conversely. . . .
- On the other hand. . . .
- Similarly. . . .

Paragraphs three and four

The third and fourth paragraphs give yet more supporting examples. You may say something like, "According to articles written by psychologists, interviews with criminals have consistently shown that the criminals did, in fact, stop to consider the consequences of their actions prior to committing the crimes and took precautions not to let their crimes develop to extremes, such as murder. In these instances, the criminals were deterred by the threat of capital punishment." List places in which you have read (or feasibly might have read, if you are not being entirely truthful) such statements.

The middle of your essay often has more "filler" than the beginning and end. I'm not suggesting that you add a bushel of babble just to fill up space, but if you know that your essay is heading toward only being about ten lines long, you have to flesh out your argument somewhere. The middle paragraphs are the place to bulk up your paper. Using quotations (even if somewhat made up, which you can ascribe to paraphrasing) can add quite a bit of information without sounding too much like filler. For example, you may want to say, "In an interview on a television news show, an expert criminologist said something roughly along these lines: 'Deterrence. . . .'" Be sure, however, to expand upon what the expert said by giving your opinion of her opinion. Don't simply quote a bunch of people; the point of the essay is to present *your* perspective on an issue. The people you quote simply support your own perspective.

Paragraphs five and six

The next few paragraphs can add additional points supporting your perspective or introduce new points that address the opposite perspective. Example: "There have been instances in which capital punishment did not serve as a deterrent. In medieval England, criminals were hanged, yet their hangings served as occasions for other criminals to work the crowds, committing even more crimes." Develop this topic a little further with one or two sentences. If possible, turn the opposition around, showing that although the counterargument has some validity, it isn't as strong a point of view as the one you are arguing. Example: "Today's executions are not social gatherings but closely monitored, private affairs that are reported upon but not shown. Would-be criminals hear about the consequences, and perhaps let their imaginations torment them with ideas of what those final few moments must have been like for the condemned. One's own imagination can perhaps be the most effective deterrent of all."

Paragraph seven

This paragraph pulls everything together. Don't merely rehash your point vaguely saying something like, "Therefore, based on these arguments, it is my opinion that capital punishment works well in civilized societies." Instead, "Tell 'em what you told 'em." Continuing with the preceding example, I'd use this statement as my concluding sentence, "Therefore, while capital punishment occasionally fails to deter criminal behavior, statistical and empirical evidence found in dropping crime rates and in interviews with the criminals themselves demonstrates that capital punishment is an effective deterrent."

Time's up

Question: How long does this writing sample have to be?

Answer: To some extent, the length of the essay depends on your typing speed. In general, I suggest a minimum of six paragraphs with at least four sentences each. If you are a quick thinker and an even quicker typist, you may come up with an essay of six to eight paragraphs. If your essay is any longer than that, you are probably just inserting a lot of extraneous filler.

Although your sentences should not be long enough for you to ramble and lose direction, do not only rely on short, declarative sentences. Don't let your essay read like, "I think capital punishment is effective. Studies have shown it can be a deterrent. There are many psychologists who agree." Vary your sentence structure. Make some sentences much longer and more complicated, and others can be short and distinct. While discussing an essay with a score of 6, one evaluator called the sentences "varied and complex."

 You have 45 minutes for your first essay and 30 minutes for your second masterpiece. That's actually quite a bit of time — especially if you have practiced writing these analytical samples previously. The more homework you do and the more essays you write in advance, the more comfortable you will get with your organization and writing within the time constraints.

Analyzing an Argument in Six Easy Steps

Ever see one of those carpets with footsteps on it that dance instructors use to show novices the steps to take to dance like Fred Astaire? Think of the following sections as steps on a carpet that can lead you to a good Analysis of an Argument essay.

Paragraph one

Paragraph one states your analysis of the argument — whether you found the argument valid and sound or completely ridiculous and unsupported by even a modicum of evidence. Suppose the passage argues that putting a 25¢ tax on every bottle and can will provide an incentive for consumers to recycle bottles and cans and thus cut down on waste. Here's a good opening line: "This author's statement that a tax on bottles and cans will cut down on their waste is unsupported by evidence and is illogical given current recycling parameters set by the government and consumer behavior."

Continue the first paragraph by telling why, in your opinion, the argument is incorrect. Perhaps the author gives no facts or statistics to buttress his argument but appears to base it on unsound assumptions. Perhaps the author argues from a personal point of view and doesn't address the broader concerns. Perhaps the author assumes an ideal state that society has not yet reached.

 I suggest that you have a grab bag of several refutations ready before you even get to the exam. The preceding examples are good; you can always attack a writer's source of facts or personal biases (although, as mentioned earlier, you do not want to attack the writer herself). Think of several tactics that you use to shoot down an argument when you debate with friends (writing is easier if you use what comes naturally) and have them handy.

Paragraphs two, three, and four

Your second, third, and fourth paragraphs address each assumption that you believe the author makes. If the author assumes that a financial incentive is more important than any other type of incentive, say so and then either support or refute that assumption. If the author makes the assumption that people will not do what is right unless a law tells them to do so, state that assumption and then argue for or against it.

 Your arguments do not express your personal point of view. You perform that bit of daring in the other essay, Present Your Perspective on an Issue. In the Analyze an Argument essay, you analyze, as the name implies, the strengths or weaknesses of the given argument.

Paragraph five

In the fifth paragraph, provide possible counterexamples, flaws in the reasoning of the author. If the author says that a tax of 25¢ per can and bottle would double the recycling rate, cite a situation in which increased taxes on bottles have not led to a significant increase in recycling. If the author states that people want to do the right thing but need a financial incentive, refute the argument by saying that a tax would have to be so large as to be prohibitive.

Even if you believe the author's argument is fundamentally sound and you support it, you should still be able to show the GRE reader that you can recognize that others may think that flaws exist in the argument. Try something like this: "Although some people who hear this proposal may think that it is flawed due to the difficulty of passing any law, it is, in fact, feasible to have such laws passed on a smaller, more local scale. . . ."

Don't fall into your own trap. If you argue that the writer's assumption is based on personal logic, unsupported by facts, be sure that your refutation is not based on personal logic, unsupported by facts. The last thing you need to do is point out the author's weakness and then make the reader chuckle as he marks you down for having the exact same weakness.

Paragraph six

In the final paragraph, give your conclusions. Once again, say whether the author makes a valid point or is just wasting everyone's time and briefly reiterate your reasons for thinking so.

If you can't think of a different way to write the material in the last paragraph so it's different than the first paragraph, skip the last paragraph. You do *not* want to parrot the first paragraph entirely. You want to summarize your writing, but not by simply repeating what you said earlier. Either put a new slant on the material, packaging it neatly, or eliminate this paragraph entirely.

Time's up

Question: How long should an Analysis of an Argument essay be?

Answer: You have less time for an Analysis of an Argument passage (30 minutes) than for a Perspective on an Issue (45 minutes) essay. Therefore, you will probably write a little less in this section. Because you go more in depth, analyzing the argument, each paragraph may be longer than the ones in the Perspective on an Issue essay, resulting in fewer paragraphs.

Keep in mind that everything you have read in this chapter about length is simply a suggested format. There is no one right or wrong length (although too short can definitely be a problem). I give you these pointers as guidelines you can use in practicing essay writing. After a few practice essays, you will know your comfort zone — the length of the passage you can write in the allotted time without going crazy.

And speaking of practice essays, go on to Chapter 19 and get ready to try a few on your own. Please write these essays using a word-processing program on a computer because that's what you'll use to write them on the test day. Don't grab some lined paper and bang these essays out when you're in the library one afternoon. Sit down at your computer, type the essays as you will be doing on the real test, and be sure to time yourself. For most people, it's not the writing itself that's difficult; the hard part is coming up with a decent essay in just 30 minutes. After you finish, ask a friend to read the grading criteria in Chapter 19, evaluate each essay on a scale of one to six (you can't get a zero because you've actually written something), and discuss his or her reasoning with you.

Chapter 19

Do You Have the Write Stuff? Analytical Writing Practice Questions

••

1 promised you in the introduction to this book that each lecture, including the practice exam, would take you about two hours. Going through the material in Chapter 18 should have taken you less than an hour. Use your remaining time to write two essays: Your Perspective on an Issue and Analysis of an Argument.

Set your timer for 45 minutes for the perspective essay and 30 minutes for the analysis essay, but if you can't finish an essay, go ahead and ignore the time constraint — just this once. Finish your writing. After you finish, check out how long you took to complete the task. If you only took 35 minutes for the 30-minute passage, you should be able to speed up your writing enough to cover that extra bit of inspiration that ate up the five extra minutes. However, if you took 40 or 50 minutes for the 30-minute essay, you have to decide how you're going to cut your time down. Here are a few suggestions:

- ✔ **Cut out a few of the middle paragraphs.** Your most important points should be in the beginning and ending of your essay. (Tell 'em what you're going to tell 'em, tell 'em, and then tell 'em what you told 'em.) Although you must provide some support for your thesis, you can present your supporting arguments in one or two paragraphs rather than three or four.

- ✔ **Limit the length of your paragraphs.** Many writers end up saying the same thing over and over. They keep making the same important point — they just say it slightly differently each time. Here's an example from one of my own students: "Community service instead of jail time serves no purpose because the criminals learn no lesson from their service. The people who commit the crimes don't take community service time seriously. There is nothing learned by the criminals who have to serve only community service time." Although the writer obviously has a point, she makes it three times — once would have been enough.

- ✔ **Have a boilerplate format and several refutations or support statements in your mind before you get to the test.** It would be nice if you came up with some astonishingly creative piece of writing that blew away the evaluators, but creativity is not as easy to come by as you may think. Besides, in the Analysis of Argument essay, your creativity is irrelevant. The graders judge your analytical abilities. The analytical writing section as a whole tests your ability to reason well and to express your thoughts cogently and clearly. If you can come up with some basic support statements at home, you'll be pleasantly surprised at how well they work into an essay. For example, I almost always put in something about financial repercussions. Everything has financial repercussions. I also write about individual rights versus the power of the government; I can find something to say about that issue for nearly every topic. If timing is a problem, have a few stock phrases in mind that you can adapt to your essay as needed.

Ready? Computer fired up and cursor blinking at you? Fingers limber? Then set your timer and go!

Give Your Perspective on an Issue

Directions: Present your perspective on the issue below using relevant reasons and examples to support your views. You have 45 minutes.

"Because society is always changing, laws should always change to reflect the times as well. In addition, laws should be open to interpretation based on the facts of each individual circumstance."

Answer explanations

Following are three sample answers to the issue topic. These essays are graded as a 5 or 6 (an evaluator would probably give the essay either a five or a six), 3 or 4, and 1 or 2.

Sample Answer One: Score 6 (outstanding) or 5 (strong)

My French grandmother was fond of saying, "Plus ça change, plus c'est la même chose," which roughly means that the more something seems to change, the more it actually remains the same. This saying is appropriate when considering the laws of our nation. By changing or updating laws and statutes, by being flexible in their interpretation, we fundamentally remain the same: We continue to be fair and just, as the creators of the laws intended. In law, considering the spirit of the law is often necessary before creating the letter of the law.

A prime example of the necessity for flexibility is the Three Strikes Law in California. This law is paraphrased as "Three strikes, you're out!" by police officials and other law-enforcement personnel who have supported it whole-heartedly. The law states that a person who previously has been convicted of two crimes will be sent to prison for life when convicted of a third crime. Newspapers are fond of reporting stories of a transient who receives a life sentence for stealing a candy bar from a gas station, or a young man who goes to prison for life for smoking a marijuana joint in public. Although one may argue there are, in fact, incorrigible criminals, ones who will continue to commit crime after crime despite all legal deterrents, common sense would dictate that spending twenty, thirty, or even fifty years in prison is not a suitable punishment for stealing a 59¢ bag of chips.

Some laws have never changed, yet they are rarely enforced. Every time a new law goes into effect, news reporters present human-interest stories about unusual laws that have officially never been repealed. There is the example of "It's illegal to walk on the sidewalks of Philadelphia carrying goldfish," or "It is a crime to sing to your horses in the hearing of others." Every state and every county has a number of these laws that newspapers and television stations trot out occasionally for the amusement of the audiences on slow news days.

And what should we make of the so-called "Blue Laws," laws that attempt to mandate morality? In certain counties, it's illegal to sell or purchase alcoholic beverages on Sunday. In the county in Indiana where I grew up, it was against the law to dance on Sundays. Of course, no one ever enforced that statute; it was simply a curiosity. The question is raised, therefore, do we need to enact new laws, rescind the old ones, or practice a policy of benign neglect, simply not enforcing those laws we consider unnecessary? And if we neglect certain laws, who gets to choose which laws are enforced and which are ignored? By being more flexible in the passage and creation of the laws, we are able to avoid this dilemma.

Many years ago, England had two court systems: The courts of law (which is why lawyers are called "attorneys at law") and the courts of equity. The courts of equity attempted to "make known the King's conscience," showing mercy and treating cases equitably even when such treatment was against the law. Both courts were merged years ago but leave a legacy of flexibility and moral justice in their interpretation of the law. A legal system that cannot change with the times *will* not survive, and a legal system that will not treat cases fairly and justly *should* not survive.

Reader comments on the 6/5 essay

This essay presents an excellent answer to the question. The writer uses interesting, intriguing comments (such as the opening with the grandmother's French saying), strong, evocative vocabulary ("incorrigible," "trot out,"), and a good variety of sentence structures. (The use of the occasional question was particularly effective.)

The writer's opinion is clear from the start and is supported by well-reasoned and thoroughly developed examples. The three examples are separated, yet they flow together well via the use of good transitions. The ending is perhaps a bit dramatic, but leaves no doubt as to the opinion of the author.

Sample Answer Two: Score 4 (adequate) or 3 (limited)

Laws must change when Society changes. This is true for all types of laws, the major laws and the minor laws. This is true for all types of Societies, the so called First World, and the so-called Third World. This is true for all types of situations, from the serious to the silly to the macabre.

An example of when a law must change is the death penalty. Many years ago, condemned prisoners were executed routinely. Such executions became major events, almost parties, with the public making an excursion to watch the hanging. The irony, of course, is that the huge crowds at the execution attracted additional criminals who then committed more crimes (theft, pickpocketing, assault) and perpetuated the cycle. Today, while there are less executions, they have become media events. We don't attend the executions in person, but we live through them vicariously, watching them on tv. When Timothy McVee, the Oklahoma City bomber, was given a lethal injection, the tv stations carried a minute-by-minute report. The amount of money and time and energy that was put into this could have been better spent elsewhere.

A second reason laws must be flexible is in time of war or social upheaval. Take, for example, the 1960's. The United States had a sea change during that decade. Many more things were acceptable socially then than had ever been before, and the laws had to change to reflect that fact. The possession of certain drugs became much less serious than it had been before. People weren't sentenced to twenty years for *using* drugs, just for *pushing* them. Today even more liberal attitudes towards drugs enable people to use them legally, as in the case of glaucoma or AIDS patients who smoke pot.

Traffic laws are a less serious, but still good, example of when laws should change. The speed limit in downtown New York must obviously be less than that in the outskirts of Podunk, Idaho (my apologies to the Podunkians!). Many people in Wyoming and other sparsely-populated Western states fought against having a federally-mandated speed limit of 55 on the freeways, argueing that in their areas, 65 or even 75 would be more logical. This is an example of the need for a change to meet the needs of a local community or Society. The same is true for the age at which youngsters can get a license, as they are more mature earlier now than before.

In conclusion, laws are not static because people are not static. We change from decade to decade, and from locale to locale. While it is important to adhere to the Declaration of Independence's statement that "all men are created equal," and thus should have equal rights, not all times are created equal, and thus should not have equal laws.

Reader comments on the 4/3 essay

This is a generally acceptable response. The writer does present an unequivocal answer to the question, and uses some good vocabulary ("macabre," "vicariously"). In addition, the length is good, with three well-organized examples.

The essay does have weaknesses that prevent it from receiving a higher score. There are mistakes in grammar ("less" instead of "fewer," "so-called" once with a hyphen and once without) and spelling ("perpetuated," "argueing,") and instances of inappropriate humor ("my apologies to the Podunkians!"). In addition, some concepts were introduced without being fully developed, such as the final sentence in the traffic paragraph.

Sample Answer Three: Score 2 (seriously flawed) or 1 (fundamentally deficient)

"Because Society is always changing, laws should always change to reflect the times as well." This is a very true statement. Nothing ever remains exacly the same, and things change all the time. Isn't it logical to think that the laws should change as people and other situations change? My example the American society. We are much more ethnical diverse than we were a generation or two ago, and our laws have guaranteed this diversity. Old laws said that, for example, African-American people were not allowed in certain clubs or given certain jobs and this of course was wrong. Now there are laws to show how Society has changed and accepted this variety of people. Maybe someday there will be laws needed to protect White people who can't get jobs neither.

"In addition, laws should be open to interpretation based on the facts of each individual circumstance." This also is true. What about car accidents? If a person has an honest accident and hits and kills someone because he just lost control, that's a lot different than if he has been drunk and lost control that way and killed someone. It's not fair to send someone to prison for life because he had one horrible minute, but maybe it is fair to send someone to prison for life because he made the choice to drink and drive, the wrong choice.

In conclusion, I agree totally with both parts of the statement above. People need to realize that our Society changes and because laws are meant to protect Society, those laws must also change, too.

Reader comments on the 2/1 essay

The writer does present a clear response to the question, both at the beginning and the end of the essay. The writer, however, simply repeats the issue and makes a general statement of agreement.

Although there are a few examples given to support the writer's opinion, the organization of the essay is not developed well. The writer makes the comment that, "Now there are laws to show how Society has changed. . . ." The quality of the essay would be improved were the writer to add more examples and explain each example more fully. The closing statement in paragraph two appears to introduce a new topic, which is not covered fully.

Poor spelling ("exacly") and grammar ("much more ethnical diverse") hurt the response as well. Although the writer's opinion is still understandable, these errors contribute to the low score.

Analyze an Argument

Directions: Discuss how well reasoned you find this argument. You have 30 minutes to write your analysis.

The following appeared in an in-house memo sent from a marketing director to the editorial department of a television news station.

"Our research shows that when the news director comes on screen at the end of the newscast to present his perspective on an issue, many viewers switch stations or turn off the television entirely. Besides losing viewers, which lowers our ability to charge top dollar for advertising spots, we are wasting extra time that we could be filling with more ads. In addition, people tell us that they feel editorials are best read in the newspaper, not heard on television. Therefore, we recommend stopping all editorials at the ends of newscasts."

Answer explanations

Following are three sample answers to the Analysis of an Argument topic. These essays are graded as a 5 or 6 (an evaluator would probably give the essay either a five or a six), 3 or 4, and 1 or 2.

Sample Answer One: Score 6 (outstanding) or 5 (strong)

The marketing director concludes that the news station should stop all editorials because viewership decreases when the news director presents his perspective on an issue at the end of the newscast. The memo argues that when people don't watch the end of the newscast, the station loses advertising revenue.

The conclusion is based on a number of questionable assumptions. First, the director recommends that the station stop all editorials at the end of newscasts because people are turning off what is currently offered. By proposing that the station eliminate *all* editorials, the memo assumes that viewers would not watch any kind of editorial. It could be that viewers simply don't like the news director or are turned off by the "perspective on an issue" format.

Second, the director claims that the time devoted to the current editorial could be sold to advertisers. He assumes, then, that people who turn off the television or switch stations when the news director comes on will not do so when an advertisement comes on in the editorial's place. If viewers stop watching the station when they know the news is over, they will probably do the same when commercials come on instead of the editorial. When advertisers find out that people are not watching their commercials, they will pay the station less.

Third, the director notes that people tell the station's marketing team that editorials are best read in the newspaper, not heard on television. As with any survey, this finding assumes that the people who are saying these things are representative of the larger population. In other words, the marketing department assumes that these "people" are representative of the station's viewers. The memo is vague about the identity of these people. Perhaps they are not viewers at all and, therefore, cannot be used to represent the television viewing audience. The director also fails to mention how numerous these people are and does not include any information about how many people may have expressed the opposite opinion to the marketing team. An analogous situation: Just because some people support a political candidate does not mean that others don't prefer somebody else. In addition, the people who said that editorials are best read in the newspaper could have been people who are more oriented towards reading and writing. There is a good chance that these people wrote letters to the station. If station employees had called viewers during the newscast, they may have received many responses claiming that editorials are better to watch on TV than read.

Finally, that director bases his argument on making money for the news station. This proposal assumes that the purpose of a news station is to make money. The editorials may not generate as much advertising revenue as other television presentations would, but the editorials are better to include if one assumes that the purpose of a news station is to inform viewers and stimulate their thinking.

To improve the argument, the news director needs to address the above issues. He needs evidence that shows that viewers would turn off any kind of editorial at the end of the newscast. He also needs to demonstrate that viewers would watch advertisements after the presentation of news. He should also clarify how the marketing team received the comments about editorials in newspapers. Ideally, the director should show that such comments were generated by a scientific survey of people who actually watch the news station. The director should also articulate that the primary aim of the news station is to attract viewers and generate revenue.

Reader comments on the 6/5 essay

This very strong response presents a coherent, well-organized, direct analysis, introducing and fully developing the various points. It identifies four central issues that weaken or even undermine the argument, and supports each point with evidence before summarizing in a brief conclusion. The language, grammar, spelling, and general writing skills also contribute to the excellence of this essay.

Sample Answer Two: Score 4 (adequate) or 3 (limited)

This editorial is relatively well reasoned, although flawed in some aspects. The primary weakness, in my opinion, is found at the beginning, where the memo states, "Our research has shown. . . ." without specifying what that research is. Did someone poll viewers who regularly watched the show? Did someone send out a questionaire which was returned only by a small percentage of people, some of whom did not regularly watch the news? How were the questions phrased by the researcher (as we all know, a question can easily beg the answer, be skewed so as to direct the response in the direction the questioner wants it to go). A good editorial will state the basis for the conclusions it makes.

The argument has inspecificity. Nowhere does the editorial say why the viewers switch stations. Maybe they don't like that particular news director. The station can experiment by having the editorials read by others on the staff, by reporters, or even by the public at large. There are some stations where I live that do that, have local people at the end of the newscasts tell their opinions. Many of my friends, at least, tune in to watch what their peers have to say.

Is the purpose of the last few minutes of a newscast to sell ads? Maybe, if there were no editorial, there would be an extra two minutes of news reporting, not of advertisements. There are already so many ads in a newscast as it is; more would possibly alienate the viewers even more than the editorial does. Also, I believe there is an FCC mandate as to how many minutes per hour or half hour can be commercials, at least in prime time. If the station didn't have the editorial, but ran commericials, they may acceed this limit.

Reader comments on the 4/3 essay

This response is adequate. The organization is acceptable, although it would be improved by the use of transitional phrases. The writer appears to have a basic understanding of the argument but does not fully develop his comments except in a personal vein. A few basic spelling errors ("acceed," "questionaire") also detract from the paper. Finally, the lack of a coherent conclusion shifts this paper from a possible 5 to a 4 or 3.

Sample Answer Three: Score 2 (seriously flawed) or 1 (fundamentally deficient)

The reasoning in this arguement is not well-reasoned. The writer didn't convince me of their point at all. He doesn't talk about the possibility of moving the editorial, maybe putting the perspective at the beginning of the newscast, when people are probly more interested than at the end when they've already heard everything they tuned in for. He doesn't say anything about maybe having the editorials paid for by an advertisement. He doesn't cover the possibility of the fact that the government considers some editorials public service anouncements. He doesn't go into enough detail to make a good case on anything.

If I was the memo-writer, I would also talk about how the editorials maybe appeal to a more educated, higher-class (to use a politically incorrect term) audience, one that maybe spends more money on the products. Like some sitcoms appeals to a different audience (some to older viewers or white viewers, some to younger more hip maybe black viewers) the newscast can appeal to more educated viewers with the editorials.

Reader comments on the 2/1 essay

This essay is seriously hurt by the lack of organization. Ideas are introduced but not fully developed before new ideas are added. No one argument or theme is developed. There are many errors in grammar (pronoun agreement, saying "The writer" and "their" and "If I was") and spelling ("arguement," "probly," "anouncements"), and the essay demonstrates a lack of variety in its sentence structure.

The writer shows little ability to analyze the argument and gives no support for the points made. Instead, the writer presents a personal opinion, giving his own views rather than analyzing and evaluating the points made by the author of the memo.

Part VI

It All Comes Down to This: Full-Length Practice GREs

The 5th Wave   **By Rich Tennant**

"THE IMAGE IS GETTING CLEARER NOW... I CAN ALMOST SEE IT... YES! THERE IT IS — THE ANSWER IS $3ab^2 \times 7d^3 - \sqrt{19L} + U\frac{3}{4}m^4 \div \pm 100. (J5) 7\frac{9}{5} \Phi Q69.$"

In this part . . .

*J*ust when you think your brain can't be stuffed with one more factoid, relief is at hand. You finally get to download some of the information you've been inputting for the past 19 chapters. Trust me; you'll feel better when you let it all out.

This unit has two verbal and quantitative exams that are as close to the actual GRE as I can get without having briefcase-bearing barristers pounding on my door. I take these tests seriously, and you should too — do them under actual test conditions, sitting in a quiet room and timing yourself. Open books are definitely out (sorry!). I have spies everywhere; I'll know if you cheat on these tests. You'll hear a knocking at your door one foggy night. . . .

After you've done your duty on these two practice exams, you'll have a good time going through the answer explanations, which are nowhere near as dry and stuffy as the exams themselves.

Chapter 20

How to Ruin a Perfectly Good Day, Part I: Practice Exam 1

You are now ready to take a sample GRE. Like the actual GRE, the following exam consists of one 30-minute verbal section, one 45-minute quantitative section, one 30-minute essay, and one 45-minute essay. The actual GRE may also include one additional verbal or quantitative section, which does not count toward your GRE score. (The test will not include an extra analytical writing essay.) Because this section will not be identified as a test that is not scored, you must give every section your best effort. You may also get an extra section that will be identified as experimental, meaning that it won't affect your score. Here, I don't include the experimental sections because I don't want to put you through any more anguish and agony than absolutely necessary. You're welcome.

You are familiar with the question formats by now, so you should not have to read the instructions for each specific question type when you take the GRE. Nevertheless, take as much time as you need to go through the computer tutorial, which precedes the timed part of the actual exam. Do not start the test until you are comfortable with how to scroll down passages, graphs, and figures, mark an answer, and turn the clock off and on. The tutorial covers these topics, along with some other basic information. Even if you are extremely comfortable with using the computer to take the GRE, use the tutorial time to block the outside world from your mind and focus on the task ahead of you.

Please take this practice test under normal exam conditions and approach it as if it were the real test. This is serious stuff here!

1. **Work when you won't be interrupted (even though you'd probably welcome any distractions).**

2. **Use scratch paper that is free of any prepared notes. (On the actual GRE, you will get blank scratch paper before your test begins. You will have a little time before the clock starts to jot down a few notes and formulas and a series of columns of numbers or letters that you may want to use to help you eliminate answer choices, but you may not whip out a ready-made version of such test-taking aids.)**

3. **Turn off the clock at the beginning of each test section and be very careful on the first five questions. Remember that these earlier questions contribute more to your score than do the later questions.**

4. **If a question is truly impossible for you, guess and move on. You do not have the option of skipping the question and coming back to it. The computer will not let you move on until you mark and confirm an answer.**

5. **Make sure that you get to the end of the test section (30th question for verbal and 28th question for quantitative). If you have to, make wild guesses to reach the end before time expires. Unanswered questions will hurt your score more than incorrect ones will.**

6. If you get to the last question before time expires, you have the option of answering it right away and finishing your test early (you can't use the time to go back and check your work) or relaxing for a while and marking your answer shortly before time expires. If you feel pumped up and you're on a roll, do the former. Give yourself the breather if you feel bombarded by the test.

7. Do not leave your desk while the clock is running on any one section.

8. You will get a one-minute break after the first section and the option to take a ten-minute break after the second section.

After you complete this entire practice test, check your answers with the answer key at the end of this chapter. Go through the answer explanations to ALL the questions, not just the ones you miss. A plethora of worthwhile information is waiting for you in the answer explanations — material that provides a good review of everything you went over in the lectures. I even tossed in a few good jokes to keep you somewhat sane.

Verbal Section

Time: 30 minutes

30 questions

Choose the best answer to each question. Blacken the corresponding oval on the answer grid.

Directions: Choose the answer choice most nearly opposite in meaning to the question word.

1. SAGACIOUS
   - (A) isolated
   - (B) erudite
   - (C) ignorant ✓
   - (D) ludicrous
   - (E) short

2. INEPT
   - (A) profane
   - (B) skilled ✓
   - (C) prolific
   - (D) thrifty
   - (E) indigenous

Directions: Each of the following questions features a pair of words or phrases in capital letters, followed by five pairs of words or phrases in lowercase letters. Choose the lowercase pair that most closely expresses the same relationship as that of the uppercase pair.

3. SWAGGER : ARROGANCE ::
   - (A) swindle : veracity
   - (B) renege : consistency
   - (C) orchestrate : harmony
   - (D) wheedle : certitude
   - (E) stagger : imbalance ✓

4. SHEAF : PAPERS ::
   - (A) discourse : arguments
   - (B) collection : items ✓
   - (C) cygnet : swans
   - (D) quiver: arrows
   - (E) quarter: dimes

Go on to next page

> *Directions:* Each of the following sentences has one or two blanks indicating that words or phrases are omitted. Choose the answer that best completes the sentence.

5. The earliest models of bicycles, - - - - in the late 1700s, were called "walking" bicycles as the only way to - - - - the vehicle was to use the feet to push both rider and bicycle forward.

   (A) constructed ... propel

   (B) introduced ... stop

   (C) advocated ... move

   (D) implemented ... steer

   (E) built ... develop

6. Reluctant to - - - - the man as the complete fraud she suspected him to be, Jill chose to attack the weaker points of his theory, - - - - them one by one.

   (A) denounce ... debunking

   (B) ridicule ... proving

   (C) castigate ... applauding

   (D) expose ... strengthening

   (E) recommend ... disseminating

> *Directions:* Each passage is followed by questions pertaining to that passage. Read the passage and answer the questions based on information stated or implied in that passage.

Line The Canyon Pintado Historic District in northwest Colorado has been occupied by pre-historic people for as long as 11,000 years, including the Fremont culture that left behind rock-art sites. Fremont rock art has recurring motifs that link it both in time and culture. Strange human-like figures with broad shoulders, no legs, and horned headdresses are similar to the Barrier Canyon style of southwestern Utah. Figures with shields or shield-like bodies are like Fremont figures from the San Rafael region of Southern Utah. Some figures have large, trapezoidal shaped bodies, stick-like legs, trapezoidal heads, and in many cases, are adorned with necklaces. Another
(15) motif of the Fremont culture is the mountain sheep with graceful curvilinear horns. Designs such as concentric circles, snake-like lines, hands, footprints, and rows of dots are also often found in Fremont art. A unique figure in
(20) Douglas Creek is Kokopelli, the humpbacked

flute player of Anasazi mythology. His presence indicates some kind of tie with the more advanced culture of the Four Corners area.

7. The author mentions the connection to the culture of the Four Corners area to

   (A) challenge the claim that the Fremont culture was the most advanced of its time.

   (B) refute the assertion that Fremont rock art merely copied art from other cultures.

   (C) suggest that the mimicking of art from other cultures may indicate contact between the cultures.

   (D) prove the relationship between art and the level of civilization.

   (E) ridicule the suggestion that there is a connection between artistic images and warfare success.

8. The passage supplies information for answering which of the following questions?

   (A) What significance is there to the lack of legs on the human-like figures?

   (B) What was the purpose of the rock art?

   (C) Were curved lines absent in Fremont rock art?

   (D) How much of the artwork was sacred and how much secular?

   (E) What other cultures besides those in the Four Corners influenced Fremont rock art?

Line The war that many people commonly refer to as the Civil War has had many appellations throughout history. While the war was being fought, the South labeled it the "War Between the States." Sundry Southerners used the term
(05) "The Second American Revolutionary War," emphasizing their belief that they were attempting to secede from what they considered a tyrannical federal government.

One primary etiology of the Civil War may
(10) have been the 1820 Missouri Compromise. The compromise admitted Missouri into the Union as a slave state, while accepting Maine as a free state. The compromise also banned slavery in all western territories. However, it wasn't until 1860
(15) when Abraham Lincoln, who was known to be against slavery, was elected President that South Carolina withdrew from the Union. At that time, the president was James Buchanan, who did not fight against the secession. By 1860, six more
(20)

Go on to next page ➡

states had withdrawn, banding together to form the Confederate States of America, which eventually was comprised of 11 states. Their president was Jefferson Davis; the Confederacy's capital,
(25) which originally was Montgomery, Alabama, moved to Richmond, Virginia.

The first battle of the Civil War was fought at Bull Run in Virginia. Schoolchildren today still are told how the local people treated the battle as if
(30) it were a social event, taking picnic baskets and sitting on top of the hill watching the fighting. The Federal troops lost the battle and had to retreat. Later, there was a Second Battle of Bull Run, which the Union lost as well.
(35) General Ulysses S. Grant, later president of the United States, gained fame as a great Civil War strategist. When he captured Vicksburg, Mississippi, he made it possible for the Union to control all the Mississippi River, a critical point
(40) given that goods were often shipped along that river. The Union, therefore, was able to prevent materials from reaching the Confederate troops, a situation which many historians considered essential to the quick termination of the war.
(45) Grant had the honor of receiving the surrender of the South from General Robert Lee at Appomattox Courthouse, near Richmond, Virginia, on April 9, 1865. It was only five days later that President Lincoln was assassinated.
(50) The Civil War was the first war to have photographers, leaving to posterity the real evidence of the battles. This war also was more industrialized than many other wars, employing railroads, iron ships, and submarines.

9. All of the following were discussed in the passage EXCEPT

(A) the causes of the Civil War.

(B) the South after the Civil War.

(C) the various names of the Civil War.

(D) great generals of the Civil War.

(E) strategies that won the Civil War.

10. The author would best strengthen his point in the first paragraph by doing which of the following?

(A) Supplying alternate names that the Northerners called the Civil War.

(B) Explaining the ambiguity of the term "Civil" War.

(C) Listing reasons the South wanted to secede from the Union.

(D) Discussing the actions the North had taken that the South considered tyrannical.

(E) Refuting the common misconception that slavery issues caused the Civil War.

11. By stating in line 48–49, "It was only five days later that President Lincoln was assassinated," the author implies that

(A) Southern troops fighting the war had made their way to the capital seeking revenge on Lincoln.

(B) The president was improperly protected because the guards believed that when the war had ended, there was little threat to Lincoln.

(C) The course of history, especially the reconstruction of the country and rehabilitation of the former slaves, would have been greatly altered had Lincoln lived to serve out his term.

(D) There may have been a connection between the end of the war and the assassination.

(E) The former Confederate government wanted a chance to place its people in positions of power.

12. Which of the following statements would most logically follow the last sentence of the passage?

(A) The photographs proved that the Civil War was the bloodiest war ever fought on American soil.

(B) The new technology, especially submarines, gave the North an advantage in the War that the less industrialized South did not possess.

(C) Many of the photographs are kept in the Smithsonian Museum in Washington, D.C.

(D) People not fighting directly in the war were, for the first time, able to comprehend the reality of the war.

(E) The railroad technology developed during this time led eventually to the expansion of the West.

Go on to next page

Directions: Choose the answer choice most nearly opposite in meaning to the question word.

13. INTRANSIGENT
    (A) tawdry
    (B) vulnerable
    ✓(C) flexible
    (D) querulous
    (E) precocious

14. EXTROVERTED
    (A) bombastic
    (B) unnecessary
    ✓(C) shy
    (D) stationary
    (E) ubiquitous

Directions: Each of the following questions features a pair of words or phrases in capital letters, followed by five pairs of words or phrases in lowercase letters. Choose the lowercase pair that most closely expresses the same relationship as that of the uppercase pair.

15. HARDY : STRONG ::
    (A) puny : grandiose
    (B) unruly : disorganized
    (C) stubborn : flexible
    (D) dubious : ineligible
    (E) lucid : clouded

16. VACILLATE : INDECISIVE ::
    (A) deliberate : certain
    (B) hesitate : steadfast
    (C) repress : straightforward
    (D) affect : candid
    (E) contemplate : incurious

Directions: Each of the following sentences has one or two blanks indicating that words or phrases are omitted. Choose the answer that best completes the sentence.

17. To criticize a new employee for working slowly may actually be ----, as the employee becomes so flustered that he slows down even further in an attempt to concentrate on his task.
    (A) counterproductive
    (B) praiseworthy
    (C) worthwhile
    (D) essential
    (E) reasonable

18. Solar power is ---- by its ---- as a way to protect the environment, increase energy independence, reduce electricity bills, and protect against blackouts and accidents within the energy grid.
    (A) derided ... supporters
    (B) denounced ... champions
    (C) touted ... advocates
    (D) lampooned ... beneficiaries
    (E) lauded ... detractors

Directions: Choose the answer choice most nearly opposite in meaning to the question word.

19. PROGNOSTICATE
    (A) recall
    (B) exasperate
    (C) curtail
    (D) abhor
    (E) confiscate

20. CRYPTIC
    (A) destructive
    (B) craven
    (C) picayune
    (D) multifaceted
    (E) frank

Go on to next page

21.   ABSTAIN

(A) sneer

(B) participate

(C) approximate

(D) meander

(E) infuriate

Directions: Each of the following questions features a pair of words or phrases in capital letters, followed by five pairs of words or phrases in lowercase letters. Choose the lowercase pair that most closely expresses the same relationship as that of the uppercase pair.

22.   STAPLE : ATTACH ::

(A) button : sew

(B) carpet : impede

(C) water : dehydrate

(D) incision : open

(E) petition : review

23.   SKULL : BRAIN ::

(A) cuticle : toe

(B) blanket : bed

(C) cover : book

(D) trinket : shelf

(E) armor : body

Directions: Each of the following sentences has one or two blanks indicating that words or phrases are omitted. Choose the answer that best completes the sentence.

24.   It is unfortunate that Heather's first day on the job was filled with so many mistakes that her supervisor felt ---- his original recommendation not to hire her.

(A) justified in

(B) discontented with

(C) objective about

(D) vituperative regarding

(E) innovative in

25.   Unable to complete the project yet ---- to admit defeat, Liz worked at the task until she was lucky enough to find a solution that nearly ---- the difficulty.

(A) proposing ... destroyed

(B) unwilling ... resolved

(C) reluctant ... worsened

(D) eager ... doubled

(E) determined ... reduced

Directions: Each passage is followed by questions pertaining to that passage. Read the passage and answer the questions based on information stated or implied in that passage.

Studies have shown that certain components (Line) of the immune system behave abnormally in people with chronic fatigue syndrome. Chemicals called interleukin-2 and gamma interferon, which the body produces during its battle against (05) cancer and infectious agents, may not be made in normal amounts. There is evidence that a low-grade battle is being waged by the immune system of CFS patients, given the slight increase in the number of white cells that usually accumu- (10) late in the blood when people are fighting off an infection. Natural killer cells, though, that also help the body in this battle are found in slightly reduced numbers. It's important to note that clin- ical depression has the identical small reduction (15) in natural killer-cell activity. In addition, some depressed patients produce higher amounts of antibodies to certain viruses. There may be more of a connection between depression, the immune system, and chronic fatigue syndrome than is (20) realized even now, which introduces the some- what controversial aspect of the syndrome, its neuropsychological features.

Go on to next page

26. Which of the following does the author mention to support his theory that the immune system may be affected by chronic fatigue syndrome?

    (A) Clinical depression may be more physical than psychological.

    (B) Interleukin-2 and gamma interferon are not produced in normal amounts.

    (C) Antibody levels are higher in depressed people than in nondepressed people.

    (D) White-cell levels in people with neuropsychological problems tend to decrease.

    (E) Natural killer cells reduce the number of white blood cells.

27. When the body battles cancer,

    (A) it produces chemicals like gamma interferon.

    (B) it turns against its own immune system.

    (C) it stimulates the condition known as clinical depression.

    (D) it reduces the number of antibodies available to battle viruses.

    (E) it develops abnormal lesions around the area of the cancer.

Directions: Choose the answer choice most nearly opposite in meaning to the question word.

28. ILLICIT

    (A) expedient

    (B) insufficient

    (C) legal

    (D) affable

    (E) coarse

29. IRRITATE

    (A) badger

    (B) soothe

    (C) pressure

    (D) scratch

    (E) dry

Directions: Each of the following questions features a pair of words or phrases in capital letters, followed by five pairs of words or phrases in lowercase letters. Choose the lowercase pair that most closely expresses the same relationship as that of the uppercase pair.

30. JITTERBUG : DANCE ::

    (A) page : book

    (B) drawer : dresser

    (C) clatter : sound

    (D) sliver : slab

    (E) mortgage : house

Go on to next page

Quantitative Section

Time: 45 Minutes

28 questions

Notes:

All numbers used in this exam are real numbers.

All figures lie in a plane.

Angle measures are positive; points and angles are in the position shown.

The answer choices are

A if the quantity in Column A is greater.

B if the quantity in Column B is greater.

C if the two quantities are equal.

D if the relationship cannot be determined from the information given.

Column A	_Column B_

1. a is an integer greater than zero

$(\frac{1}{2}a)^2$	$\frac{1}{2}a^2$

2. $\boxed{x} = (3x)^2 - \frac{1}{3}x$

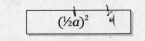

$\boxed{-3}$	$\boxed{3}$

3. $0 > a > b > c$

$a - c$	$a + b$

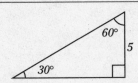

4.
Area of the triangle	$25\sqrt{3}$

Column A	_Column B_

5. $16a + 5b = 37; 3b - 8a = -21$

$a + b$	2

6.
Area of a rectangle of perimeter 20	Area of a triangle of perimeter 20

7. $a \neq 0, 1$

a^2	1

8. $3a + 5b = 12; 3b + 5a = 28$

$3(a + b)$	15

9. A right cylinder of volume 200π cubic units has a height of 8.

Circumference of the base	10

Go on to next page ➡

Column A	_Column B_

10. $2^{25} - 2^{24}$ | 2^{23}

11.   A sequence repeats as shown:
$-5, 0, 5, -5, 0, 5, -5, 0, 5.$

| Sum of 250th and 251st terms | 5 |

12. $x < 1 < y; \; x^2 > y^2$

| $(x+y)^2$ | $x^2 + y^2$ |

13. $a + b + c = 47; \; a + b - 2c = 14$

| $a + b$ | 33 |

14. Bob traveled 40 percent of the distance of his trip alone, went another 20 miles with Anthony, and then finished the last half of the trip alone. How many miles long was the trip?

(A) 240

(B) 200

(C) 160

(D) 100

(E) 50

15. Square RSTU has a perimeter of 48. If A, B, C, and D are the midpoints of their respective sides, what is the perimeter of square ABCD?

(A) 32

(B) $24\sqrt{2}$

(C) 24

(D) $12\sqrt{3}$

(E) $12\sqrt{2}$

16. Gigi and Neville, working together at the same rate, can mow the estate's lawn in 12 hours. Working alone, what fraction of the lawn can Gigi mow in three hours?

(A) ½₄

(B) ½₂

(C) ⅛

(D) ¼

(E) ⅓

The answer choices are

A if the quantity in Column A is greater.

B if the quantity in Column B is greater.

C if the two quantities are equal.

D if the relationship cannot be determined from the information given.

Column A	_Column B_

8

17.

| Number of square units in the shaded portion of the square | 20 |

Go on to next page

Use the following graphs to answer questions 18–20.

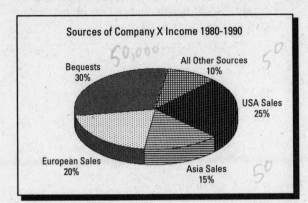

Sources of Company X Income 1980-1990

Bequests
30%

All Other Sources
10%

USA Sales
25%

European Sales
20%

Asia Sales
15%

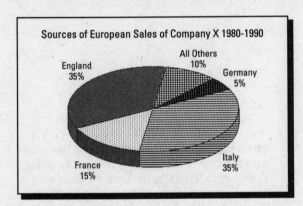

Sources of European Sales of Company X 1980-1990

England
35%

All Others
10%

Germany
5%

France
15%

Italy
35%

18. If Company X received $50,000 in bequests from 1980 through 1990, how much money did it receive from sales to France?

(A) $16,666

(B) $3,333

(C) $5,000

(D) $333

(E) $250

19. From the information given, the 1980 sales to England were what percent of the sales to Italy?

(A) 100

(B) 50

(C) 35

(D) 25

(E) It cannot be determined.

20. From the information given, if sales to Italy accounted for $1 million more than sales to France, how much income came from U.S. sales?

(A) $200,000

(B) $6,250,000

(C) $5 million

(D) $25 million

(E) It cannot be determined.

21. If $x \neq -1$ or 0 and $y = \frac{1}{x}$, then $\frac{1}{(x+1)} + \frac{1}{(y+1)} =$

(A) 1

(B) 3

(C) x

(D) $x + 1$

(E) $\frac{(x+1)}{(x+2)}$

22. If a is six greater than b, and the sum of a and b is -18, then $b^2 =$

(A) 144

(B) 36

(C) 16

(D) 4

(E) 0

Go on to next page

Questions 23 and 24 refer to the following graphs.

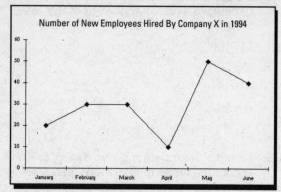

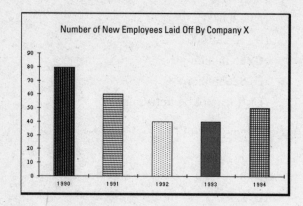

23. If new employees hired in May 1994 were ⅕ of the total employees, new employees laid off in 1994 would be what percent of the total employees in the company?

(A) 60

(B) 50

(C) 33⅓

(D) 24

(E) 20

24. In 1995, the increase in the percentage of new employees laid off over that of the previous year was the same as the increase in the percentage of new employees hired between January and February of 1994. How many new employees were laid off in 1995?

(A) 10

(B) 20

(C) 50

(D) 60

(E) 75

25. If ten plums cost a cents and six apples cost b cents, what is the cost of two plums and two apples in terms of a and b?

(A) $\dfrac{3a + 5b}{15}$

(B) $3a + 5b$

(C) $15ab$

(D) $5a + \dfrac{3b}{15}$

(E) $\dfrac{1}{15ab}$

26. If $x \neq 4$, solve for $\dfrac{\sqrt{x} + 2}{\sqrt{x} - 2}$

(A) -1

(B) $\dfrac{x + 4}{x - 4}$

(C) $-\sqrt{x} - 1$

(D) $\sqrt{x} + 4$

(E) $\dfrac{x + 4\sqrt{x + 4}}{x - 4}$

27. Two cans each have a height of 10. Can A has a circumference of 10π. Can B has a circumference of 20π. Which of the following represents the ratio of the volume of Can A to the volume of Can B?

(A) 1:10

(B) 1:8

(C) 1:4

(D) 1:2

(E) 1:1

28. A plane flies from Los Angeles to New York at 600 miles per hour and returns along the same route at 400 miles per hour. What is the average (arithmetic mean) flying speed for the entire route?

(A) 460 mph

(B) 480 mph

(C) 500 mph

(D) 540 mph

(E) It cannot be determined from the information given.

Go on to next page

Analytical Writing: Present Your Perspective on an Issue

Time: 45 minutes

One essay

Directions: Present and explain your view on the following issue. Although there is no one right or wrong response to the issue, be sure to consider various points of view as you explain the reasons behind your own perspective.

"Complete disclosure of facts by a country's leaders is not always in the best interest of the public."

Which point of view do you agree with — that complete disclosure of facts by a country's leaders is or is not always in the best interest of the public? Justify your position using examples from your personal or professional experience, reading, or general observation.

Analytical Writing: Analyze an Argument

Time: 30 minutes

One essay

Directions: Critique the following argument. Identify evidence that will strengthen or weaken the argument, point out assumptions underlying the argument, and offer counterexamples to the argument.

The following appeared in a memo sent by an outside efficiency expert hired by a firm to evaluate employee performance.

"In the six months that I have been watching the employees, their productivity has increased by over 12 percent. Therefore, my recommendation is that the employees either be watched by, or think that they are watched by, an outside evaluator at all times from this point on."

Discuss the merits of the previous argument. Analyze the evidence used as well as the general reasoning. Present points that would strengthen the argument or make it more compelling.

Answers to Practice Exam 1

Verbal section		*Quantitative section*	
1.	C	1.	B
2.	B	2.	A
3.	E	3.	A
4.	B	4.	B
5.	A	5.	C
6.	A	6.	D
7.	C	7.	D
8.	C	8.	C
9.	B	9.	A
10.	A	10.	A
11.	D	11.	B
12.	B	12.	B
13.	C	13.	A
14.	C	14.	B
15.	B	15.	B
16.	A	16.	C
17.	A	17.	B
18.	C	18.	C
19.	A	19.	E
20.	E	20.	B
21.	B	21.	A
22.	D	22.	A
23.	E	23.	E
24.	A	24.	E
25.	B	25.	A
26.	B	26.	E
27.	A	27.	C
28.	C	28.	B
29.	B		
30.	C		

Chapter 21
Practice Exam 1: Answers and Explanations

Verbal Section

1. **C.** *Sagacious* means wise. If you have more degrees than a thermometer, you are sagacious. Try to think of a word in another, more common form. You probably know that a sage is a wise person. (H.L. Mencken was nicknamed "The Sage of Baltimore" for his wit.) If you chose erudite, you fell for the trap: You selected a synonym rather than an antonym. *Erudite* means educated, scholarly. Choice E may have trapped you, had you confused sagacious with a *saga* — a long tale.

2. **B.** *Inept* means bungling or foolish. An inept person makes a mess of anything he attempts. The prefix *in-* means not; someone inept is not adept, or not skillful. Choice C, *prolific,* means abundant or producing much. An inept person is prolific at creating chaos. Choice E, *indigenous,* means native to. Long-legged blondes are indigenous to California beaches.

3. **E.** To *swagger* is to walk with arrogance or to strut your stuff. Remember all those bad war movies you watched on Saturday afternoons back in the good old days when all your time wasn't spent studying for this exam? The evil commandant often had a short stick tucked under his arm. That little piece of hardware was called a swagger stick because it was a symbol of his authority and *arrogance* (conceit). To *stagger* is to teeter, to walk with difficulty, or to have trouble maintaining your balance. (Don't confuse *swagger* with *stagger.* You swagger off the football field when you score the winning touchdown. You stagger out of the locker room after drinking too much champagne while celebrating your winning touchdown.)

To *swindle* is to cheat. *Veracity* is truthfulness (*ver-* means truth; *-ity* makes the word a noun). You don't cheat someone with truthfulness — you cheat someone with dishonesty.

 If a word in English is difficult, try pronouncing it with the accent of your native language. You may find that the word pronounced in your native accent will sound like a word in your own language that is similar in meaning. For example, *verdad* in Spanish means truth. Knowing that fact, you may be able to make a connection with *veracity*.

To *renege* is to go back on your word or to not be consistent at all. (If you tell your friends that you'll split your lottery winnings with them, and then a miracle happens, and you actually do win ten gazillion dollars, would you *renege* on your promise? That all depends on your *veracity* in making the statement in the first place.)

To *orchestrate* is to arrange to achieve a maximum effect. For example, a good hostess orchestrates a dinner party by arranging the seating and the entertainment to give the maximum pleasure to the guests. If you fell for this answer, hang your head in shame. The connection between orchestra and harmony is just a little too hokey, don't you think? One of my goals is to get you thinking the GRE way (don't worry, the condition is not permanent) so that you can recognize cheap tricks like this one.

And finally, to *wheedle* is to beg or flatter. It has nothing to do with *certitude,* which is just what it looks like (certainty, confidence, or assurance). Someone sure of himself or herself probably wouldn't have to beg or wheedle.

4. **B.** A *sheaf* is a collection or bundle of papers. (You may have heard the lyric, "Bringing in the sheaves," referring to harvesting sheaves, or bundles, of wheat.) A *collection* is a bundle of items. A *discourse* is conversation. A *cygnet* is a baby swan. A *quiver* contains arrows. A *quarter* is not a collection of dimes. ***Bonus trivia:*** A quarter has exactly 119 grooves on its circumference. A dime has 118.

5. **A.** The second blank is the key to this question. If the feet were used to push both rider and bicycle forward, the vehicle was not being stopped or developed or steered; only choices A and C work. Choice C doesn't fit the first blank. *Advocated* means defended or supported a cause. You may advocate the abolishment of all GRE testing.

6. **A.** You can predict the types of words you need to fill in the blanks. Jill was reluctant to show the man to be a fraud, so she attacked or put down or criticized the weaker points of his theory. To *denounce* is to criticize, to speak harshly of. To *debunk* is to disprove (*de-* = down from, away from, to put down). The first words in choices B, C, and D fit well; the second do not. To *castigate* is to criticize or punish. (For you men who are crossing your legs, relax. *Castigate* does not mean castrate, although both are certainly punishing!) In choice E, to *disseminate* is to spread, to disburse.

7. **C.** First, use the verbs to help eliminate wrong answers. Passages are rarely negative and don't ridicule anything (choice E). This very factual passage does not *refute* (deny or disprove) anything, eliminating choice B. A strong word like "prove" (choice D) is rarely correct (and how much can be proven in two paragraphs, anyway?). Just by examining the verbs, you have narrowed your answers down to a 50-50 guess.

On the GRE, you must guess before the computer permits you to go to the next question. A 50-50 shot is a real gift.

Choice A would be tempting except that the author never makes the claim that the Fremont culture was the most advanced, so how can that claim be challenged? Choice C fits: Recurring motifs between cultures may indicate connections between those cultures.

8. **C.** Choice A sounds like something that would be interesting to know (Hmmm . . . just why *didn't* the figures have a leg to stand on?), but the passage doesn't supply the answer. Choice B is the trap. Logically, you'd think that a passage about rock art would discuss the purpose of the art, but this very short passage doesn't provide that information. You may be tempted to throw out choice C after you read that sheep were depicted with curvilinear lines and that circles were a frequent motif. However, this information serves to answer the question in choice C with a definitive "no." The question simply asks which question can be answered. It makes no difference whether the answer is *yes* or *no.* Choice D is completely irrelevant; nothing was said about religion. Choice E may have tempted you. The author did mention a possible connection between the Fremont artists and people of the Four Corners area, but you should not take the information further. Nothing was said about people from other cultures beyond those of the Four Corners area.

9. **B.** A negatively phrased question, such as "all of the following are true EXCEPT" or "which of the following is NOT true" is often a time waster. You may have to go back to the passage again and again and again, eliminating answers one by one until you have only one left. If time is short for you, this question would be a good one to guess on quickly. In the passage, nothing was mentioned about the South after the Civil War.

10. **A.** The key to this question is to identify the purpose of the first paragraph. The main idea of paragraph one was to discuss the names of the Civil War. The material listed names that the South called the War; supplying names used by the North as well would strengthen the point.

11. **D.** When something is implied, it is indirectly stated meaning that the author may not be making a very strong point. Choose a wishy-washy, "possibly" or "maybe" style answer. The other choices go too far. Nothing was said about Southern troops going to the capital, about the protection of Lincoln (or threats made against him), or about a conspiracy by the Confederate government. Choice C is a logical answer, and it may be true, but the statement in the passage does not imply it.

    Just because a statement is true does not mean it is a correct answer.

12. **B.** The theme of the paragraph is the new technology. The rest of the paragraph would probably discuss the impact of that technology on the war. Choices A, C, and D, dealing with photography, are too specific. Choice E may be true but is probably not the point of the passage. Industrialization in general and its effect on the war is the important part, not the photography or railroads per se.

13. **C.** Use your roots to help you define this word. *In* usually means not. *Trans* means change, as in transferring from one place to another. An *intransigent* person does not change. He or she is stubborn and not flexible. Choice A, *tawdry,* means tacky, gaudy, or cheap. *Bonus trivia:* Do you know the origin of the word tawdry? It is a corruption of *St. Audrey's lace,* referring to a lace collar worn by a holy woman and copied in a cheaper form by the common people. *Querulous* means complaining and peevish. (Note that it doesn't mean quarreling, although certainly enough complaining may lead to a quarrel.) *Precocious* means advanced for one's age.

14. **C.** *Extroverted* means outgoing. The opposite is shy. *Bombastic* means big talking or grandiloquent. *Ubiquitous* means everywhere at once. After you learn these words, you'll be surprised how ubiquitous they are. You will start to see these words in advertisements, editorials, even love letters — well, maybe not every love letter (only the letters from your more bombastic companions!).

    Fun Fact: You won't see this word on the GRE, but *ubiety* is a great word to use with your friends — especially the bombastic ones who think their vocabularies are superior to yours. Although ubiquitous means everywhere at once, *ubiety* means having the property of being in one particular place at one particular time. For example, the planets have ubiety. If you're so wedded to routine that your friends can set their clocks by you, you have ubiety.

15. **B.** *Hardy* means strong. You'd get this question right even if you didn't know the words, assumed that they are synonyms, and made the *is* sentence: "Hardy is strong." (When you were young, did you ever read the adventure-book series about the Hardy boys? That name expressed the type of young men the main characters were.) *Unruly* means unable to be ruled or uncontrollable. A group of elementary school kids is unruly when a substitute teacher tries to take over the class. Roots could help you to define choices D and E. *Dubious* means doubtful: *dub-* means doubt; *-ous* means full of. *Lucid* means clear: *luc-* means light or clear. Unless someone has a lucid explanation of why he wants to borrow your car, it's dubious you'll let him take it.

16. **A.** This was a difficult question. If you don't know what vacillate means, assume the words are synonyms and make the *is* sentence: "To vacillate is to be indecisive." In fact, that's correct. To *vacillate* is to waver, to show indecision. You vacillate over whether to take the GRE or the GMAT. You can also get this question correct by process of elimination. In choice A, *deliberate* is to be certain, not uncertain. To *hesitate,* choice B, is to be uncertain, wavering, or vacillating — just the opposite of *steadfast* (holding steady, holding fast). To *repress* is to hold back, not to be straightforward. To *contemplate* is to be thinking about something or to be curious, not incurious. All three of these answers have the same relationship — they're antonyms — so all three must be wrong. You may know choice D, *affect,* in another form, affected or affectatious, meaning pretentious, artificial, or doing something just for show. *Candid,* which means open and sincere, is just the opposite.

17. **A.** The gist of the sentence is that criticizing the employee for working slowly makes him work even more slowly. The action, therefore, hurts rather than helps the situation and is counterproductive, meaning having a different result or consequence than what was intended. For example, staying up late studying the night before the GRE may actually be *counterproductive;* you will be so tired that you may do worse on the exam than you would have had you studied less and slept more.

Try to predict whether the word that you'll place in the blank should be a "good" or positive word or a "bad" or negative word. You know that if the employee gets flustered and slows down, something bad has happened. Looking for a negative word allows you to eliminate choices B, C, D, and E.

18. **C.** Given all the good things the sentence says about solar power, it's logical to assume that both blanks will be filled with positive words. Go through the answer choices and eliminate anything with a negative word: A (*deride* means to put down), B (*denounce* means to put down), and E (*detractors* are people who put something down or criticize). Note that all these words with *de* mean to put down, to criticize. (If you don't know your roots yet, be sure to go back and review them, along with prefixes and suffixes, in Chapters 3 and 7.) Choice D may have been difficult, but to *lampoon* is to ridicule or slander (think of *National Lampoon,* the magazine and the movies). By process of elimination, choice C is correct. To *tout* is to praise highly: I tout learning roots, prefixes, and suffixes. To *advocate* is to support or champion (the prefix *ad-* means toward; if you *advocate* something, you go toward it, you like it). A *beneficiary* benefits or gets something good (*ben* means good). To *laud* is to praise (think of applaud).

19. **A.** This question rewards you for learning your roots. *Gnos* means knowledge. One of the three meanings of *pro* is before. The suffix *–ate* means to make. To *prognosticate* is "to make knowledge before," or to predict. I prognosticate that your score on this exam will be excellent. To *recall* is to remember, as in, "I recall that once upon a time I didn't know what prognosticate meant." To *exasperate* is to annoy. To *curtail* is to shorten. (Think of this word as "to cut the tail off," which makes something shorter.) To *abhor* is to hate. (The prefix *ab-* means away from; when you abhor or hate something, you stay away from it.) Choice E is the trap. Did you think that *con* in confiscate is the opposite of *pro* in prognosticate? Sorry, not this time. To *confiscate* is to take like when a teacher confiscates a child's bubblegum in school.

20. **E.** *Cryptic* means hidden, mysterious, or baffling. (*Crypt* means hidden.) The opposite is *frank,* meaning open, straightforward, and concealing nothing. *Craven* in choice B means cowardly. Choice C, *picayune* (yes, that's how you spell the word that is pronounced pick-a-yune) means small, trivial, or petty. *Multifaceted* means complex, having a variety of features or parts. Most relationships are multifaceted and fall apart because of a spat over some picayune point.

21. **B.** To *abstain* is to refrain or to hold back (*ab-* means away from). You may abstain from voting in the student elections if you don't like any of the candidates. The opposite is to participate. In choice D, to *meander* is to wander aimlessly, to ramble. To *infuriate* is to annoy greatly, to make furious. A good public speaker will abstain from meandering too much because rambling can infuriate the audience.

22. **D.** The purpose of a staple is to attach something; the purpose of an *incision* (a cut) is to open something. A surgeon makes an incision to get into your chest, for example.

If you chose A, you fell for a trap. Although a button is sewn on, the purpose of a button is not to sew. Don't fall for a trap answer by looking at the meanings of the words. The fact that buttons and staples both attach items doesn't have any relevance here. You need to look at the relationships between the words, not at their meanings.

The purpose of a carpet is not to *impede,* which is to hold back or to hinder. If you want to go roller-skating, then roller-skating across a carpet would impede your progress; but impeding progress is not a carpet's primary function. The purpose of water is to *hydrate* (moisten something), not to *dehydrate* (dry something out). The purpose of a petition is to suggest or demand that something happen, not to review what happened. If you create a petition against the GRE, your purpose is to suggest that the exam be abolished from polite society, not to review the status of the exam.

23. **E.** This should have been a relatively easy question. Make the sentence: A *skull* protects the brain; *armor* protects the body. A *cuticle* is part of a toe, but it doesn't offer much protection when you drop a GRE book on your foot. A blanket covers, but doesn't protect, a bed. A cover of a book affords some protection, but not much. A *trinket* goes on a shelf. Speaking of what's inside your skull, here's some bonus brain trivia: How old are you right now? If you're over 20, I've got some bad news. You're heading downhill from the nose up. The brain reaches its maximum weight — about 3 pounds — at age 20. Over the next 60 years, the brain loses about 3 ounces as billions of its nerve cells die. The brain begins to lose cells at a rate of 50,000 per day by the age of 30.

24. **A.** If the supervisor was afraid to hire the worker who *bungled* (messed up) badly on her first day, it appears the supervisor's fears were well founded or justified.

    In choice C, *objective* means neutral or unbiased — just the opposite of what the supervisor was. Choice D, *vituperative,* means violently abusive. And *innovative* means new and original. A vituperative person may come up with some innovative *epithets* (names, titles) to call the object of his *wrath* (anger).

25. **B.** The only excuse for missing a question such as this one is laziness or carelessness. So many of the Sentence Completion questions test very hard vocabulary that when you get to one like this with very easy vocabulary, you should take your time and go through each answer choice carefully to ensure that you find the correct one.

    To resolve a difficulty is to solve the problem. If Liz kept working, she was unwilling to abandon the project. Only choices B and C work for the first blank; the second word in answer choice C is just the opposite of what the sentence intends to say.

26. **B.** The first two sentences of the passage tell you that " . . . certain components of the immune system behave abnormally in people with chronic fatigue syndrome" and " . . . interleukin-2 and gamma interferon . . . may not be made in normal amounts." This one is a simple detail or fact question.

    Choice C is a trap answer. The author does in fact say that antibody levels are higher in depressed people; however, he does not make that statement to support the theory that the immune system may be affected by chronic fatigue syndrome. Just because a statement is true does not mean that it is the correct answer; be sure to address what the question is asking.

    Questions usually go in order through the passage — especially science passages (which require you to find specific facts rather than make inferences). Because this is the first question, go back to the first sentence or two.

27. **A.** This is a very simple, detail or fact question. Lines 3–6 tell you that the body produces chemicals such as interleukin-2 and gamma interferon during its battle against cancer.

    As you have probably noticed by now, the questions on science passages are often easier than questions on other types of passages. Even if the science passages themselves are boring or difficult to understand, the questions relating to them are usually quite straightforward; frequently, you just have to skim for a specific fact or detail.

28. **C.** *Illicit* means illegal. The opposite is legal. *Affable* means friendly. (I like to think of *affable* as "af-friend-able.")

29. **B.** To *irritate* is to annoy. The opposite is to soothe. Choice A, *badger,* is to harass, bother, or annoy. Occasionally, the answer choices feature a word that is a synonym to the question word. It's easy to choose this answer because uppermost in your mind is the definition. "Badger, hmmm. That means to annoy or to irritate. Oh, there it is!" Keep in mind that the name of the game is *antonyms,* not synonyms.

30. **C.** A *jitterbug* is a type of dance; a *clatter* is a type of sound. A *page* is a part of a book, not a type of book. A *drawer* is a part of a dresser, not a type of dresser. A *sliver* is a small part of a slab. A *mortgage* is usually necessary to buy a house, but it isn't a type of house.

Quantitative Section

1. **B.** Plug in numbers. Suppose that $a = 1$. Then Column A is $\frac{1}{2} \times 1$, which is $\frac{1}{2}$, and then $\frac{1}{2}^2$, which is $\frac{1}{4}$. Column B requires you to square the 1 first, which is simply 1, and then multiply by $\frac{1}{2}$ to get $\frac{1}{2}$. So far, Column B is bigger. Try a different number. Suppose that $a = 2$. Then Column A is $\frac{1}{2}$ of 2, which is 1. You know that $1^2 = 1$. Column B is $\frac{1}{2}$ of 4 (because $2^2 = 4$) and Column B is still greater. No matter what you plug in (and you should always plug in more than one number, or you'll never know whether the answer depends on what you plug in), Column B is larger.

   Do you remember the Sacred Six you need to plug in for variables? They are 1, 2, 0, –1, –2, and $\frac{1}{2}$. Usually, just plugging in 1 and 2 gets the job done. Turn back to Chapter 14 for more info.

2. **A.** Ah, if you chose C, you got careless.

   Whenever you see a choice C, double- and triple-check it. More traps lie in the C answers than in most of the rest of the answers. If your first instinct is to choose C, you're probably just making some nasty test-maker's day by falling for his trap.

   First, you have to say to yourself in English what the symbols mean. Say, "I have something in a triangle. First, I multiply that something by 3. Then I square that answer. Then I take a third of that something. Then I subtract the second from the first." In other words, substitute the number in the triangle for the x in the equation. For Column A, you have 3×-3, which is –9. Then $-9^2 = 81$. Next, $\frac{1}{3}$ of $-3 = -1$. Finally, $81 - (-1)$ means $81 + 1 = 82$. For Column B, you have $3 \times 3 = 9$. Then $9^2 = 81$. Next, $\frac{1}{3}$ of $3 = 1$. Finally, $81 - 1 = 80$. You had to keep your negatives and positives straight.

   Whenever a problem has a negative variable, double-check your signs. You can easily make a careless mistake with them.

3. **A.** You have absolutely no excuse for missing this problem, even if you did get a brain cramp when you first looked at it. Remember my tip from Chapter 14: Cancel quantities that are identical in both columns. Slash off the a in both columns. That leaves you with $-c$ and $+b$. Because c is negative, a negative c is a double negative, which is actually a positive. In Column B, b remains negative (because a positive times a negative is negative). Because any positive is greater than any negative, Column A is larger.

   Did you look at all the variables and choose D, thinking the answer depended on what you plugged in? That's a very good first reaction, but be sure to do the actual plugging. Say that the numbers are –1, –2, and –3. (Be careful not to get messed up and put –3, –2, –1. With negatives, everything is backwards: –1 is greater than –2.)

   Column A is $-1 - (-3) = -1 + 3 = 2$. Column B is $-1 + (-2) = -3$. Please, please be careful not to overuse and abuse my tips. They are glorious tips and will help you if you treat them with respect. When you use a tip, make a commitment to it: Work it through to the end. If you decide that the answer is going to depend on what you plug in, *actually plug in the numbers* and work the problem through.

   Usually, choice D is valid in three instances. You think D when you have a geometry problem with no picture. You think D when a picture specifically says that it is not drawn to scale (something that is very rare on the GRE). And you choose D when you have *actually* plugged in different values for variables, *actually* done the work, and *actually* gotten different answers.

4. **B.** If you chose D, you fell for the trap. You probably looked at the question, saw that only one side was given, and figured that you didn't have enough info to answer the question. Wrong. You should have reminded yourself of the tip — when a figure is given, the answer is rarely D. (This is the flip of the tip that when a geometry problem gives words but no pictures, it is usually D.)

Do you remember your Pythagorean triples? I discuss these threesomes in Chapter 11. For many right triangles, the sides have a special ratio. For a 30:60:90 triangle, that ratio is side : side $\sqrt{3}$: 2 side. The side opposite the 30-degree angle is the shortest side — the 5 in this case. The side opposite the 60-degree angle is the next shortest side, the "side $\sqrt{3}$" side. With this question, that's $5\sqrt{3}$. Although you don't need to know this to find the area of the triangle, the *hypotenuse* (the side opposite the 90-degree angle) is the longest side — the "2 side" side. Here, it's 10.

The area of a triangle is ½ base × height. The base is $5\sqrt{3}$; the height is 5. Therefore, the area is $½(25\sqrt{3})$. Don't bother finding the exact number; it is certainly less than $25\sqrt{3}$. If you chose C, you did *allllll* that work and, because you forgot the very last step, missed the stupid question anyway.

How can you prevent making a careless mistake like forgetting to multiply by ½ in this problem? Simple. Immediately write down the formula for the problem on the scratch paper. Writing the formula may seem childish or like extra work, but it only takes a nanosecond and can prevent careless errors. When you see the formula, you plug the numbers into it and work it through.

5. **C.** It's amazing how many questions that require you actually to do the work and solve the problem turn out to be choice C. I'm not saying that you should choose C as soon as you start shoving the pencil around, but the more calculations a question requires, the more often the answer seems to be C. (That's the flip of the tip in the lecture that if the quantities appear to be equal at first glance, without doing any work, a trap is probably lurking.) Here, set the equations up vertically:

$$16a + 5b = 37$$

$$-8a + 3b = -21$$

You want to either add or subtract to get the same numerical coefficient (the number that goes in front of the variable) for the *a* and the *b*. When you add the equations here (and notice how I've moved the *a* to the front of the second equation to make the variables add up neatly), you get $8a + 8b = 16$. Divide both sides by 8 to get $a + b = 2$.

You didn't have to go through the whole mess of substitution. That is, you didn't have to say for the first equation that $16a = 37 - 5b$, and then say that $a = \frac{37}{16} - \frac{5b}{16}$, and then substitute that for the value of *a* in the second equation. I'd call that *gratuitous* (uncalled for, unearned, or unnecessary) violence. When you have two equations, line them up vertically and work so that one of the variables drops out (for example, you may have $3b - 3b$) or the variables have the same numerical coefficients.

6. **D.** When a geometry problem has no figure drawn, the answer is often choice D because it *de*pends on how the figure is drawn. A rectangle of perimeter 20 can have, for example, sides of 1 and 9 and 1 and 9, making the area 9. Or it can have sides of 6 and 4 and 6 and 4, making the area 24. (The area of a rectangle is *length times width*. If you forgot this formula, turn to Chapter 11.) A triangle of perimeter 20 can have sides of 4, 7, and 9, or a *plethora* (abundance) of other combinations. And because you don't know whether the triangle is a right triangle, you have no idea what the height is. That height could be a leg of the triangle, be inside the triangle, or be outside the triangle. There is not enough information to compare the quantities.

7. **D.** If you chose A, you fell right for my cunningly devised trap (okay, so it was a cheap trick). Don't forget that a negative squared is a positive. If *a* were -2, for example, then $-2^2 = 4$, and Column A is larger. And what if *a* is a fraction? If $a = ½$, then $½^2 = ¼$, and B is bigger. If the answer could be A or B, it *de*pends on what you plug in — choice D.

Remember the Sacred Six that I asked you to get into the habit of plugging in? These numbers are 1, 2, 0, -1, -2, ½. You don't need to plug in 0 or 1 this time, but you do need to plug in the fraction. You should chant this phrase to yourself as if it were a mantra: "Positive, negative, zero, fraction. Positive, negative, zero, fraction." Got it?

8. **C.** Line the equations up vertically and either add or subtract them to get the same numerical coefficients (the numbers before the variables). In this case, you add:

$$3a + 5b = 12$$
$$5a + 3b = 28$$
$$\overline{8a + 8b = 40}$$

Now divide both sides of the equation by 8 to get $a + b = 5$. Finally, $3 \times 5 = 15$.

9. **A.** The volume of any figure is *area of the base × height*. Because the base of a cylinder is a circle, the volume of a cylinder is $\pi \ radius^2 \times height$. Divide the volume, 200π, by the height, 8, to find that the area of the base is 25π. Because the base is a circle of area = $\pi radius^2$, the radius is 5. But don't choose B; you're not finished yet.

The circumference of a circle is 2π radius, which here is 10π. If you chose C, you fell for the trap. You forgot your π! The circumference of 10π is actually $10 \times$ approximately 3.14, which is more than 10 (don't bother to figure it out exactly). The moral of the story: Keep your eye on the π.

If your first thought when you look at a problem is that the columns are equal, think again. Usually — not always — you have to do actual calculations to get a C.

Usually, when a geometry problem is all words and no pictures, the answer is choice D because the comparison will depend on what the picture looks like. This is an exception to the tip. I included it here just to keep you from using the tips automatically instead of actually thinking the problem through.

10. **A.** Why would I give you a problem like this without allowing you access to your calculator? Well, you have two choices (and murder and mayhem are not among them). You can make a quick guess at the answer to this problem and pretty much blow it off entirely. Or you can be very smart and realize that if a principle is valid with a large number, it is usually valid with a small number. In other words, instead of 2^{25} or 2^{24}, make it 2^5 or 2^4. You can quickly figure 2^5 as $2 \times 2 \times 2 \times 2 \times 2 = 32$. Then 2^4 is 16, and $32 - 16 = 16$. Therefore, $2^5 - 2^4$ is 2^4, just as $2^{25} - 2^{24}$ is 2^{24}, not 2^{23}.

11. **B.** There are three terms in the sequence. That means that every third term is 5. Divide 250 by 3 to get 83 with a remainder of 1. That means that the 249th number is 5 (because 249 divides evenly by 3), the 250th number is -5, and the 251st number is 0. Add $-5 + 0 = -5$.

The people who devise the GRE put questions like this one in to get you to waste your time. Oh sure, you could have counted on your fingers up to the 250th term, but who has that sort of time? Find the closest number that divides by 3 and then work from there.

Did you choose D for this problem? If so, you probably confused "It depends" with "Don't have a clue — duuuh!" Choice D does not mean *you* don't know how to do the problem but rather that no one could do the problem with the *paucity* (lack) of information presented in the problem. In other words, don't take the question personally. Just because you can't do a problem yourself does not indicate it is undoable, or a choice D.

12. **B.** Did you fall for trap answer A? Choice A is wrong because $(x + y)^2 = (x + y)(x + y) = x^2 + 2xy + y^2$. Column A has $2xy$, which Column B doesn't have. Don't jump on choice A in this case just because you see that Column A has something extra. You know that y is positive because $y > 1$, but for x^2 to be greater than y^2 while $x < y$, x must be negative. With a negative x and a positive y, $2xy$ will be negative, making Column A with the extra $2xy$ less than Column B.

Don't like algebra? Try a simple way to do this problem: Plug in numbers. You need to be absolutely sure that the numbers you plug in fit the constraints given by the centered information. For example, you could not say $x = 1$ because the problem states $x < 1$. Why don't you try $x = 0$ and $y = 2$? Wait, wait: Those numbers don't work with the second equation. 0^2 is NOT larger than 2^2. Try some different numbers. How about $x = -1$, $y = 2$? No, -1^2 is NOT larger than 2^2. Try -3 for x and 2 for y. Ah, that works: -3^2, which is 9, IS larger than 2^2, which is 4. (Note that this "plug 'n' chug" technique, although easy, can be tricky and time consuming.) Now plug these values into the question: $(-3+2)^2 = -1^2 = 1$. Column B: $-3^2 + 2^2 = 9 + 4 = 13$. Column B is correct. BUT you need to plug in again, just to be sure. Try -4 and 3. $(-4+3)^2 = 1^2 = 1$. $-4^2 + 3^2 = 16 + 9 = 25$. Column B is still greater.

13. **A.** Line up the equations vertically and subtract so that a and b fall out.

$$a + b + c = 47$$
$$-(a + b - 2c = 14)$$
$$a - a = 0$$
$$b - b = 0$$
$$c - (-2c) = 3c$$

Don't forget that you are subtracting a negative: A negative negative is a positive. In other words, "minus minus $2c$" is $+2c$.

$$47 - 14 = 33$$
$$3c = 33$$
$$c = 11$$

If $a + b + 11 = 47$, then $a + b = 47 - 11 = 36$. If you chose C, you probably got confused on the negative signs and said $-(-2c) = c$, then $c = 33$.

14. **B.** If Bob traveled the last half of his trip alone, then the 40 percent and the 20 miles are the first half, or 50 percent. Because 50 percent – 40 percent = 10 percent, 20 miles = 10 percent. It may be easier to think in terms of fractions: 10 percent = $\frac{1}{10}$. One-tenth of *something* is 20; that *something* is 200. (Arithmetically: $\frac{1}{10}x = 20$. Divide both sides through by $\frac{1}{10}$, which means inverting and multiplying by $\frac{10}{1}$, and $20 \times 10 = 200$.) This was a good problem to talk through; you needed reasoning, not arithmetic.

15. **B.** The four sides of a square are equal, such that one side of square RSTU is 12. If the points are midpoints, each one divides the large square's sides into two parts, each part consisting of 6 units. The new inner square has equal sides of 6 and forms four isosceles right triangles. The ratios of the sides of an isosceles right triangle are side : side : side $\sqrt{2}$. That means the hypotenuse of triangle DRA, for example, is $6\sqrt{2}$. Add the four sides to get $24\sqrt{2}$.

If you chose A, you said that four "root 2's" equaled 8, and added $24 + 8 = 32$. You can't add square roots like that. (If you're confused, go back to the roots section in Chapter 12.)

16. **C.** The key to this problem is knowing that Gigi and Neville work at the same rate. If they finish the lawn in 12 hours, each did $\frac{1}{2}$ of the job in 12 hours. Therefore, Gigi working alone would have taken 24 hours to finish the lawn. Because 3 hours is $\frac{1}{8}$ of 24 hours, she could have done $\frac{1}{8}$ of the job in that time.

17. **B.** Think of a shaded area as a leftover. It's what's left over after you have subtracted the unshaded area from the figure as a whole. Because Column A tells you that the figure is a square, you find its area by multiplying side times side: $8 \times 8 = 64$. The diameter of the circle is the same as the length of the square, 8. The radius of a circle is half the diameter, or 4. The area of a circle is π radius^2, or 16π. Find the shaded area by subtracting $64 - 16\pi$.

Do not, I repeat, do not bother actually figuring out how much 16π is. You know that π is slightly larger than 3.14, but I wouldn't even make things that complicated. Just say that π is bigger than 3. Multiply $16 \times 3 = 48$. Subtract $64 - 48 = 16$. The actual area will be even smaller than that because you'll be subtracting some number larger than 48 (whatever you get when you multiply 3.14×16, which I am not about to do, and neither should you). Because 16 is smaller than 20, and the "real" answer will be even smaller than 16, Column B is bigger.

If you've forgotten how to do shaded areas, return to Chapter 11, where I discuss a simple three-step approach.

18. **C.** Bequests account for 30 percent of total income. ***Hint:*** Ignore the zeros; just let the equation be $50 = .3x$. Divide both sides through by .3 to get x (total income)= 166.67. European sales were 20 percent of total income, or $166.67 \times .20 = 33.3$. Sales to France were 15 percent of that figure: $.15 \times 33.3 = 5$.

Estimate wildly. The answer choices are so far apart that you can get away with murder here. Say that Bequests are about a third of the total, making the total 15. Then European sales are 20 percent or a fifth of the total, or 3. Then French sales are 15 percent of that, or .45. The only answer even remotely close to that is choice C. If this question really slows you down, just guess.

19. **E.** Read the titles on the graphs: They show income and sales from 1980 through 1990. You cannot figure out sales in one particular year. If you chose A, you fell for the trap. And shame on you for being so ***credulous*** (gullible). You should have been more paranoid than that. If something looks too good to be true, it probably is.

20. **B.** Good problem. If you got this question right, ***kudos*** and ***accolades*** and ***encomium*** (praises) to you. This question takes a lot of backtracking.

Sales to Italy are 20 percent more than sales to France (35 percent − 15 percent) meaning that 20 percent = 1 million, or $\frac{1}{5}$ = 1 million; thus, 100 percent = 5 million. But this is 100 percent of the second graph, which is still only 20 percent of the first graph. In other words, the total 5 million in the second graph is 20 percent or $\frac{1}{5}$ of the first graph; therefore, the total of the first graph is 25 million. (Are you totally confused yet? Just keep reading and no one will get hurt.) U.S. sales are 25 percent or $\frac{1}{4}$ of that: $.25 \times \$25$ million is — hey, stop right there; don't actually do all the work. Estimate. A fourth of 25 is just over 6; the only possible correct answer is B. Don't do all the work until you've checked out the answer choices; often, you can do just a rough estimate and get the correct answer.

21. **A.** There's an easy way, and there's a hard way to approach this problem. I'll start with the easy way: Plug in numbers. Substitute numbers for the variables.

Let $x = 3$. (It doesn't make much difference what number you substitute; I just choose 3 because it's small and easy to deal with. I did not want to use 1 because of the fractions: $\frac{1}{1}$ doesn't help much.) If $x = 3$, then $y = \frac{1}{3}$.

Now plug these numbers into the entire equation:

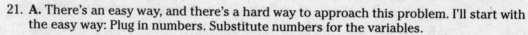

$$\frac{1}{(x+1)} + \frac{1}{(y+1)} = \frac{1}{(3+1)} + \frac{1}{(\frac{1}{3}+1)} = \frac{1}{4} + \frac{1}{(\frac{4}{3})} = \frac{1}{4} + \frac{3}{4} = 1$$

Although in this case, choice A is correct, you MUST go through the final step of checking every answer choice. Here, choice B is obviously wrong. Choice C, $x = 3$, is wrong (remember, you're looking for a final answer of 1). In choice D, $3 + 1 = 4$. Choice E is $\frac{(3+1)}{(3+2)} = \frac{4}{5}$. Why bother with this last step of checking every answer? Depending on what number you plug in, more than one answer could work. In that case, you'd have to change your numbers and try again.

If you are a more abstract thinker and prefer to use basic algebra, think of this as a substitution problem. Substitute $y = \frac{1}{x}$ for the y in the expression $\frac{1}{(y+1)}$:

$$\frac{1}{(x+1)} + \frac{1}{(\frac{1}{x}+1)}$$

To get rid of that ugly second part of the expression, multiply $\frac{1}{(\frac{1}{x}+1)}$ by $\frac{x}{x}$ (Don't forget to distribute.):

$$\frac{1}{(x+1)} + \frac{1}{(\frac{1}{x}+1)} \times \frac{x}{x} = \frac{1}{(x+1)} + \frac{x}{(1+x)}$$

Now you have a common denominator (remember that $x + 1$ is the same as $1 + x$), so add the fractions:

$$\frac{(1+x)}{(x+1)} = 1 \text{ (choice A)}$$

22. **A.** Set up the equations: $a - b = 6$ (because a is six greater than b, the difference between them is 6) and $a + b = -18$. Line them up vertically, and add:

$$a - b = 6$$
$$\underline{a + b = -18}$$
$$2a = -12$$
$$a = -6$$
$$-6 + b = -18$$
$$b = -12$$
$$-12^2 = 144$$

The key to this problem is lining up the equations vertically and then adding them so that one variable (in this case, the b) drops out. Solve for the other variable and then substitute that number back into one of the equations.

23. **E.** This relatively simple problem takes two steps. In May there were 50 new employees hired. 50 = 20 percent or ⅕ of the total (250) employees. If there were 250 employees and 50 of them were laid off, then ⅕ (back to that same number!) were laid off.

Did you see the shortcut in this problem? The 50 in the top graph is the same as the 50 in the bottom graph. Therefore, whatever percent you have for the top graph is the same as the percent for the bottom graph. You did not need to go through all of that work.

24. **E.** First, figure out the percent increase in new hires between January and February. Twenty new employees were hired in January and 30 were hired in February. To find a percent increase or decrease, you use the formula: *Number increase or decrease ÷ original whole* (the number you began with). Here, that's ¹⁰⁄₂₀ = ½ = 50 percent.

The number of employees laid off in 1994, according to the bottom graph, was 50. The number laid off in 1995 was 50 percent greater than this. Fifty percent of 50 is ½ of 50, or 25. Add 50 + 25 = 75.

Did you fall for choice D? The increase in new hires between January and February was 10, but this does not mean that the number of layoffs in 1995 was 10 higher than the number in 1994. You must figure the *percentage*.

25. **A.** If 10 plums cost a cents, then each plum costs ¹⁄₁₀ a and 2 plums cost ²⁄₁₀ or ⅕ a. If 6 apples cost b cents, then each apple costs ⅙ b cents, and 2 apples cost ²⁄₆ b or ⅓ b cents. Now use 15 as a common denominator for 5 and 3. Convert: ⅕ a = ³⁄₁₅ a, and ⅓ b = ⁵⁄₁₅ b.

This pretty confusing problem assumes you have some sort of sick fetish for fractions. You can work out the problem without stooping so low as to deal with those nasty little things. The easy way to do this problem is to substitute numbers for the variables. Let $a = 10$, such that each plum costs 1 cent and two plums cost 2 cents. Let $b = 6$ such that each apple costs 1 cent and 2 apples cost 2 cents. Then the total is 4 cents. Plug the same values into the answer choices to see which one comes out to be 4. In a, you have $3(10) + 5(6) = 60$ divided by 15 = 4.

You must check all the answer choices when you plug in your own numbers. Did you get as far as choice E? If you did, you got 4 there as well (¹⁄₁₅ × 10 × 6 = ¹⁄₁₅ × 60 = 4). What now? If you get more than one correct answer based on the terms you plug in, plug in different terms and try again.

Suppose that this time $a = 20$ and $b = 6$. Now the cost of each plum is 2 cents, making the cost of two of them 4 cents. The cost of the apples remains the same. Two plums (4 cents) plus 2 apples (2 cents) = 6 cents. The new answer you're looking for is 6.

Don't bother going through all of the answer choices again. You've already narrowed the field down to A or E; try just those two.

Now choice A is $(60 + 30) \div 15 = 90 \div 15 = 6$. It works. Choice E is $\frac{1}{15} \times 20 \times 6 = \frac{1}{5} \times 120$, which does not equal 6. Throw E away; A is correct.

I was incredibly kind with this problem by making A the correct answer. A less magnificent human being would have switched answers A and E. Then, if you didn't bother plugging in the answers for every single answer choice and stopped at A, you would fall for the trap.

26. **E.** Does this problem make you think of Egyptian hieroglyphics? Join the crowd. Instead of just saying, "That's History, babe!" and guessing at this problem, make it easy to work through by *plugging in numbers.* Choose a number that has an easy square root. Make $x = 9$ (because $\sqrt{9} = 3$). Now solve the question:

$$(\sqrt{9} + 2) \div (\sqrt{9} - 2) = (3 + 2) \div (3 - 2) = \frac{5}{1} = 5$$

Keep in mind that 5 is the answer to the problem. It is not the value of x. Jot the 5 down to the side, draw a circle around it, put arrows pointing to it, or do whatever it takes to remind yourself that the answer you want is 5. Now go through each answer choice and see which one comes out to be 5. Only choice E works:

$$(9 + 4\sqrt{9} + 4) \div 9 - 4(9 + 4 \times 3 + 4) \div 5 = (9 + 12 + 4) \div 5 = \frac{25}{5} = 5$$

Be very, very careful not to put 3 in for x in the problem. Remember $x = 9$ — the square root of $x = 3$. I suggest you make a chart to the side, simply writing down $x = 9$ and ANSWER = 5.

When you plug in numbers, go through every single answer choice, *soporific* (sleep-inducing) though that may be. If you started with choice E, for example, and made a careless mistake, you would find that choices D, C, and B didn't work either . . . and probably choose A by process of elimination. If you take just a second to work out A, you'll see that it too is wrong, alerting you to the fact that you made a careless mistake somewhere.

For you algebra addicts who can't live without your fix: Simplify the denominator by multiplying each side through by $(\sqrt{x} + 2)$.

$$\left[(\sqrt{x} + 2) \div (\sqrt{x} - 2)\right] \times \left[(\sqrt{x} + 2)(\sqrt{x} + 2)\right]$$

The numerator is $(\sqrt{x} + 2)(\sqrt{x} + 2)$. Use FOIL (First, Outer, Inner, Last) to multiply these: $\sqrt{x} \times \sqrt{x} = x$. Then $\sqrt{x} \times 2 = 2\sqrt{x}$. Next, $2 \times \sqrt{x} = 2\sqrt{x}$. Finally, $2 \times 2 = 4$. Add: $x + 4\sqrt{x} + 4$.

The denominator is $(\sqrt{x} - 2) \times (\sqrt{x} + 2)$. Use FOIL again to multiply these: $\sqrt{x} \times \sqrt{x} = x$. Then $x \times 2 = 2x$. Next, $\sqrt{x} \times 2 = 2\sqrt{x}$. Next, $\sqrt{x} \times -2 = -2\sqrt{x}$.

The $2\sqrt{x}$ and $-2\sqrt{x}$ cancel each other out, leaving you with $x - 4$.

If you took my advice in Chapter 12 and memorized some basic FOIL problems, you knew immediately that $(a + b)(a + b) = a^2 + 2ab + b^2$ (just substitute x for the a, and 2 for the b). You knew that $(a + b)(a - b) = a^2 - b^2$ (substitute the x for the a and the 2 for the b). If you haven't memorized these handy pieces of FOIL, go back to Chapter 12 and do so now.

27. **C.** The volume of any figure is (area of base) × height. The base of a cylinder is a circle. Because the area of a circle is πr^2, the volume of a cylinder is $\pi r^2 h$.

The circumference of a circle is $2\pi r$. Therefore, the radius of Can A = 5; the radius of Can B = 10. Volume Can A = $5^2 \pi \times 10 = 250\pi$. Volume Can B = $10^2 \pi \times 10 = 1000\pi$. Finally, $250\pi : 1000\pi = 1:4$.

You may — *or may not* — be given the necessary formulas to solve this type of question. Don't take any chances: Have the geometry formulas memorized. They're all given in the math review chapters (Chapters 11, 12, and 13).

28. **B.** If you chose C, my work here has been in vain. To find an average, you add up the terms and then divide by the number of terms. But this is a Time-Rate-Distance problem and the terms here aren't simply 600 and 400. You have to find the length of time spent flying at 600 mph and the length of time spent flying at 400 mph, and then, you add *those* numbers and divide.

If you think logically about this problem, you know the answer can't be C, but if you don't want to spend time working it out, you can eliminate a few more answers. You know that the plane must go more time at the slower rate and less time at the faster rate. That means the average is going to be less than half of the "average" 500 mph. Immediately narrow your answers down to A and B. If you're in a hurry, guess and go.

You probably wanted to make a simple Time-Rate-Distance chart for this problem, right? Good thinking . . . but it won't work here. To make a chart of that sort, you have to have at least two of the three variables. For example, if you know rate and distance, you can find time. But here, you have only one variable — rate. You cannot solve for time and distance. What do you do now? Find a ratio.

Use a common multiple of 12 (actually, 1,200) miles. In 2 hours, the plane traveling at 600 mph will go 1,200 miles. In 3 hours, the plane traveling at 400 miles will go 1,200 miles. To find the average, add 600 twice and 400 three times . . . and then divide by 5, not by 2. $600 + 600 + 400 + 400 + 400 = 2400$. $2400/5 = 480$.

Did the words "arithmetic mean" confuse you? They're put there to prevent any lawsuits over confusion of terms. The "average" can mean different things to different people; the "arithmetic mean" is the precise term. Don't worry about it. The info in parentheses is usually there to cover fundamental anatomical regions in case of litigation. You can ignore it.

Analytical Writing Sections

Give your essay to someone to read and evaluate for you. Refer that helpful person to Chapter 18 for scoring guidelines.

Chapter 22

How to Ruin a Perfectly Good Day, Part II: Practice Exam 2

• •

Are you bloody but unbowed and ready to have another go at it? The following exam consists of four sections — one 30-minute verbal section, one 45-minute quantitative section, one 30-minute essay, and one 45-minute essay. (You were kind enough to laugh at my jokes; I'm kind enough to leave out the experimental section.) You are familiar (practically *intimate*) with the question formats by now.

Please take this test under normal exam conditions and approach it as if it were the real test. This is serious stuff here!

1. **Work with your computer when you won't be interrupted (even though you'd probably welcome any distractions).**

2. **Use scratch paper that is free of any prepared notes. (On the actual GRE, you will get blank scratch paper before your test begins. You will have a little time before the clock starts to jot down a few notes and formulas and a series of columns of numbers or letters that you may want to use to help you eliminate answer choices, but you may not whip out a ready-made version of such test-taking aids.)**

3. **Turn off the clock at the beginning of each test section and be very careful on the first five questions. Remember that these earlier questions contribute more to your score than do the later questions.**

4. **If a question is truly impossible for you, guess and move on. You do not have the option of skipping the question and coming back to it. The computer will not let you move on until you mark and confirm an answer.**

5. **Make sure that you get to the end of the test section (30th question for verbal and 28th question for quantitative). If you have to, make wild guesses to reach the end before time expires. Unanswered questions will hurt your score more than incorrect ones will.**

6. **If you get to the last question before time expires, you have the option of answering it right away and finishing your test early (you can't use the time to go back and check your work) or relaxing for a while and marking your answer shortly before time expires. If you feel pumped up and you're on a roll, do the former. Give yourself the breather if you feel bombarded by the test.**

7. **Do not leave your computer while the clock is running on any one section.**

8. **You will get a one-minute break after the first section and the option to take a ten-minute break after the second section.**

After you finish, check your answers with the answer key. Take a few minutes to go over the answer explanations to all the questions, not just the ones you miss. This is your last chance to pick up one more nugget of knowledge — that final bit of information that could put you over the top.

Answer Sheet

Begin with Number 1 for each new section. If any sections have fewer than 50 questions, leave the extra spaces blank.

Verbal Section

1. Ⓐ Ⓑ Ⓒ Ⓓ Ⓔ	26. Ⓐ Ⓑ Ⓒ Ⓓ Ⓔ
2. Ⓐ Ⓑ Ⓒ Ⓓ Ⓔ	27. Ⓐ Ⓑ Ⓒ Ⓓ Ⓔ
3. Ⓐ Ⓑ Ⓒ Ⓓ Ⓔ	28. Ⓐ Ⓑ Ⓒ Ⓓ Ⓔ
4. Ⓐ Ⓑ Ⓒ Ⓓ Ⓔ	29. Ⓐ Ⓑ Ⓒ Ⓓ Ⓔ
5. Ⓐ Ⓑ Ⓒ Ⓓ Ⓔ	30. Ⓐ Ⓑ Ⓒ Ⓓ Ⓔ
6. Ⓐ Ⓑ Ⓒ Ⓓ Ⓔ	31. Ⓐ Ⓑ Ⓒ Ⓓ Ⓔ
7. Ⓐ Ⓑ Ⓒ Ⓓ Ⓔ	32. Ⓐ Ⓑ Ⓒ Ⓓ Ⓔ
8. Ⓐ Ⓑ Ⓒ Ⓓ Ⓔ	33. Ⓐ Ⓑ Ⓒ Ⓓ Ⓔ
9. Ⓐ Ⓑ Ⓒ Ⓓ Ⓔ	34. Ⓐ Ⓑ Ⓒ Ⓓ Ⓔ
10. Ⓐ Ⓑ Ⓒ Ⓓ Ⓔ	35. Ⓐ Ⓑ Ⓒ Ⓓ Ⓔ
11. Ⓐ Ⓑ Ⓒ Ⓓ Ⓔ	36. Ⓐ Ⓑ Ⓒ Ⓓ Ⓔ
12. Ⓐ Ⓑ Ⓒ Ⓓ Ⓔ	37. Ⓐ Ⓑ Ⓒ Ⓓ Ⓔ
13. Ⓐ Ⓑ Ⓒ Ⓓ Ⓔ	38. Ⓐ Ⓑ Ⓒ Ⓓ Ⓔ
14. Ⓐ Ⓑ Ⓒ Ⓓ Ⓔ	39. Ⓐ Ⓑ Ⓒ Ⓓ Ⓔ
15. Ⓐ Ⓑ Ⓒ Ⓓ Ⓔ	40. Ⓐ Ⓑ Ⓒ Ⓓ Ⓔ
16. Ⓐ Ⓑ Ⓒ Ⓓ Ⓔ	41. Ⓐ Ⓑ Ⓒ Ⓓ Ⓔ
17. Ⓐ Ⓑ Ⓒ Ⓓ Ⓔ	42. Ⓐ Ⓑ Ⓒ Ⓓ Ⓔ
18. Ⓐ Ⓑ Ⓒ Ⓓ Ⓔ	43. Ⓐ Ⓑ Ⓒ Ⓓ Ⓔ
19. Ⓐ Ⓑ Ⓒ Ⓓ Ⓔ	44. Ⓐ Ⓑ Ⓒ Ⓓ Ⓔ
20. Ⓐ Ⓑ Ⓒ Ⓓ Ⓔ	45. Ⓐ Ⓑ Ⓒ Ⓓ Ⓔ
21. Ⓐ Ⓑ Ⓒ Ⓓ Ⓔ	46. Ⓐ Ⓑ Ⓒ Ⓓ Ⓔ
22. Ⓐ Ⓑ Ⓒ Ⓓ Ⓔ	47. Ⓐ Ⓑ Ⓒ Ⓓ Ⓔ
23. Ⓐ Ⓑ Ⓒ Ⓓ Ⓔ	48. Ⓐ Ⓑ Ⓒ Ⓓ Ⓔ
24. Ⓐ Ⓑ Ⓒ Ⓓ Ⓔ	49. Ⓐ Ⓑ Ⓒ Ⓓ Ⓔ
25. Ⓐ Ⓑ Ⓒ Ⓓ Ⓔ	50. Ⓐ Ⓑ Ⓒ Ⓓ Ⓔ

Quantitative Section

1. Ⓐ Ⓑ Ⓒ Ⓓ Ⓔ　　26. Ⓐ Ⓑ Ⓒ Ⓓ Ⓔ
2. Ⓐ Ⓑ Ⓒ Ⓓ Ⓔ　　27. Ⓐ Ⓑ Ⓒ Ⓓ Ⓔ
3. Ⓐ Ⓑ Ⓒ Ⓓ Ⓔ　　28. Ⓐ Ⓑ Ⓒ Ⓓ Ⓔ
4. Ⓐ Ⓑ Ⓒ Ⓓ Ⓔ　　29. Ⓐ Ⓑ Ⓒ Ⓓ Ⓔ
5. Ⓐ Ⓑ Ⓒ Ⓓ Ⓔ　　30. Ⓐ Ⓑ Ⓒ Ⓓ Ⓔ
6. Ⓐ Ⓑ Ⓒ Ⓓ Ⓔ　　31. Ⓐ Ⓑ Ⓒ Ⓓ Ⓔ
7. Ⓐ Ⓑ Ⓒ Ⓓ Ⓔ　　32. Ⓐ Ⓑ Ⓒ Ⓓ Ⓔ
8. Ⓐ Ⓑ Ⓒ Ⓓ Ⓔ　　33. Ⓐ Ⓑ Ⓒ Ⓓ Ⓔ
9. Ⓐ Ⓑ Ⓒ Ⓓ Ⓔ　　34. Ⓐ Ⓑ Ⓒ Ⓓ Ⓔ
10. Ⓐ Ⓑ Ⓒ Ⓓ Ⓔ　　35. Ⓐ Ⓑ Ⓒ Ⓓ Ⓔ
11. Ⓐ Ⓑ Ⓒ Ⓓ Ⓔ　　36. Ⓐ Ⓑ Ⓒ Ⓓ Ⓔ
12. Ⓐ Ⓑ Ⓒ Ⓓ Ⓔ　　37. Ⓐ Ⓑ Ⓒ Ⓓ Ⓔ
13. Ⓐ Ⓑ Ⓒ Ⓓ Ⓔ　　38. Ⓐ Ⓑ Ⓒ Ⓓ Ⓔ
14. Ⓐ Ⓑ Ⓒ Ⓓ Ⓔ　　39. Ⓐ Ⓑ Ⓒ Ⓓ Ⓔ
15. Ⓐ Ⓑ Ⓒ Ⓓ Ⓔ　　40. Ⓐ Ⓑ Ⓒ Ⓓ Ⓔ
16. Ⓐ Ⓑ Ⓒ Ⓓ Ⓔ　　41. Ⓐ Ⓑ Ⓒ Ⓓ Ⓔ
17. Ⓐ Ⓑ Ⓒ Ⓓ Ⓔ　　42. Ⓐ Ⓑ Ⓒ Ⓓ Ⓔ
18. Ⓐ Ⓑ Ⓒ Ⓓ Ⓔ　　43. Ⓐ Ⓑ Ⓒ Ⓓ Ⓔ
19. Ⓐ Ⓑ Ⓒ Ⓓ Ⓔ　　44. Ⓐ Ⓑ Ⓒ Ⓓ Ⓔ
20. Ⓐ Ⓑ Ⓒ Ⓓ Ⓔ　　45. Ⓐ Ⓑ Ⓒ Ⓓ Ⓔ
21. Ⓐ Ⓑ Ⓒ Ⓓ Ⓔ　　46. Ⓐ Ⓑ Ⓒ Ⓓ Ⓔ
22. Ⓐ Ⓑ Ⓒ Ⓓ Ⓔ　　47. Ⓐ Ⓑ Ⓒ Ⓓ Ⓔ
23. Ⓐ Ⓑ Ⓒ Ⓓ Ⓔ　　48. Ⓐ Ⓑ Ⓒ Ⓓ Ⓔ
24. Ⓐ Ⓑ Ⓒ Ⓓ Ⓔ　　49. Ⓐ Ⓑ Ⓒ Ⓓ Ⓔ
25. Ⓐ Ⓑ Ⓒ Ⓓ Ⓔ　　50. Ⓐ Ⓑ Ⓒ Ⓓ Ⓔ

Verbal Section

Time: 30 minutes

30 questions

Choose the best answer to each question. Blacken the corresponding oval on the answer grid.

Directions: Choose the answer choice most nearly opposite in meaning to the question word.

1. LUCID

    (A) turbid

    (B) vivacious

    (C) minuscule

    (D) domineering

    (E) spicy

Directions: Each of the following questions features a pair of words or phrases in capital letters, followed by five pairs of words or phrases in lowercase letters. Choose the lowercase pair that most closely expresses the same relationship as that of the uppercase pair.

2. TONSORIAL : HAIR ::

    (A) professorial : job

    (B) medical : disease

    (C) stentorian : throat

    (D) sartorial : apparel

    (E) canine : teeth

3. CHATTER : MONKEYS ::

    (A) pride : lions

    (B) fawn : deer

    (C) snake : viper

    (D) low : cattle

    (E) pelt : fox

Directions: The following sentence has one blank indicating that a word is omitted. Choose the answer that best completes the sentence.

4. Although often - - - -, James Michael realized the importance of proceeding slowly with his task and deliberately forced himself to examine all the options available to him before making the decision on the best way to proceed.

    (A) impetuous

    (B) pensive

    (C) uncouth

    (D) dilatory

    (E) unenthusiastic

Directions: Choose the answer choice most nearly opposite in meaning to the question word.

5. INDIGENOUS

    (A) foreign

    (B) amiable

    (C) satisfactory

    (D) lustrous

    (E) pallid

6. HACKNEYED

    (A) belligerent

    (B) mercenary

    (C) flexible

    (D) fresh

    (E) passive

Go on to next page

Directions: Questions 7 and 8 pertain to the following passage. Read the passage and answer the questions based on information stated or implied in the passage.

Line   Community property is a legal concept that is growing in popularity in the United States. A few years ago, only the western states had com-munity property laws, and few people east of the
(05) Mississippi had ever heard the expression "com-munity property." Now several states have adopted or modified laws regarding community property.
    Both wife and husband jointly own commu-
(10) nity property. Generally, the property that a spouse owned before the marriage is known as separate or specific property. It remains the prop-erty of the original possessor in case of a separa-tion or divorce. Community property is anything
(15) gained by the joint effort of the spouses.
    Gifts specifically bestowed upon only one party, or legacies to only one spouse, are sepa-rate property. However, courts often determine that a donor had the intention to give the gift to
(20) both parties, even though his words or papers may have indicated otherwise. Community prop-erty goes to the surviving partner in case of the death of one spouse. Only that half of the prop-erty owned by the testator can be willed away.

7.   In which of the following instances would a gift to one party become community property?

  I. When the court determines the intent of the donor was to make a gift to the couple.

  II. When the property is real (land) rather than personal (possessions).

  III. When the court determines that the intent to give the gift was formed by the donor prior to the party's marriage.

    (A) I only

    (B) II only

    (C) I and III only

    (D) II and III only

    (E) I, II, and III

8.   You may infer that the author would most likely agree with which of the following?

    (A) Community property is the fairest set-tlement concept for marital property.

    (B) Community property laws currently discriminate against the working spouse in favor of the homemaker spouse.

    (C) Community property laws will probably continue to increase in number throughout the U.S.

    (D) Community property laws will be expanded to include all property acquired during the marriage, regard-less of its source.

    (E) All inheritances received by one party during the marriage are in theory, if not in fact, community property.

Directions: Choose the answer choice most nearly opposite in meaning to the question word.

9.   HAPLESS

    (A) saturnine

    (B) fortunate

    (C) cacophonous

    (D) mordant

    (E) ambiguous

10.   BURGEON

    (A) garble

    (B) purchase

    (C) aggravate

    (D) wither

    (E) dominate

Directions: Questions 11–14 pertain to the following passage. Read the passage and answer the questions based on information stated or implied in the passage.

Line A key study has shown that the organic matter content of a soil can be altered to a depth of 10 cm or more by intense campfire heat. As much as 90 percent of the original organic matter
(05) may be oxidized in the top 1.3 cm of soil. In the surface 10 cm, the loss of organic matter may reach 50 percent if the soil is dry and the temperature exceeds 250°C. The loss of organic matter reduces soil fertility and water-holding capacity
(10) and renders the soil more susceptible to compaction and erosion.

Sandy soils attain higher temperatures and retain heat longer than clay soils under similar fuel, moisture, and weather conditions. From this
(15) standpoint, it is desirable to locate campgrounds in an area with loam or clay-loam soil. Sandy soils are less susceptible to compaction damage, however, and are more desirable for campgrounds from this standpoint.

(20) A water-repellent layer can be created in a soil by the heat from the campfire. This condition was noted only in sandy soils where the temperature remained below 350°C during the campfire burn. Campfires often produce temperatures above this
(25) level. By comparison, forest fires are a shorter-duration event, and soil temperatures produced are more likely to create water repellency-inducing conditions. The greater extent of forest fires makes them a more serious threat than campfires in
(30) terms of causing soil water repellency.

If the soil remained moist for the duration of the campfire, the increased heat capacity of the soil and heat of water vaporization kept the soil temperature below 100°C. At this temperature,
(35) little loss of organic matter occurred, and no water repellency was created. For areas where the soil remains very moist, campfires probably have little effect on the soil properties.

Studies show that softwood fuels burn faster
(40) and produce less heat flow into the soil than do hardwood fuels under the same conditions. Elm and mesquite were the hottest burning and longest lasting fuels tested. In areas where some choice of fuels is available, the use of softwood
(45) fuels should be encouraged in an effort to minimize the effect of campfires on soil properties.

By restricting the fire site to the same area, the effects of campfires on the soil in a campground can be lessened, even if permanent con-
(50) crete fireplaces are not installed. In this manner, any harmful effects are restricted to a minimum area. If campfires are allowed to be located at random by the user, the harmful effects tend to be spread over a larger part of the campground.
(55) The placement of a stone fire ring in the chosen location is one way to accomplish the objective.

These data support the decision to install permanent fireplaces in many areas and to restrict the use of campfires elsewhere in the
(60) park. This eliminates the harmful effects of camp-

fires on the soil and allows the campground to be located on sandy soil with low compactibility and good drainage.

11. It can be inferred from the passage that campfire users generally

(A) evaluate the amount of soil damage that can result before they build a campfire.

(B) are concerned with the possibility that their campfire can cause a forest fire.

(C) have no regard for the biological consequences that result from their campfires.

(D) consider many areas of a campground to be suitable for a campfire.

(E) favor sandy soil over clay-loam soil as a campfire site.

12. The main idea of this passage is that

(A) excessive campfires will eventually make it impossible to grow crops.

(B) soil temperature affects soil fertility.

(C) only certain woods allow for high-quality campfires.

(D) soils must be able to absorb water to sustain organic matter.

(E) steps can be taken to minimize soil damage from campfires.

13. Long-lasting campfires are more likely than short-lived ones to

(A) create water repellency-inducing conditions.

(B) maintain soil fertility.

(C) occur with softwood fuels.

(D) restrict damage to the top 1.3 cm of soil.

(E) produce higher soil temperatures.

14. It can be inferred from the passage that the author would be most likely to agree with which of the following?

(A) Campfires should be banned as destructive to campfire soil.

(B) Organic matter decreases soil erosion.

(C) Clay-loam soil is preferable to sandy soil for campsites.

(D) The longer the duration of the fire, the higher the resistant soil temperatures.

(E) Campfires will not burn in areas with moist soil.

Go on to next page

Directions: Choose the answer choice most nearly opposite in meaning to the question word.

15. EQUIVOCAL

    (A) shy

    (B) direct

    (C) vapid

    (D) incongruous

    (E) obtuse

16. SANGUINE

    (A) supple

    (B) stygian

    (C) doting

    (D) morose

    (E) voracious

17. ABJURE

    (A) tamper

    (B) placate

    (C) exacerbate

    (D) advocate

    (E) extirpate

Directions: The following sentences have one or more blanks indicating that words are omitted. Choose the answer that best completes the sentence.

18. Although he lacked the ---- that he would like to have in the field, Dr. Dickstein felt confident enough of his premise to continue arguing ---- against the physician, whom he considered to be a dangerous quack and a charlatan.

    (A) fidelity ... exhaustively

    (B) grace ... indifferently

    (C) skill ... lackadaisically

    (D) expertise ... vehemently

    (E) ability ... tentatively

19. The feeling that one is being watched is not always mere paranoia; indeed, the ---- and random viewing of citizens by some governmental bureaus is quite probably more ---- than is commonly known.

    (A) intermittent ... widespread

    (B) haphazard ... ironhanded

    (C) arbitrary ... fly-by-night

    (D) flagrant ... surreptitious

    (E) unauthorized ... banal

Directions: Each of the following questions features a pair of words or phrases in capital letters, followed by five pairs of words or phrases in lowercase letters. Choose the lowercase pair that most closely expresses the same relationship as that of the uppercase pair.

20. ANTHEM : SONG ::

    (A) picture : portfolio

    (B) score : instrument

    (C) bellow : whisper

    (D) prologue : epilogue

    (E) panegyric : speech

21. HEIRLOOM : ANCESTOR ::

    (A) red herring : magician

    (B) bequest : testator

    (C) instrument : musician

    (D) rules : renegade

    (E) throne : usurper

22. INCITE : STIFLE ::

    (A) exorcise : remove

    (B) stymie : confuse

    (C) begrudge : deny

    (D) abscond : return

    (E) verify : prove

Go on to next page

Directions: The following sentences have one or more blanks indicating that words are omitted. Choose the answer that best completes the sentence.

23. At the - - - - of his career, Ken basks in the kudos and - - - - of judges and audiences alike.

    (A) apogee ... plaudits

    (B) lapse ... reproofs

    (C) apex ... fecklessness

    (D) genesis ... effrontery

    (E) nascency ... perjury

24. Purchasing lengthy, often incomprehensible - - - - for the sole purpose of displaying them in one's bookcase has been labeled by some - - - - "intellectual vanity."

    (A) collages ... pundits

    (B) maxims ... writers

    (C) brochures ... sages

    (D) scores ... teachers

    (E) tomes ... wags

Directions: Each of the following questions features a pair of words or phrases in capital letters, followed by five pairs of words or phrases in lowercase letters. Choose the lowercase pair that most closely expresses the same relationship as that of the uppercase pair.

25. THIN : EMACIATED ::

    (A) happy : ecstatic

    (B) reclusive : solitary

    (C) sentimental : apathetic

    (D) relevant : immaterial

    (E) fickle : constant

26. ANGRY : INCENSED ::

    (A) noticeable : flamboyant

    (B) obdurate : stubborn

    (C) ancient : outmoded

    (D) melodious : euphonious

    (E) calm : pacific

Directions: Questions 27– 29 pertain to the following passage. Read the passage and answer the questions based on information stated or implied in the passage.

In many ways, a Cherokee woman in the time of the "Wild West" had more power within her social group than did a European woman. It was through the mother of the family that membership in clans and general kinship were (05) determined. A Cherokee (the name comes from a Creek Indian word "Chelokee" meaning "people of a different speech"; however, today many Cherokee prefer to be called Tsalagi from their own name for the Cherokee Nation, Tsalagihi (10) Ayili) woman was not forced to marry someone whom her family had chosen in advance for her, as was the practice in European families. Instead, the Cherokee woman had the right to choose her own mate. That mate then had the job to build a (15) house for the woman, which was considered the woman's property. If the woman already had a house of her own, the man would go live there. Should the man be unable or unwilling to build a house, the couple would live with the woman's (20) parents.

A Cherokee house was wattle and daub. Often described as looking like an upside-down basket, it was a simple circular frame with interwoven branches. The house was plastered with (25) mud and sunken into the ground. Although many people do not associate log cabins with Native Americans, these dwellings became common among the Cherokee later in their history. They also built large council houses to keep the sacred (30) fire, which was never allowed to go out.

Divorce was very simple. The woman would place her husband's possessions outside of the house, which was considered sufficient notice to free both the woman and the man to remarry. (35) The woman kept the house her husband built for her. It was accepted for a woman to have one husband after another. Adultery in the marriage, therefore, was relatively uncommon.

Any children born to the couple were considered the woman's as well. The father had very few (40) child-rearing responsibilities; instead, the mother and her brothers took charge of the children, showing them the tribal ways. The woman also controlled how many children would survive. She (45) had the legal right to destroy any children who were not born healthy or give away any children she felt were beyond the number she was capable of feeding and caring for. The father had no such right. (50)

Go on to next page

Rights for women were just one aspect of the Cherokee civilization. During the early 1800s, the Cherokee developed a formal written constitution. Cherokees had their own courts and (55) schools, considered by some to be of a higher standard than those of their White counterparts. Even today, the Cherokee level of education and living standard ranks among the highest of all Native American tribes.

27. The passage serves primarily to

    (A) ridicule the idea that Cherokee women were less advanced than White women.

    (B) compare and contrast the educational systems of Cherokees and Whites.

    (C) praise the advances that Cherokees made in the face of White resistance.

    (D) inform the reader of the rights of Cherokee women.

    (E) refute the theory that Cherokee women were less capable of fighting than were Cherokee men.

28. Which of the following questions is NOT answered in the passage?

    (A) When did the Cherokee nation begin following a written constitution?

    (B) What do the Cherokee people call themselves?

    (C) How is a Cherokee house constructed?

    (D) Who educated Cherokee children?

    (E) How did a Cherokee woman choose a mate?

29. The author's strategy in this passage is best described as

    (A) presenting a chronological history of events.

    (B) presenting and then refuting a theory.

    (C) proposing a theory and then anticipating a countertheory.

    (D) stating an idea and then giving supporting examples.

    (E) refuting a controversial idea.

Directions: The following sentence has one or more blanks indicating that words are omitted. Choose the answer that best completes the sentence.

30. Experts - - - - that dog carvings and statues found in such - - - - places as Egypt, Mexico, and China were of the dachshund, whose German name means badger hound.

    (A) conjecture ... ancient

    (B) hypothesize ... disparate

    (C) refute ... similar

    (D) insist ... geographic

    (E) deny ... inauspicious

Go on to next page

Quantitative Section

Time: 30 Minutes

28 questions

Notes: All numbers used in this exam are real numbers.

All figures lie in a plane.

Angle measures are positive; points and angles are in the position shown.

The answer choices are

A if the quantity in Column A is greater.

B if the quantity in Column B is greater.

C if the two quantities are equal.

D if the relationship cannot be determined from the information given.

Column A	Column B

1. In Debittown, the roller rink is 10 kilometers from the school, which is 3 kilometers from the coffee shop.

Distance from the roller rink to the coffee shop	13 kilometers

2. $a = \frac{2}{3}b; \; b = \frac{3}{4}c$

Fraction that a is of c	$\frac{1}{3}$

3.

$x^{-y} \, y^{-x}$	1

4.

$a^{10} \times a^{5} \times \frac{1}{a^{3}}$	a^{12}

N   P

45°

O

Area of circle O=36π

5.

Length of arc *NP*	36π

Column A	Column B

6. $-2 \le x < 0$

Greatest possible value of x^{3}	0

7. $a * b * c = 3a + 4b - \frac{1}{2}c$

$3 * 6 * 12$	27

8. The test scores of a group of five students are 72, 70, 68, 75, and 80.

The median test score	73

20°

$x°$ $y°$

9.

y	110

Go on to next page

Column A	Column B
10. 300% of 30	60% of 15

11. $a \times b = c$

c	b

12. 20 percent of 120	120 percent of 20

13. The number of days in four years	The number of years in forty decades

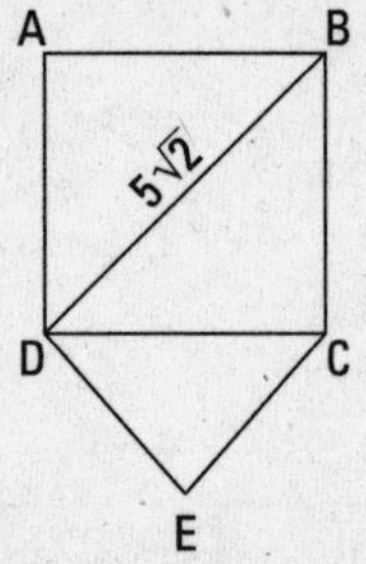

Square ABCD and
Equilateral triangle CED
are as shown.

14. Perimeter of the figure above	25

15. The average scores of students on a final exam are as shown on the chart below.

Student	Average score
Dustin	75
Kristiana	82
Leoni	79
Tim	91
Deidre	93

What is the positive difference between the mean and the median of their scores?

(A) 84

(B) 82

(C) 12

(D) 5

(E) 2

16. An equilateral polygon (not shown) has a total interior angle measure of 1260. If one side of the figure is 6, what is the perimeter of the figure?

(A) 60

(B) 54

(C) 42

(D) 9

(E) 7

Questions 17–18 are based on the following graph.

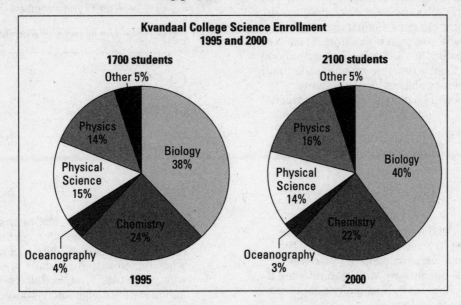

Kvandaal College Science Enrollment
1995 and 2000

17. To the nearest whole percent, the 2000 biology enrollment was what percent greater than the 1995 biology enrollment?

(A) 2

(B) 5

(C) 8

(D) 24

(E) 30

18. A switch from physics to chemistry of how many students in 2000 would have produced a physics to chemistry ratio equal to that of 1995?

(A) 22

(B) 42

(C) 44

(D) 84

(E) 114

19. A number of friends are at a party. At 11:00 p.m., ¼ of the friends leave. At midnight, ⅓ of the remaining friends leave. At 1:00 a.m., as many people leave as left at 11:00 p.m. Exactly 30 people remain. How many people were at the party to begin with?

(A) 60

(B) 90

(C) 120

(D) 160

(E) 180

20. $\dfrac{6a^{10}b^5c^7}{3a^5b^9c^7}$

(A) $2a^2b^4c$

(B) $\dfrac{2a^2b^4}{c}$

(C) $\dfrac{2a^5b^4}{c}$

(D) $2a^5b^4$

(E) $\dfrac{2a^5}{b^4}$

21. A box of candy contains three types of candy: 20 creams, 15 chews, and 12 nuts. Each time LaVonne reaches into the box, she pulls out a piece of candy, takes a bite out of it, and throws it away. She pulls out a cream, a nut, a chew, a nut, a cream, and a chew. What is the probability that on the next reach, she will pull out a nut?

(A) ¹⁵⁄₄₇

(B) ¹³⁄₄₁

(C) ¹⁰⁄₄₁

(D) ¹³⁄₁₅

(E) ¹¹⁄₁₅

Go on to next page

22. Barb, Jim, Angie, Mike, Laura, Carissa, and Sara enter a tournament. Each contestant must compete once against every other contestant, one match at a time, in each of the following five activities: hot air balloon race, golf, mile run, one-on-one basketball, and a talent competition. How many matches will be played in the tournament?

    (A) 125

    (B) 105

    (C) 50

    (D) 42

    (E) 21

23. One hundred job applicants show up in response to a classified ad. If 60% of the applicants are female and if 75% of the female applicants are willing to relocate if the job demands it, how many people are not willing to relocate?

    (A) 60

    (B) 55

    (C) 45

    (D) 15

    (E) It cannot be determined from the information given.

24. If line segment XY (not shown) goes from (–2, 6) to (4, 6), what are the coordinates of the midpoint of XY?

    (A) (–1,6)

    (B) (0,0)

    (C) (1,6)

    (D) (3,0)

    (E) (3,6)

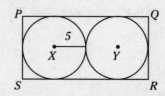

25. Area of circle X = area of circle Y

    What is the area of rectangle *PQRS* above?

    (A) 200

    (B) 180

    (C) 150

    (D) 100

    (E) 25

26.

    > $\boxed{x} = x + x^2$ for all prime numbers.
    >
    > $\boxed{x} = x^2 - x$ for all composite numbers.

    $\boxed{4} + \boxed{5} =$

    (A) 50

    (B) 42

    (C) 40

    (D) 20

    (E) 19

27. At a warehouse store, eight cans of frozen concentrated orange juice cost d dollars. If each can makes m milliliters of orange juice when mixed with three cans of water, what will be the total cost, in dollars, to make 400 milliliters of orange juice if one can of water costs c cents?

    (A) $3200md + 96c$

    (B) $\dfrac{(md + 3c)}{400}$

    (C) $\dfrac{(d + 3c)}{50m}$

    (D) $\dfrac{(8d + 96c)}{m}$

    (E) $\dfrac{(50d + 12c)}{m}$

28. Circle B is perfectly inscribed in the semi-circle A (not shown). If the area of circle A is 16π, what is the circumference of circle B?

    (A) 16π

    (B) 12π

    (C) 8π

    (D) 4π

    (E) 2π

Go on to next page

Analytical Writing: Present Your Perspective on an Issue

Time: 45 minutes

One essay

Directions: Present and explain your view on the following issue. Although there is no one right or wrong response to the issue, be sure to consider various points of view as you explain the reasons behind your own perspective.

"Television and videos are going to leave a more lasting and valid perception of our society to future generations than is literature."

Which point of view do you agree with — that television and videos will leave a more lasting and valid perception of our society to future generations or that literature will? Justify your position using examples from your personal or professional experience, reading, or general observation.

Analytical Writing: Analyze and Argument

Time: 30 minutes

One essay

Directions: Critique the following argument. Identify evidence that will strengthen or weaken the argument, point out assumptions underlying the argument, and offer counterexamples to the argument.

The following appeared in a letter to the editor of the Flint Herald newspaper.

"School board elections are coming up in a few months. Voters should vote for Martinez Westwood for school board member, rather than for the incumbent Harris Black because the current school board is doing a poor job. In the past two years since the current board was elected, the dropout rate has increased by 30 percent, voters did not approve the necessary tax increase to raise teacher salaries, and the morale of both educators and students is down. By electing Martinez Westwood, these problems will be resolved quickly and correctly."

Discuss the merits of the previous argument. Analyze the evidence used as well as the general reasoning. Present points that would strengthen the argument or make it more compelling.

Answer Key for Practice Exam 2

Verbal section

1. A
2. D
3. D
4. A
5. A
6. D
7. A
8. C
9. B
10. D
11. D
12. E
13. E
14. B
15. B
16. D
17. D
18. D
19. A
20. E
21. B
22. D
23. A
24. E
25. A
26. A
27. D
28. E
29. D
30. B

Quantitative section

1. D
2. A
3. D
4. C
5. B
6. B
7. C
8. B
9. C
10. A
11. D
12. C
13. A
14. C
15. E
16. B
17. E
18. B
19. C
20. E
21. C
22. B
23. E
24. C
25. A
26. B
27. E
28. D

Chapter 23

Practice Exam 2: Answers and Explanations

● ●

Verbal Section

1. **A.** You probably got this question right by the process of elimination. *Lucid* means clear (*luc* means light or clear). A lucid explanation **elucidates,** or makes clear, the material. *Turbid* means thick, cloudy, dense. When you stir up waters that are muddy, they become turbid. If you put ice cubes into a glass of ouzo (Greek liqueur), the liquid becomes turbid. *Vivacious* means lively, full of life (*vi* means life; *-ous* means full of). *Minuscule* means very small.

   Do not confuse *turbid* with *turgid. Turgid* means swollen or distended. A corpse floating in turbid waters after a few days would become turgid. (Where else but in *The GRE® Test For Dummies,* 5th Edition can you read answer explanations that manage to work in both Greek liqueurs and floating corpses?)

2. **D.** *Tonsorial* means pertaining to hair. No one really expects you to know this word. Instead, assume that unknown words are synonyms and make your sentence, "Tonsorial is hair." Then you can probably narrow the answers down to the two words you don't know (stentorian and sartorial) and make a quick guess. (If I'm underestimating your genius and your vocabulary, I abjectly apologize.) *Sartorial* means pertaining to clothing or apparel. If you want to get your money's worth out of this book, tell your mother that she is looking sartorially resplendent when she asks how her new outfit looks on her. And to be sure that she gets the message, bellow your praise in a *stentorian* (loud) voice. In Homer's poetry, Stentor was a character who "has the voice of 50 men." In other words, he was a loudmouth. (I once had a less-than-erudite boyfriend who pouted when I talked about Homer's poetry, telling me that it wasn't polite to discuss former sweethearts and their love poems in front of him!)

   Professorial does not mean pertaining to a job. That word would be *professional,* pertaining to a profession or job. *Professorial* means like a professor. In B, *medical* means pertaining to medicine, not pertaining to a disease. Choice E may have made you pause for a moment. Yes, we have canine teeth, but *canine* actually means pertaining to a dog, not pertaining to teeth. Our canine teeth are called that because they are pointed like dogs' teeth.

3. **D.** Unless you're a cowboy or cowgirl, you probably answered this question by the process of elimination. *Chatter* is the sound that monkeys make. *Low* is the sound that cattle make. A *pride* is a group of lions. A *fawn* is a baby deer. A *viper* is a type of snake. A *pelt* is the skin of a fox.

 If you think the GRE is a beastly exam, you're right. There are often questions in the analogies requiring you to know the terms for the young of animals, groups of animals, or where animals live; therefore, I'd advise you to learn the terms. Use flash cards. Label one *young animals,* and write on it such terms as kit, joey, and cygnet. Label a second card *habitats* and write things such as den, corral, and sty. Label a third card *groups of animals* and write down pride, pod, and flock. A few minutes of memorization can pay off here because there are no roots, prefixes, or suffixes to help you define these types of words.

4. **A.** The "although" alerts you to the fact that you want a word meaning the opposite of "proceeding slowly." Because someone *unenthusiastic* probably *would* proceed slowly (how fast do *you* go when you approach a task unenthusiastically?), eliminate it. Scratch off *pensive*, meaning thoughtful or meditative. A pensive person would naturally slow down and examine all aspects of a situation. Eliminate *dilatory*, or slow. A slow person would not have to *force* himself to slow down. You have the answers narrowed down to two. *Uncouth* means unsophisticated or ill mannered and has no connection to the sentence. *Impetuous* means hasty, rash, precipitate. An impetuous person would usually rush into things and would have to force himself to slow down and examine the situation more carefully.

5. **A.** *Indigenous* means native to. Monsters are indigenous to the spaces under children's beds. Something not native to an area is *foreign* to it.

    Amiable means friendly (*Hint:* think of *ami*, which is *friend* in French, or *amigo*, which is *friend* in Spanish). *Lustrous* means shiny (*lus* means light or clear). *Pallid* means pale.

6. **D.** *Hackneyed* means made trite by overuse. A phrase like, "Have a happy day!" is hackneyed. Most slang becomes hackneyed after a few months. Choice A, *belligerent*, means warlike, ready to fight (*belli* means war or fight). *Mercenary* means greedy, done for money.

7. **A.** The passage states in lines 18–21 that a court may deem a gift community property if the donor's intent was to give it to both parties, even if the donor did not state so specifically. Because statement I is correct, eliminate answers B and D. Statement II is wrong; it brings in the distinction between real and personal property, which was not covered in the passage. (For those of you who have gone through *acrimonious* — bitter — divorces and are all too familiar with the concept of community property, shelve your knowledge while answering these questions. Answer them based only on information stated or implied by the passage.) Statement III is also wrong but very tricky. Nothing in the passage stated that the time of the intent to make the gift was important, only the intent of the donor. If you chose C, you read too much into the question.

8. **C.** The author mentions early in the passage that there used to be just a few community property states, but that the number has been steadily increasing. From this, you may infer that this increase will continue.

    Choice A is definitely a judgment call. Who is to say whether the community property concept is fair, not fair, the fairest, or the least fair? Passages (unless they are editorial or opinion types, which are infrequently included on the GRE) rarely give personal opinions or push one person's theories or philosophies.

    Choice B is well outside the scope of this passage; nothing was mentioned about homemakers. Choice D goes overboard. Just because the author believes there will be more community property states does not mean states will turn *all* possessions to community property.

    You learned in the reading lecture in Chapter 8 to be wishy-washy, not dramatic. Eliminate answers with "strong" words, such as *all, every, never,* and *none*. Choice E has the same problem: It features the excessive word *all*.

9. **B.** *Hapless* means unlucky. (*hap* means luck; a mishap is bad luck; *haphazard* means depending on luck or chance; hapless is without luck, unlucky.) Choice A, *saturnine*, means gloomy or morose. Choice C, *cacophonous*, means bad sounding or raucous. (*caco* means bad; *phon* means sound; *-ous* means full of.) My friends who have to listen to my cacophonous singing voice are saturnine (actually, they become *sanguinary*, which means bloodthirsty, but that's another story). Choice D, *mordant*, means sarcastic or caustic. Choice E, *ambiguous*, means uncertain, able to be interpreted in two or more ways. (*ambi* means both; *-ous* means full of. Ambiguous is "full of both," unclear.)

10. **D.** To *burgeon* is to blossom and grow. The opposite is to *wither*. To *garble* is to distort or jumble. A student may garble her words and mispronounce this question as "surgeon" or even (my favorite) "sturgeon." Pretty hard to find the opposite of sturgeon, wouldn't you say? (To whom do you complain when you get a bad batch of caviar? The sturgeon general!)

11. **D.** The last two paragraphs of the passage urge measures to restrict campfire location. Without such measures, the author claims that campfires will be built just about everywhere and that soil damage will be widespread. It can be inferred from this that campfire users, when left to their own devices, will build a campfire just about anywhere. This leads to choice D as the answer. Because the opposite of choice A appears to be true, eliminate this choice. Choice B is plausible, but the author does not mention a connection between campfire users and forest fires. Forest fires were discussed briefly in paragraph three in relation to water repellency. Choice C goes overboard. There is no information to indicate whether campfire users favor a certain type of soil, eliminating choice E. The scientific findings discussed in paragraph two point to an advantage of one type or the other, but you can't tell whether the campfire users actually consider this evidence.

12. **E.** This passage contains a lot of dry detail about how certain campfire factors damage soil and its ability to support life. Throughout the passage, the author uses these details to recommend a certain action. The author is concerned that campfires damage soil and wants to minimize this damage. Choice E fits this perfectly. Choice A is too extreme. Choices B and D are true statements, but these are just two of several factors mentioned by the author.

    Just because a statement is true does not mean it is the correct answer; in a main idea question, all five choices may in fact be true. Choice C is also a detail but is wrong primarily because the author is concerned that certain woods will lead to soil damage, not with how well the woods will work with the campfire per se.

13. **E.** Common sense suggests that E is the right answer. Paragraph three helps to confirm this. This paragraph mentions that short-lived forest fires are more likely than campfires to create water-repellency-inducing conditions (knocking out choice A). This information implies that campfires last longer. Combine this reasoning with the explicit mention that campfires typically exceed 350 degrees and you've got your answer. Choice C is directly contradicted by paragraph five. Choices B and D don't make sense. The passage often mentions that heat flow into the soil damages it. A long-lasting campfire will produce more heat flow than a short-lived one.

    Although you certainly do not need to have any background knowledge to answer Reading Comprehension questions (all information necessary is given or implied in the passage), don't hesitate to use your common sense, especially with science passages. Common sense is a good place to start, but do be sure to check your "logical" answer with the facts given in the passage.

14. **B.** The last sentence of the first paragraph states that the loss of organic matter reduces water-holding capacity and renders the soil more susceptible to erosion.

    Note that this question basically required you to truly understand the whole passage. If you didn't read this passage carefully but just skimmed for specific answers to specific questions, this question would have been a good question just to guess at.

15. **B.** *Equivocal* means misleading, ambiguous, uncertain. When you ask your parents whether they'll buy you a fire engine red Ferrari should you finish your Ph.D., their "We'll see" is an equivocal response.

    You may be more familiar with this word in its negative sense, *unequivocal,* which means absolutely direct, certain, no doubt about it. When you ask your parents to let you use your college fund to backpack around the world, their response will be an unequivocal "NO!"

Vapid means lifeless, dull, boring. It can also mean literally tasteless as in vapid soda that has gone flat. (Vapid is akin to the word *vappa,* which means stale wine.) *Incongruous* means inconsistent or not in agreement. You know that congruent angles in geometry are equal; incongruent angles are not equal. *Obtuse* can mean blunt, or it can mean dull metaphorically as in slow to understand. An obtuse boyfriend buys his girlfriend a new car battery for her birthday, even though she has been leaving jewelry store ads in his room, backpack, and car.

16. **D.** *Sanguine* means cheerful, optimistic, and confident. Do not confuse sanguine with *sanguinary,* meaning bloodthirsty. The opposite is *morose,* which means gloomy, or sullen. Choice A, *supple,* means flexible, lithe. Choice E, *voracious,* means greedy, ravenous. Are you voracious for yet more vocabulary, or has this section sated you?

17. **D.** To *abjure* is to give up (*ab* means away from; when you abjure your rights, you go away from them, you give them up). To *advocate* (*ad* means toward) is to support, be in favor of. After you've aced the GRE, you'll abjure studying this material and advocate making it into confetti to celebrate your excellent score. To *tamper* is to interfere or meddle with. As an April Fool's joke, you may tamper with the bathroom scale so that your sorority sister thinks that she's ten pounds heavier than she is. To *placate* (*plac* means peace or calm) is to mollify, appease, pacify, or stop from being angry. To placate your friend who is furious about your April Fool's joke, you turn the scale back ten pounds, to make her think that she's thinner than she is. To *exacerbate* is to aggravate, to make more intense, to irritate. Your second prank just exacerbated the situation, making it worse. To *extirpate* is to destroy or remove (*ex* means out of or away from), to abolish. Your more mature friends extirpate the bathroom scale, tossing it in the trash to avoid any more crises.

18. **D.** Focus on the second blank. If Dr. Dickstein felt that the man against whom he was arguing was dangerous, he would argue pretty strongly against him. Eliminate choice B (*indifferently* means not caring one way or the other), choice C (*lackadaisically* means in a mellow, laid-back, nonenergetic way), and choice E (*tentatively* means hesitantly or uncertainly). The second word in choice A is possible; *exhaustively* means thoroughly. (It does not mean the same thing as exhausted, although an exhaustive search of the house for your missing car keys may leave you exhausted.) The first word, however, doesn't fit. *Fidelity* means faithfulness as in fidelity among a loving couple (or the fidelity exhibited by Fido the faithful companion). That leaves choice D. *Vehemently* means strongly-felt and powerfully.

Do you know the words *charlatan* and *quack* in the question? A *charlatan* or a *quack* is a fraud or nonexpert. A GRE tutor who tells you that you'll get a 1600 if you stand naked in the light of the full moon and bury a toad in your backyard is a charlatan.

19. **A.** Vocabulary is the key to this sentence. You probably could predict relatively easily what types of words go in the blanks; the trouble is finding the words with those definitions. Start with the second blank. Say: The practice is probably more *common* than realized. *Widespread* means common, spread about everywhere.

Ironhanded means severe, strong. Have you heard the expression "rules with an iron fist"? That type of ruler is ironhanded.

Throughout this book, I use clichés and expressions common to English, like "rules with an iron fist." If you don't understand those expressions or aren't comfortable with them, get someone to explain them to you. Many vocabulary words on this exam are parts of sayings or proverbs, *aphorisms* (sayings), or *adages* (sayings). I suggest that you pull out an index card and write the cliché or saying on the card along with an explanation of how it is used and what words are related to it (such as ironhanded). *Fly-by-night* is another cliché. It means temporary, not permanent. This came from the idea that a less-than-honest company would pack up in the middle of the night and leave town, taking its customers' money with it. It would, in effect, fly away in the middle of the night: fly-by-night.

Surreptitious means secretive, concealed. *Banal* means dull or stale from overuse. A cliché is banal.

Here's the vocabulary for the first blanks. *Intermittent* means off and on, not constant. Don't confuse this word with *interminable,* which means endless, or seemingly endless. A lecture can be interminable; a good lecturer will use jokes intermittently to try to keep the listeners' attention. *Haphazard* means nonsystematic, unplanned. *Arbitrary* means dependent on individual discretion and not fixed by law. You make an arbitrary choice when you buy a grab bag.

20. **E.** An *anthem* is a song, usually one of praise. A *panegyric* is a speech (or a piece of writing), usually one of praise. *Bonus trivia:* Did you know that Sir Walter Scott wrote the words to the American presidential anthem, "Hail to the Chief"?

Choice B is a trap. A trap answer often has the same general meaning (music, score, anthem, song) as the question. Remember to create and use a sentence that expresses the relationship between the words. An anthem is a type of song; a *score* is not a type of instrument. A *bellow* is the opposite of a whisper. A *prologue* (*pro* meaning before, *log* meaning speech) comes before the main speech and is the opposite of the *epilogue,* which comes at the end.

21. **B.** Now this is a hard question because so many of the answer choices are similar. The best sentence is that an *heirloom* is something left to you by an ancestor. A *bequest* (a gift to an heir) is left to you by a *testator* (one who makes the last will and testament). Although a magician may incorporate a *red herring* (something that tries to mislead or trick) into his act, he doesn't leave you one. While a musician uses an instrument, he doesn't leave you one. A *renegade* is a person who breaks the rules, a rebel. He leaves you with nothing. A *usurper* is one who takes without authority or right. He takes the throne; he doesn't leave it to you.

22. **D.** To *incite* is to stir up or rouse something, as in inciting a riot. To *stifle* is to hold back, suppress, or inhibit. With the help of this book, you will be unable to stifle your cheers when you see your excellent GRE scores. The relationship is opposites. To *abscond* is to run away quickly, the opposite of to return.

Knowing your roots can help you here: *ab* means away from. Choice A, to *exorcise* is to take away (*ex* means out of, away from). To *stymie* is to confuse or bewilder. To *begrudge* is to give with reluctance as in begrudging a friend a bite of your favorite dessert. To *verify* (*ver* means truth) is to prove true.

23. **A.** Start with the second blank. If Ken is *basking* in something, he is enjoying it immensely; it must be good. You could deduce the same thing by knowing that *kudos* means praise, glory, fame. The second word that goes with *kudos and* . . . must be positive as well. *Plaudits* are praises. An *apogee* is the zenith, the highest point. Winning one night on *Jeopardy!* was the apogee of my television career (don't ask what happened the next night; it was my career *nadir,* or low point).

Choice B, a *lapse,* is a pause or break. I had a brain cell lapse the second night on *Jeopardy!* and was full of self-reproof. *Reproofs* are criticisms or condemnations. (To reprove does not mean to prove again; it means to criticize or condemn. People often misdefine this word.) In choice C, an *apex* is the top point, the zenith, the apogee — it would work for the first blank. But the second blank lets you down. *Fecklessness* is feebleness, irresponsibility. In choice D, the *genesis* of something is the beginning. *Effrontery* is audacity, shameless boldness. And finally, choice E, *nascency,* is birth, the process of being brought into existence. *Perjury* is false testimony, lying under oath.

24. **E.** A *tome* is a lengthy, ponderous, scholarly book. The word usually refers to the type of heavy book that could serve as a foundation stone in a skyscraper. A *wag* is a wit, a clever person. A *collage* is a collection of images, like a photo collage. You don't think of a collage as lengthy or incomprehensible. A *pundit* is a learned person; a *sage* is an intelligent person.

25. **A.** Someone very, very thin is *emaciated.* Someone very, very happy is *ecstatic.* Choice B is backwards. *Solitary* does mean reclusive, but *reclusive* (a recluse is a hermit) has the connotation of being very, very solitary, of not wanting anything to do with the world. Choice C is antonyms; someone *sentimental* is full of feeling (*senti* means feeling); someone *apathetic* has no feeling (*a* means not or without; *path* means feeling). Choice D is antonyms. *Immaterial* (*im* means not) means not relevant — learning most languages (especially Spanish and French) can help you with the GRE, but learning sign language is immaterial. Choice E is also antonyms. Someone *fickle* is not constant.

When three answers all have the same relationship, all three must be wrong. Therefore, even if you didn't know what emaciated meant, you could eliminate choices C, D, and E and assume that emaciated was a synonym, not an antonym, of thin.

26. **A.** The relationship is from lesser degree to greater degree. First, you're angry, and then you become *incensed,* which means furious, or burning mad (think of burning incense). Choice A also moves from a lesser to a greater degree. Something may be *noticeable,* like a new haircut; however, when you dye your hair neon green, the hairdo turns from noticeable to *flamboyant,* very noticeable or showy.

The pair of words in choice B are synonyms: *obdurate* means stubborn. You can remember this by pairing obdurate with a more familiar *ob* word, *obstinate* (also meaning stubborn). *Outmoded* means out of fashion. Something ancient may or may not be out of fashion; as the song says, "Everything old is new again." In choice D, *melodious* and *euphonious* are synonyms. You can figure out *euphonious* with roots: *eu* means good; *phon* means sound; *-ous* means full of. Something *euphonious* is full of good sound, or melodious. Choice E also lets you use your roots: *pac* means calm.

27. **D.** Because the "primary purpose" or "main idea" question is so common in Reading Comprehension passages, you should read the passage with an eye toward identifying those points. Although the passage gets more general at the end, it is primarily about the rights of the Cherokee women.

28. **E.** A negatively-phrased question, such as "Which is NOT true" or "All of the following are true EXCEPT" is often very difficult or tricky or just plain time-consuming. Good test-takers often just "guess and go," guessing quickly on this type of question and going on to the next question. Here, although the passage said the Cherokee woman has the right to choose her own mate, the procedure for this decision was not discussed anywhere in the passage.

29. **D.** The best way to answer this question is through the process of elimination. There is no *chronology* (time line) of events (choice A). There is no *refutation* (disproving) of a theory (choice B) or counterexample to a theory (choice C). There is no proof or disproof of a controversial theory (choice E). All the author does is state his idea and then give examples to support what he's said.

30. **B.** The key to this question is the second blank. The countries of Egypt, Mexico, and China are neither similar nor *inauspicious* (unfavorable). They are geographic, but that word makes no sense in the context of the sentence. The countries are ancient, but they still exist, making choice A illogical. *Disparate,* meaning distinct or different, makes sense. Choice A, *conjecture,* means to hypothesize.

Quantitative Section

1. **D.** Please tell me you didn't fall for this trap. Did you pick up your pencil and start to draw a picture of the roller rink, the school, and the coffee shop? As soon as you have to draw a picture, you should be thinking choice D. The answer *de*pends on how you draw the picture. If you put the roller rink, the school, and the coffee shop all in a straight line in that order, then the coffee shop and the rink are in fact 13 kilometers apart. But (and this is a big but, because whenever you see a C answer, you should be paranoid and double-check it) what if you put the coffee shop three kilometers to the other side of the school, between the rink and the school? Then the distance from the rink to the coffee shop is only 7 kilometers, and now the answer is B. If the answer changes *de*pending on how you draw the figure, choose D.

   TIP

   Problems that require you to find a distance between places or people are often D because the distance depends on the sequence those places or people are in. When you see a "line 'em up" problem, think D.

2. **A.** Are you a fraction-phobe like most people? Then avoid fractions altogether and simply plug in numbers. Work backwards and plug in a number for c that will be divisible by both 4 and 3. Try 12. If $c = 12$, then $b = \frac{3}{4} \times 12 = 9$. If $b = 9$, then $a = \frac{2}{3} \times 9$, or 6. Now $\frac{a}{c} = \frac{6}{12}$, or $\frac{1}{2}$. Because $\frac{1}{2}$ is greater than $\frac{1}{3}$, A is the answer. Although this will work no matter what number you plug in for c, why not make life easy and plug in a nice round number? If you plug in something like 10, then $b = \frac{3}{4} \times 10$ or $\frac{30}{4}$ and that's a pain in the fundament (that portion of your body upon which you are sitting even as we speak).

   If you want to do the problem "the real way," it's not hard. You just have to know that *of* means *times* and multiply the whole shebang. $\frac{2}{3}$ of $\frac{3}{4}$ of $c = \frac{2}{3} \times \frac{3}{4} \times c = \frac{6}{12} \times c = \frac{1}{2} \times c$. It comes out the same.

3. **D.** If you chose C, you fell for the trap. You cannot simply multiply the exponents of two unlike bases. For example, if you were to multiply 5^{-2} (which is $\frac{1}{5^2}$ or $\frac{1}{25}$) $\times\ 2^{-5}$ (which is $\frac{1}{25}$ or $\frac{1}{32}$), the answer would not be 1. The answer depends on the values of x and y: are they positive? Negative? Fractions? With this many possibilities, the answer is D.

   TIP

   The more variables you have, the better your chances of getting a D answer. Don't immediately choose D when you see a lot of x and y variables, but you should entertain the possibility that the answer will depend on the numbers you plug in.

   Will the end of the QC's have a lot of D answers like this? Not necessarily. However, because questions go from easier to harder and because the hard or tricky questions often have answer D, don't be surprised if you do have what seems a disproportionate number of D's at the end of the exam.

4. **C.** To multiply like bases, add the exponents. One over a^3 is the same as a to the negative third power. Add: $a^{10} \times a^5 \times a^{-3} = a$ to the $(10 + 5 - 3) = a^{12}$.

   Did you choose D because you don't know what a is? The value of a here, although unknown and unknowable given the information you have, is irrelevant. $a^{12} = a^{12}$, no matter what the value of a. If this question ***befuddled*** (confused) you, return to Chapter 12.

5. **B.** This problem is rather lengthy *unless* you see the shortcut. Here's the long way first: An arc is a fraction of the circumference of the circle. The circumference is 2π *radius.* Because the area of a circle is πradius^2, the radius here is 6. The circumference, therefore, is 12π. The arc is the same fraction of the circle that the central angle is of 360. Here, put $\frac{45}{360}$ and reduce it to $\frac{1}{8}$. That means the arc is $\frac{1}{8}$ of the circumference of the circle. $\frac{1}{8}$ of 36π is certainly less than 36π.

Ready for the shortcut? You can cut off the last step entirely. You still have to break down the area to find the radius and then work back up to find the circumference. (You should be so comfortable with formulas that you can do this step without even breathing hard.) You can see by looking at the figure that the arc is not the entire circumference, but only a part of it. That means that the arc is less than 36π, and B is larger. You don't need to — and certainly don't want to — find the exact measure of the arc.

If you're getting brain cramps, go back to the circles section of Chapter 11 and look for the arc info.

6. **B.** When a negative is cubed, it remains a negative. For example, $-2^3 = -2 \times -2 \times -2 = -8$. Therefore, whatever Column A is, it's negative. Stop right there and don't strain the brain any more.

As you go through the QC questions, keep reminding yourself that the name of the game is Quantitative Comparisons, not Problem Solving. More times than not, you don't have to solve the problem. You work until you see which column is going to be greater, and then you stop. The actual solution is irrelevant and unnecessary. Every second that you save by not working on the QCs is another second that you can use on the regular multiple-choice problems where you *do* need to do all that drudge work.

7. **C.** This is a symbolism problem. It looks more intimidating and difficult than it actually is. Substitute the numbers for the variables in the "explanation." Use the numbers in the same order as the variables. That is, 3 is in the first position, and *a* is in the first position, so substitute a 3 for an *a*. 6 is in the second position, and *b* is in the second position, so substitute a 6 for a *b*. 12 is in the third position, and *c* is in the third position, so substitute a 12 for a *c*. That gives you $3(3) + 4(6) - \frac{1}{2}(12) = 9 + 24 - 6 = 27$.

The more calculations you do, the less surprised you should be when the answer comes out to be choice C. This does not mean that, as soon as you find yourself doing a lot of pencil pushing, you should give up and choose C, hoping for the best. It does mean that if you do no work, and you just think the columns are equal, you've probably fallen for a trap because you frequently have to perform the actual calculations and prove that the columns are equal.

8. **B.** If you chose C, you fell for the trap. The mean (average) of the scores is 73, but the median is 72. A median is the middle term when all terms are arranged in order: 68, 70, 72, 75, 80.

To remember a median, think of the median strip when you're driving down the road: It's in the middle. If you're rusty on the three M's, mean (average), median (middle term), and mode (most occurring term), check out the math review in Chapter 13.

9. **C.** There are two ways you can approach this problem. The sum of the angles in any triangle is 180 degrees. Because you know two angles are 90 degrees (the box indicates a right or 90-degree angle) and 20 degrees for a sum of 110 degrees, you know the remaining angle must be 70 degrees ($180 - 110 = 70$). That angle and the *y* angle are along a straight line, which means they are supplementary and add up to 180 degrees. Subtract 70 from 180 and you get 110.

There's an even easier way to do this problem. The exterior angle is equal to the sum of the two remote interior angles. In simple speech, that means an angle outside the triangle is the same as the sum of the two angles away from it inside the triangle. In this problem, angle $y = 90 + 20 = 110$.

Most geometry problems simply require you to know the properties of angles and figures. I can't emphasize enough the importance of memorizing everything you can wrestle your brain cells around in geometry. Learn the rules until you can mutter them in your sleep and they'll return to you in your hour of need.

10. **A.** This problem is easy if you convert the percentages to decimals (all right-thinking people despise percentages) and remember that *of* means *times*. Column A, therefore, is 3.0 (300 percent is the same as 3, or 3.0) $\times 30 = 90$. Column B is $.60 \times 15 = 9$.

Did you fall for the trap and choose C? Don't be *disheartened* (sad); it happens to the best of us. You were thinking of only the numerals and forgetting your decimal places. You could have avoided all this grief by using your brain instead of your yellow #2. You know quickly that 300 percent of 30 is more than 30. You know just as quickly that 60 percent of 15 is less than 15. Because more than 30 is greater than less than 15, Column A is greater. Whenever possible, try to talk the problem through rather than solving it precisely. No one really cares what the answer is.

11. **D.** If you chose A, you fell for the trap. What if $a = 1$ and $b = 1$? Then $c = 1$, and the columns are equal. What if $a = 2$ and $b = 2$? Then $c = 4$, and A is the answer. If the answer DEEEE-pends on what you plug in, choose D.

12. **C.** Please tell me you didn't actually work out this problem. You know that the word *of* means times, or to multiply. If you were to do this problem as a decimal, you'd have $.20 \times 120$ and 1.20×20. Because the number of decimal places is the same, the solution is the same as well.

This problem is very common. However, don't get complacent, see this sort of thing, and immediately choose C. What if Column A said 0.20 percent rather than 20 percent? That would make the multiplication $.0020 \times 120$, a very different answer indeed. Keep a wary eye on the decimal point.

13. **A.** You didn't actually work this problem out either, did you? One of the things the QC questions tests is your knowledge of when to pick up your pencil and when just to guesstimate. This problem is a definite guesstimate. With 365 days per year (366 in a leap year), Column A would be $365 \times 3 + 366$. Don't actually work it out. Column B is 40×10 because a decade has ten years. You can see at a glance that Column A is much larger.

Although it's not a trap in this particular problem, often a question can getcha if you forget about leap year. For example, if a question asks you how much money Mark makes if he earns $200 a day every single day for four years, your answer will be $200 off unless you remember that one of those years has 366, not 365, days.

If you didn't grow up in the United States, you may be accustomed to different units of measurement such as metric units rather than standard units. It's important that you take a few minutes to go back to the units of measurement portion of Chapter 13 and make sure that you know, for example, how many inches are in a foot, and how many pounds are in a ton.

14. **C.** A diagonal divides a square into two 45:45:90 triangles. The ratio of the sides of a 45:45:90 triangle are $s : s : s\sqrt{2}$ (this concept is discussed in Chapter 11). If the diagonal or hypotenuse is $5\sqrt{2}$, each side of the square is 5. If the bottom of the square (side DC) is 5, then each side of the triangle is also 5. Add up all the sides to get 25.

If you got a number greater than 25, you probably added side DC. The perimeter is the outside of the figures.

15. **E.** This question is as much vocabulary as it is math. A *mean* is the average of numbers: Add the numbers together (420) and divide by the number of numbers ($420 \div 5 = 84$). A *median* is the middle number when the numbers are put in order.

If you chose D, you fell for the trap of thinking that 79 was the median because it was the "middle number." You have to put the numbers in numerical order first: 75, 79, 82, 91, 93. Now you can see that 82 is the median. Subtract the median from the mean: $84 - 82 = 2$. ***Bonus:*** As long as I'm talking vocabulary, do you know what the *mode* is? A mode is the most repeated term — the one that shows up the most. For example, if the numbers were 2, 3, 2, 4, 5, the mode would be 2.

16. **B.** The formula (given in Chapter 11, in case you forgot it) for the interior angle measure of a polygon is $(n - 2)180$, where n stands for the number of sides. In other words, take the number of sides, subtract 2, and multiply by 180. (Why? There are two fewer triangles in any polygon than sides. For example, a square, which has 4 sides, can

make 2 triangles. A hexagon, which has 6 sides, can make 4 triangles, and so on. Each triangle has 180 degrees.) Therefore, your equation here is: $(n-2)180 = 1260$. $180n - 360 = 1260$. $180n = 1620$. $n = 9$.

If you chose D, you didn't answer what the question asked. It wants the perimeter of the figure if each side measures 6. Finish the problem: $9 \times 6 = 54$. If you chose E you got the $(n-2)$ and if you chose C, you multiplied 7 by 6, rather than 9 by 6.

17. **E.** If you simply subtracted $40 - 38$ and got choice A, you fell for the trap. Very few questions on the GRE will be that simple.

You have a formula in the math review that tells you how to find an increase or decrease in percent. It's a fraction. The numerator (top) is the change in the number. The denominator is the starting number — what you began with.

Did you simply say 38 to 40 is 2, and $\frac{2}{38}$ is about 5%? If so, you fell for trap answer B. You did the math correctly, but missed the whole point of having two graphs. You still have work to do.

The amount greater is 40% of 2100 minus 38% of 1700. Note that the numbers at the top of each graph, which represent the totals, are different. Now do the work (remembering that *of* means *times*): 40% of $2100 = .40 \times 2100 = 840$, and 38% of $1700 = .38 \times 1700 = 646$. The increase, therefore, is not merely from 38 to 40, but from 646 to 840, or 194. Divide 194 by 646 (the starting number) to get approximately .30, which equals 30% (choice E).

18. **B.** The fastest way to figure this problem is to realize that 2000 physics must drop from 16% to 14% while chemistry must rise from 22% to 24% to produce the 1995 ratio of 14% to 24%. So, you'll get the right answer if you move 2% of the total number of students in the year 2000 from physics to chemistry: 2% of $2100 = .02 \times 2100 = 42$ (choice B).

Choice D is a tempting answer because there is a 6% difference between physics and chemistry for 2000 and a 10% difference for 1995. Although this difference in percents is 4%, you don't want to take 4% of 2100 (which is 84) because taking 2% from physics and giving 2% to chemistry will produce the required 4% change.

Confused? Think of this another way: If you and I both have $100, and I give you $5, how much more money do you have than I have? It's not $5, but $10. You have $5 more ($105) while I have $5 less ($95) for a difference of $10.

Some mathletes might figure that in 1995, 238 students took physics (14% of 1700) while 408 students took chemistry (24% of 1700). This difference is 170 students, but don't just try to make the chemistry total for 2000 exceed the 2000 physics total by 170. Choices A and C could each, by various irrelevant methods of calculation (don't worry, I won't make you suffer through them), produce a difference of 170, but you must remember that a ratio involves a difference that is related to division, not subtraction.

Choice E would produce the required 24 to 14 ratio if 114 additional students changed from being enrolled in no class to being enrolled in chemistry. The question, however, requires you to move students from physics to chemistry.

19. **C.** Figure out the fraction of people who left. First, ¼ of the people left. That means ¾ remain. Then ⅓ of the remaining people leave: ⅓ of ¾ = ⅓ × ¾ = ³⁄₁₂ = ¼. At 1:00 a.m. another ¼ of the people leave.

Be sure not to say ¼ of the *remaining* people leave. If as many people leave at 1:00 a.m. as left at 11:00 p.m., then ¼ of the original number left. Add all the fractions: ¼ + ¼ + ¼ = ¾. If ¾ of the people have left, then only ¼ remain. The new equation is: $30 = ¼T$ (T standing for total). Divide both sides through by ¼, which is the same as multiplying by ⁴⁄₁ (invert the fraction). $30 \times 4 = 120$.

20. **E.** If you chose A, you fell for a trap. (Are you getting totally sick and tired of hearing that expression? Don't fall for so many traps, and you won't have to hear it.) Dividing like bases means subtracting the exponents. For a^{10} divided by a^5, subtract: $10 - 5 = 5$. Divide 6 by 3 and get 2. You know that the first term is $2a^9$, so you can narrow the answers down to C, D, and E.

b^5 divided by b^9 is b^{-4} or $\frac{1}{b^4}$. That result eliminates answers C and D; you can stop now.

Just for fun, though, I'll finish this calculation. c^7 divided by c^7 is 1. Any number divided by itself is 1. (Or you could think of it as being $7 - 7 = 0$; any number to the 0 power is 1.) The answer 1 doesn't change in the multiplication; ignore it.

Answers A and B were traps for people who tried $10 \div 5 = 2$ instead of subtracting exponents.

Answers C and D were traps for people who forgot that a negative exponent is in the denominator, not the numerator. 2^{-3} really is $\frac{1}{2^3}$. If you forgot this, return to the thrilling math review chapters.

21. **C.** You can find the probability by using this formula:

$$\frac{\text{\# of possible desired outcomes}}{\text{\# of total possible outcomes}}$$

The first thing to do is find the denominator. How many candies will be left after LaVonne has chomped into the others? She starts with 47 candies ($20 + 15 + 12$). You know that she throws some of them away. You can eliminate choice A immediately because the denominator must be less than 47.

She throws away a cream (down to 46), a nut (down to 45), a chew (down to 44), a nut (down to 43), a cream (down to 42), and a chew (down to 41). The denominator for the probability of the next candy that she pulls out will be 41 because she'll have some chance out of 41 of pulling out a nut. That narrows the answers down to B and C.

As a shortcut, subtract 6 (the number of candies that she already pulled out) from 47, the number of candies that originally were in the box. I solved the problem the long way to show you where the 41 really comes from.

Now find the numerator. She starts out with 12 nuts, pulls out one (down to 11), and then pulls out another (down to 10). The probability that her next candy will be a nut is $\frac{10}{41}$. (This type of problem is discussed in the probability section of Chapter 12.)

22. **B.** Take this one step at a time. If you are Barb, you need to take on 6 people in a hot-air balloon race. Because each of the 7 contestants has to race 6 other people, it's tempting to say that 42 hot-air balloon races (7×6) will take place — trap answer D. The problem with this thinking is that it counts each match twice. Barb's race against Jim is the same as Jim's race against Barb. So although each contestant has 6 races, the total number of hot-air balloon races is 7×6 (42) divided by 2, or 21 (watch out for trap answer E). The last step is to multiply 21×5 to account for all the different activities. There are 21 matches in each activity and 5 activities. $21 \times 5 = 105$.

23. **E.** If you chose B, C, or D, you fell for a trap. If there are 100 applicants and 60% are female, there are 60 females . . . and 40 males. You can figure out that 75%, or 45, of the females will relocate and 15 won't relocate, but what about the males? The question asks for the number of people who are not willing to relocate. If you chose B, you just assumed that all the men will not relocate, when in fact, you have no information whatsoever about what men will or won't do (story of my life). *Note:* "It cannot be determined" answers are rare on the GRE, but if you see one, consider carefully whether there is a trap in the problem.

24. **C.** Line segment XY must be a horizontal line parallel to the *x*-axis because the *y* coordinate does not change. If the line segment goes from –2 to +4, it is 6 units long. The midway point would be 3 units along. Start at –2 and count: From –2 to –1 is one unit. From –1 to 0 is two units. From 0 to 1 is 3 units.

If you said E, you fell for the trap. Yes, you're moving three units to the right, but you're moving *from* –2. You go only from –2 to 1, not to 3.

25. **A.** This problem is easier than it looks. If two circles have the same area, they have the same radius because the area of a circle = πradius^2. The radius of circle Y is 5 as well. The diameters of the two circles are 10 each because the diameter of a circle is twice its radius. Therefore, the length of the rectangle is 20, and the width is 10.

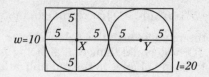

The area of a rectangle is *length × width:* 20 × 10 = 200.

26. **B.** Understand what the explanation means. (The explanation is made up for this particular problem. There is no such thing as a "circle" operation in the real world — only in the little universe of the GRE. Lucky you.) The explanation says that you have a number in the circle. If that number in the circle is a prime number (meaning that it can be divided only by itself and 1), you add the number in the circle to the square of the number in the circle.

    If the number in the circle is a composite number (one that can be divided by something other than just 1 and itself), you square that number and subtract the number in the circle from the square.

    Ugh. You may have to repeat those instructions to yourself a few times. You're really just substituting the number in the circle for the *x* in the appropriate equation.

    Because 4 is composite, you use the second line of the explanation. Square 4: $4^2 = 16$. Subtract from that the number in the circle: 16 − 4 = 12.

    Because 5 is prime, you add it to its square: 5 + 25 = 30.

    Add the two results: 12 + 30 = 42.

    This problem has all sorts of trap answers. If you used the first line ($x + x^2$) for both terms, you got 50. If you used the second line ($x^2 − x$) for both terms, you got 32. If you confused prime and composite numbers using the composite rule for 5 and the prime rule for 4, you got 40.

27. **E.** Did you get brain cramp just reading the problem? If you're totally confused, you may want to guess quickly on this advertisement for aspirin and get on to something better.

    A good test-taker knows which problems are worth investing time in, and which ones are not.

    When dealing with variables, I suggest you plug in numbers. In this case, try:

    d = 16 I chose that number so that 8 cans of juice cost $16, meaning each can costs $2.

    m = 800 so that each can makes 800 milliliters.

    c = 2 so that each can of water cost 2 cents.

    Take this one step at a time. One can of juice costs $2. One can of water costs 2 cents. You need to add three cans of water, or 6 cents' worth of water. Your grand total is now $2.06.

    This $2.06 is the cost for 800 milliliters. The problem asks for the cost of 400 milliliters; divide by 2 to get $1.03, the cost for 400 milliliters. (Why didn't I let *m* = 400? Sometimes when dealing with 1, several of the answer choices come out correct, and you have to substitute new numbers anyway. I like using a 2 in these longer, harder problems.)

    Next, plug *d* = 16, *m* = 800, and *c* = 2 into each choice and eliminate those choices that don't yield 1.03 dollars:

    (A) 3200(800)(16) + 96(2). You can tell without doing all the work that this answer will be much too large.

    (B) $\dfrac{[(800)(16) + 3(2)]}{400} = \dfrac{12,806}{400}$. This one is also certainly more than 1.03.

(C) $\dfrac{\left[16 + 3\,(2)\right]}{50\,(800)} = \dfrac{22}{40,000}$. This number is going to be a fraction.

(D) $\dfrac{\left[8\,(16) + 96\,(2)\right]}{800} = \dfrac{320}{800}$. This fraction is less than 1. The answer had better be choice E, or we're in trouble.

When you get to this point, where you've decided the answer HAS to be E, still go ahead and solve choice E. Why? What if you've made a careless mistake in one of the earlier answers (something easy to do with all these numbers)? When choice E doesn't come out right, you'll realize you bungled somewhere and you have to go back and check your work.

(E) $\dfrac{\left[50\,(16) + 12\,(2)\right]}{800} = \dfrac{824}{800} = 1.03$. At last!

Some of you algebra whizzes may find it easier to do the straightforward algebra, so this is for you.

Write down the units to make sure that you are left with dollars. For the cans of orange juice:

$$\left(\dfrac{d\,\text{dollars}}{8\,\text{cans}}\right) \times \left(\dfrac{1\,\text{can}}{m\,\text{milliliters}}\right) = \dfrac{d\,\text{dollars}}{8m\,\text{milliliters}}\,(\text{the cans cancel})$$

Because you want 400 milliliters, multiply as follows:

$$\left(\dfrac{d\,\text{dollars}}{8m\,\text{milliliters}}\right) \times 400\,\text{milliliters} = \dfrac{50d\,\text{dollars}}{m}\,(\text{the milliliters cancel})$$

Now for the water, remembering that you must convert the cents to dollars:

$$\left(\dfrac{3c\,\text{cents}}{\text{can}}\right) \times \left(\dfrac{1\,\text{dollar}}{100\,\text{cents}}\right) = \dfrac{3c/100\,\text{dollars}}{\text{can}}\,(\text{the cents cancel})$$

Work in the milliliters:

$$\left(\dfrac{3c/100\,\text{dollars}}{\text{can}}\right) \times \left(\dfrac{1\,\text{can}}{m\,\text{milliliters}}\right) = \dfrac{3c/100m\,\text{dollars}}{\text{milliliter}}\,(\text{cans cancel})$$

As with the juice, multiply by 400:

$$\left(\dfrac{3c\,\text{dollars}}{\text{milliliters}}\right) \times 40\,\text{milliliters} = \dfrac{12c}{m\,\text{dollars}}\,(\text{milliliters cancel})$$

You now have $50d/m$ for the cost of the juice and $12c/m$ for the cost of the water, so add to get $\dfrac{(50d + 12c)}{m\,\text{dollars}}$ (choice E).

28. **D.** Draw yourself a diagram as shown:

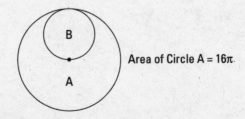

Area of Circle A = 16π

The area of a circle is πr^2. This means that $16\pi = \pi r^2$; $r^2 = 16$; $r = 4$. If the radius of circle A is 4, the diameter of circle B is 4. The circumference of a circle is $2\pi r$ or πd. The circumference of circle B is 4π.

Analytical Writing Sections

Give your essay to someone to read and evaluate for you. Refer that helpful person to Chapter 18 for scoring guidelines.

Part VII
The Part of Tens

In this part . . .

What would any *For Dummies* title be without the famous Part of Tens? This unit is your reward for surviving the previous 23 chapters. These final few chapters require no brainpower. You don't have to work through math problems, you don't have to memorize new vocabulary, and actually, you don't have to stimulate your synapses at all. These chapters are just for fun, but they do provide invaluable information such as relaxation techniques to help you get through the GRE. Read on.

Chapter 24

Ten False Rumors about the GRE

Sure, you've heard them: the horror stories about the GRE. Rumors abound, growing wilder with each telling: "You have to know calculus!" (Absolutely not.) "It's an open book test this year!" (You *wish!*)

As a test-preparation tutor, I get calls all the time from students trying to check out the latest scuttlebutt. Here are ten common stories that make the rounds every year — they're as dependable as oversleeping the morning of your most important final.

You Can't Study for the GRE

Why would I be writing this book if that were so? Studying can be done in two ways, each advantageous in its own right. First is the last-minute cram, a review in a few weeks of the types of questions, the approach to each question, the tricks and traps involved in the questions. (Sound familiar? This method is what you've been working on throughout this book.) Second is the long-range study program, in which you learn vocabulary and work on math questions from your freshman year in college on. Obviously, if you've got a year or two to put into this, you should get a dynamite score. Most people, however, benefit greatly from even a few weeks or months of intense study.

Your GRE Score Will Be About the Same as Your High-School SAT Score

Are you the same person you were in high school? No. You have matured, learned better study habits, and suddenly come to the shocking realization that no one is going to spoon-feed you anymore. You may not have studied much for the SAT figuring that you could always get into *some* college, somewhere, no matter what your score. You were probably right. But getting into graduate school is not as easy. There aren't as many graduate programs as undergraduate programs, which makes for a more cutthroat competition. Because you realize this fact of life, you study harder and study smarter. Besides, your vocabulary almost certainly has improved significantly after four years of college, and vocabulary is usually the most difficult portion of the exam for students.

The GRE Tests IQ

Nope. The GRE supposedly tests your ability to do well in graduate school. Some cynics say that all the GRE tests is your ability to take the GRE. Getting into a debate over that point is rather futile because you're stuck with taking the GRE and worrying about it just wastes brainpower you can use for other things. But be reassured that the GRE is not an IQ test. You can learn to improve your GRE score with all sorts of tricks, traps, and techniques; that's *much* harder to do on IQ tests.

 Have you ever heard of MENSA, the national high-IQ society? Although the GRE is not actually a measure of IQ, if you do well on the GRE, you can sometimes get automatic membership in MENSA (something that looks great on resumes and impresses the socks off dates' parents). Call the local MENSA chapter to find out what the qualifying score is. Hey, you put the effort into getting the score; scarf up all the benefits from the score that you can get.

You Must Pass Certain Classes to Take the GRE

Although taking classes like advanced logic or linguistics is useful, let's get real here: Not many people take those courses today. If you are reading this book as a freshman or sophomore and have the option of taking logic classes, excellent. Doing so will help you with the analytical ability portion of the GRE. But you certainly don't *have* to have a class like that to do well on the GRE. (That's a relief; who has room for that class in an already overcrowded curriculum?) As far as math goes, the GRE tests basic algebra, geometry, and arithmetic. A year of algebra and a year of geometry are sufficient. In short, the GRE has no "required courses" or "prerequisites."

Your Score Won't Improve if You Keep Retaking the GRE

Although having your score jump hundreds of points is uncommon, it has happened. Your improvement depends on the reason your score was low in the first place and on how much you study before retaking the exam. If your score was low because you didn't understand the format of the exam (for example, you looked at a Quantitative Comparison question and wondered where the answer choices were!), you can certainly improve that score by taking a few practice exams and becoming more comfortable with the question styles. If your score was low because you fell for all the traps set in the GRE, you can improve your score by going through these materials, learning to recognize those traps, and studying the tips and tricks for avoiding those traps. But it is unrealistic for a slow reader to think that a few weeks of study is going to double her reading speed or for someone who doesn't understand algebra at all to think she can get a year's worth of algebra instruction in an afternoon. You do need *some* basics under your belt.

The study time you put into preparing for the second exam is also important. If you take the exam, get back your scores, register for another exam, and then just a few days before the second exam begin studying again, you may as well forget it. Although experience helps, your score won't soar simply because you've done this before. You have to study for the second test, or you'll repeat the mistakes of the first.

The GRE Has a Passing Score

You can't pass or fail the GRE, but a particular graduate school may have a cutoff score that you must get to be considered for admission. This score is often based on your grade point average (GPA). A school may decree, for example, that if your GPA is in the 3.0 to 3.5 range, you can get an 1100 (combined verbal and math), but if your GPA is in the 2.5 to 3.0 range, your GRE must be at least a 1200. You will want to find out the GRE ranges considered acceptable by the schools you are considering.

You Can Take the GRE on Your Own Computer at Home

Oh sure, suuuuuuure. You can take the test at home, with your computer, your dictionary, your reference books, and your cousin Morty the Math Genius all standing by, ready to help you! And while we're at it, I'll be glad to come by and stand at your shoulder, pointing out all the traps as well. Sorry. You cannot take the GRE anywhere but at a recognized testing center, usually a Sylvan Learning Center.

You Can Bring Your Own Laptop to the Testing Center

Wouldn't taking your laptop be nice? You could load all sorts of programs into your computer, such as math formulas and algorithms or pages and pages of vocabulary, and taking the GRE would be a snap. Unfortunately, the GRE people are way ahead of you on this one. Not only do you have to take the exam at a special testing center, but you also have to take it on their computers. The only things you supply are the brainpower and the aspirin.

Missing the First Few Questions Gives You an Easier Test and Better Score

Right and wrong. The first five questions do indeed determine the difficulty level of the whole exam. For all practical purposes, you start off with a score of 500 — right in the middle of the score range (your score can go from 200 to 800). If you get the first question right, you get about +100 and have a 600-level exam going. If you miss the first question, you get about –100 and have a 400-level exam going. The second question is worth about 70 points. If you get it right and you got the first question right, the computer thinks you're smart enough to be working at a 670+ level, and you get a nice hard test. If you miss the second question and you missed the first question, you're working down in the 300s. You'll get an easy test, but you have almost no way to bring your score back up into the 600s. The moral of the story is: The first few questions are that "first impression" the computer gets about you. You never have a second chance to make a good first impression.

Computer Geniuses Have an Unfair Advantage on the GRE

Computer geniuses have an unfair advantage over all of the rest of us in this high-tech age; why should the GRE be any different? Let's get real here. Sure, students who are very comfortable with a computer may have a little advantage because they have one less stress factor going into the test, but the advantage ends there. The computer skills required for taking the GRE are so minimal that they're almost irrelevant. Hey, if it makes you feel any better, computer geniuses tell me they feel at a disadvantage on this test because of the "annoyingly simplistic technology."

Chapter 25

Ten Stupid Things You Can Do to Mess Up Your GRE

Throughout this book, you learned techniques for doing your best on the GRE. I'm sorry to say, however, that there are just as many techniques for messing up big time on this test. Take a few minutes to read through them now to see what crazy things people do to blow the exam totally. By being aware of these catastrophes, you may prevent their happening to you.

And no — no booby prize is awarded to the student who makes the greatest number of these mistakes.

Losing Concentration

When you're in the middle of an excruciatingly boring Reading Comprehension passage, the worst thing you can do is let your mind drift off to a more pleasant time (last night's date, last weekend's soccer game, the time you stole your rival school's mascot and set it on the john in the dean's private bathroom). Although visualization (picturing yourself doing something relaxing or fun) is a good stress-reduction technique, it stinks when it comes to helping your GRE score. Even if you have to pinch yourself to keep from falling asleep or flaking out, stay focused. The GRE is just a few hours of your life. You've had horrible blind dates that lasted longer than that, and you managed to survive them. This too shall pass.

Panicking over Time

Every section of the GRE has a specified time limit. The on-screen clock (which you do have the option of turning off, in case it's driving you crazy) displays the time you have remaining. You know going into the test exactly how many questions are in each section and, therefore, how many minutes you have per question. It's not as if this is some big mystery.

Cheating

Dumb, dumb, *dumb!* Cheating on the GRE is a loser's game — it's just plain stupid. Apart from the legal, moral, and ethical questions, let's talk practicality: You can't predict what types of vocabulary words will show up in the questions. What are you going to do, copy a dictionary on the palm of your hand? All the math formulas you need can't fit onto the bottom of your shoe. Copying everything that you *think* you may need would take more time than just learning it. Besides, the GRE tries very hard to test critical reasoning skills, not just rote memorization. The test never asks a question as straightforward as, "How many degrees in a triangle?" The questions require thinking and reasoning, not just copying down a formula. Short of having a brain transplant, cheating is impractical.

Worrying about the Previous Sections

Think of the GRE as three separate lifetimes. You are reborn twice and get two more chances to "do it right." Every time the computer prompts you to go to a new section, you get a fresh start. You have one verbal section, one math section, and one analytical writing section. (I cover the breakdown in much more detail in Chapter 1.) The computer is inexorable. You can't go back to a previous section if you suddenly recall a vocabulary word that had eluded you (such as *inexorable*, in the previous sentence!) You can't double-check your arithmetic on a math question. Forget one section as soon as you enter the next. You can't even go back to a previous question in the same section, let alone an entirely different section. Think of this as you would a new boyfriend or girlfriend in your life: Out with the old and in with the new.

Worrying about the Hard Problems

The GRE contains some incredibly hard problems. If you get the first few questions on the exam correct, the computer assumes that you're a genius and confidently offers you real mind-bogglers later on. If you miss the first few questions, the computer takes it easy on you and gives you a kinder, gentler exam (and, alas, a lower, wimpier score). Suppose that you ace the first few questions and then get some super-hard questions. Of course, you have to answer them because the computer doesn't let you go on until you punch in an answer. But if the question is just way, way beyond you, make a quick guess (emphasis on quick!), go on, and don't fret. A ridiculously few students get total 800s every year. If you get into the 700s or even the 600s, you are in a super-elite club of only a few of the thousands of students who take the GRE annually. Just accept the fact that you can't be sure of your answer on some of the questions and learn to live with your imperfections.

Rushing through the Confirm Step

When you answer a question, the computer gives you a second chance. Your screen offers you a Confirm button that you have to click on before your answer becomes permanent. Life has so few second chances; take advantage of this one. Sure, you may feel rushed; everyone does, but take those few extra seconds. Keep reminding yourself that the exam is not like a paper-and-pencil test, in which you can come back at the end and double-check for careless mistakes. You make a choice, confirm that choice, and that's all she wrote. Take the few extra seconds before clicking on the Confirm button.

Stressing Out over Your Computer Skills (Or Lack Thereof)

The GRE, in and of itself, is stressful enough. The last thing you need to do is add more anxiety to the whole nerve-racking experience of taking the test by worrying about your computer expertise. Can you type, even a little bit, in a one-finger style? If so, you have mastered all of the computer skills that the GRE requires of you. Before you begin taking the test, you complete a very brief tutorial (no, the time spent on that does not count as actual testing time) that refreshes your computer abilities, and you have the Help key available to you at all times during the actual test.

Trying to Keep Track of the Question Breakdown

Keeping track of your own (mental, emotional, and psychological) breakdown is a good idea. Keeping track of the question breakdown is not. By "the question breakdown," I mean the number of each type of question you've answered. You know that in the verbal portion, for example, you have questions in four formats: Antonyms, Analogies, Sentence Completions, and Reading Comprehension. These questions can be in any order. In other words, don't say to yourself, "Well, I've finished three Sentence Completion questions; I know it's time for Reading Comprehension." The computer makes those decisions — not you. Worrying about which type of question comes next is the high-tech equivalent of flipping forward to see how many pages you have left to read of a novel. All you do is waste your time; you don't shorten the number of pages.

Ignoring the Five-Minute Breaks Offered

You are offered a short break (usually 5 minutes) between sections (Verbal, Math, and Analytical Writing). If you don't take those breaks between the sections, you'll be sitting still for hours. I see students often pass on the breaks, especially the first one, wanting to get this whole ordeal over with as soon as possible. Although I sympathize with the desire, I strongly, strongly suggest that you take all the rest breaks that are offered. Even just standing up, swinging your arms, and grumbling a little bit will make you feel better.

Scheduling the Test at the Same Time as Your Best Friend

Depending on the size and availability of the test center, you and your buddy may be able to take the test at the same time. Big mistake. It's only human to try to compare your progress with your friend's. Unfortunately, you and your friend won't get the exact same exam. Your questions will be different. If you see your buddy zooming through the material with a big smile on her face, you may depress yourself unnecessarily. (Maybe she missed the first few questions and now is getting a much easier exam than yours. You never know.) The GRE is one place where the buddy system just doesn't work.

Chapter 26

Ten Relaxation Techniques to Try before and during the GRE

Most people are tense before the test, and butterflies dance in their stomachs. The key is to use relaxation techniques that keep your mind on your test and not on your tummy.

Breathe Deeply

Breathing is grossly underrated. Breathing is good. Take a deep breath until your belly expands, hold your breath for a few counts, and then expel the air through your nose. (Be careful not to blow anything but air, especially if your boyfriend or girlfriend is sitting next to you.) Try not to take short, shallow breaths, which could cause you to become even more anxious by depriving your body of oxygen. Try breathing in and out deeply while reciting something in your mind such as your favorite line from a movie or a totally stupid, mindless rhyme.

Rotate Your Head

Try to see behind your head. Move your head as far as possible to the right until you feel a tug on the skin on the left side of your neck. Then reverse it and move your head all the way to the left until you feel a tug on the skin on the right. Move your head back, as if you're looking at the ceiling, and then down, as if looking at your feet. You'll be surprised how much tension drains out of you as you do this a few times.

Be careful that you perform this exercise with your eyes closed and make what you're doing obvious. You don't want a suspicious proctor to think you're craning your neck to look at someone else's computer screen.

Hunch and Roll Your Shoulders

While breathing in, scrunch up your shoulders as if you're trying to touch them to your ears. Then roll them back and down, breathing out. Arch your back, sitting up super-straight, as if a string is attached to the top of your head and is being pulled toward the ceiling. Then slump and round out your lower back, pushing it out toward the back of your chair. These exercises relax your upper and lower back. They are especially useful if you develop a kink in your spine.

Cross and Roll Your Eyes

Look down at your desk as you're doing this so that people won't think you're even stranger than they already know you are. Cross your eyes and then look down as far as you can into your lower eyelids. Look to the right and then up into your eyelids and then look to the left. After you repeat this sequence a few times, your eyes should be refreshed.

Shake Out Your Hands

You probably do this automatically when you need to get rid of writer's cramp. Do it more consciously and more frequently. Put your hands down at your sides, hanging them below your chair seat, and shake them vigorously. Imagine all the tension and stress going out through your fingers and dropping onto the floor.

Extend and Push Out Your Legs

While you're sitting at your desk, straighten your legs out in front of you; think of pushing something away with your heels. Point your toes back toward your knees. You feel a stretch on the backs of your legs. Hold for a count of three and then relax.

Cup Your Eyes

Cup your hands, fingers together. Put them over your closed eyes, blocking out all the light. You're now in a world of velvety-smooth darkness, which is very soothing. Try not to let your hands actually touch your eyes. (If you see stars or flashes of light, your hands are pushing down on your eyes.)

Rotate Your Scalp

Put your open hand palm-down on your scalp. Move your hand in small circles. Feel your scalp rotate. Lift your hand and put it down somewhere else on your scalp. Repeat the circular motions. You're giving yourself a very relaxing scalp massage.

Curtail Negative Thoughts

Any time you feel yourself starting to panic or thinking negative thoughts, make a conscious effort to say to yourself *"Stop!"* Don't dwell on anything negative; switch over to a positive track. Suppose that you catch yourself thinking "Why didn't I study this math more? I saw that formula a hundred times but can't remember it now!" Change the script to "I got most of this math right. No sense in worrying now. Overall, I think I'm doing great."

Before the Test or during a Break, Visualize

Don't do this *during* the test; you just waste time and lose concentration. Before the exam, however, or at the break, practice visualization. Close your eyes and imagine yourself in the exam room, seeing questions you know the answers to, cheerfully punching the Confirm button. Picture yourself leaving the exam room dancing in the parking lot because you got your unofficial score right off the computer and eagerly rushing home to begin your mailbox vigil for the official good news. Think of how proud your parents are of you. Imagine the acceptance letter you get from the graduate school of your dreams. Picture yourself driving a fire-engine-red Ferrari ten years from now, telling the *Time* magazine reporter in the passenger seat that your success started with your excellent GRE scores. The goal is to associate the GRE with good feelings.

Chapter 27

Ten Math Concepts You Absolutely Must Know

1f you got the news that the world would end in two hours, what would you do? Order a pizza? Go surfing or play hoops with your friends? Life has its priorities. If someone were to tell you that your GRE math study time was to end in two hours, what would be your priorities? Here are my suggestions (although pizza doesn't sound half bad).

Ratios

The total possible is a multiple of the sum of the numbers in the ratio. A ratio is written as OF/TO or OF:TO.

Common Pythagorean Ratios

In a right triangle, sides may be in the following ratios:

3:4:5 $s:s:\sqrt{2}$ (or $s/\sqrt{2} : s/\sqrt{2} : s$)

5:12:13 $s:s\sqrt{3}:2s$

7:24:25

FOIL Method of Algebra

To multiply algebraic expressions, use FOIL: *First* - *Outer* - *Inner* - *Last*. To reduce algebraic equations, use FOIL backwards.

Linear Algebraic Equations

Isolate the variable; get the variables on one side of the equal sign and the nonvariables on the other side (remembering to change from a positive to a negative or vice versa when crossing over the equal sign). Add like terms. Divide both sides by what is next to the variable.

Symbolism

The GRE tests two basic types of symbolism: Plugging the numbers into the expression, and talking through the symbolism explanation in English.

Exponents

Know how to add, subtract, multiply, and divide like bases. Remember that a number to the zero power equals one and that a number to a negative power is the *reciprocal* (upside-down version) of that number.

Square Roots

Know how to multiply and divide like radicals and how to simplify radicals.

Plotting Points on a Graph

Know how to find a point on a graph given its (x,y) coordinates. Remember that the point of origin is $(0,0)$ and that points along a line with the same (x,y) coordinates form a 45-degree angle.

Angles

Understand the various types of angles, especially how to identify exterior angles and how to solve for the sum of interior angles of any polygon.

Circles

Be able to find circumference, area, sectors, and arcs of circles, and degree measures of central and inscribed angles.

Appendix
Grammar Review

• •

"**Y**ou never get a second chance to make a good first impression," as the saying goes. Although the GRE doesn't specifically test grammar, you should keep in mind that real human beings will score your Analytical Writing essays, and you don't want them to (unconsciously, of course) lower their assessment of your ideas due to careless grammar mistakes. The following is a very brief grammar review covering the most important concepts. You should memorize all these rules. Burn them in your brain, carve them in your heart, and imprint them on the very fiber of your being. Study them until they become second nature, because during the actual GRE, you won't have time to stop and think, "Now, wait a minute. Wasn't there some special rule for *neither/nor?*" You have to know and go.

Subject-Verb Agreement

1. **A singular subject takes a singular verb.**

   My <u>pencil</u> *is* (not *are*) dull.

2. **A plural subject takes a plural verb.**

   My brain <u>cells</u> *are* (not *is*) dull.

3. **A compound subject — two or more subjects often connected by the word *and* — takes a plural verb.**

   My <u>pencil</u> and my brain <u>cells</u> *are* (not *is*) dull.

4. **The following words are always plural and therefore require plural verbs:**

   few: <u>Few</u> people *score* (not *scores*) perfectly on the GRE.

   both: <u>Both</u> the GRE and the GMAT *are* (not *is*) entrance exams to graduate school.

   several: <u>Several</u> of my friends *have* (not *has*) taken the GRE.

   many: <u>Many</u> of my friends *wish* (not *wishes*) they had never heard of the GRE.

5. **The following words are always singular and require singular verbs:**

   each: <u>Each</u> question on the GRE *has* (not *have*) the potential to be a trick question.

   every: <u>Every</u> question *is* (not *are*) to be approached with trepidation and paranoia.

   The *every* words — *every*one, *every*body, *every*thing, *every*where — are always singular.

6. **The following words may be singular or plural, depending on what follows them: *some, any, most, all, none (S.A.M.A.N.).***

   some, plural: <u>Some</u> of the <u>jokes</u> in this book *are* (not *is*) beyond hope and should be given a decent burial.

   some, singular: <u>Some</u> of the <u>humor</u> in this book *is* (not *are*) inexcusable.

You can remember these words with the acronym S.A.M.A.N., the first letters of the words. Think of the sentence, "S.A.M.A.N. (say, man), can you tell me which words are sometimes singular and sometimes plural?"

7. The following collective nouns look plural but are singular and require a singular verb: *group, public, club, government, union, organization, collection.*

The <u>group</u> *is* (not *are*) interested in hearing how my studying is coming along; the <u>club</u> *is* (not *are*) going to hire me to give a speech on preparing for the GRE.

8. A prepositional phrase does not affect subject-verb agreement.

When you have a prepositional phrase, mentally draw a line through it, and simply read the noun (subject) next to the verb.

That irate <u>group</u> ~~of test takers~~ *is* (not *are*) bombarding the proctor with tomatoes.

(Did you remember from Rule #7 that *group* is singular even though it may look plural?)

Five words are exceptions to Rule #8: the S.A.M.A.N. words. Do not ignore prepositional phrases with the S.A.M.A.N. words.

<u>All</u> of my friends *are* (not *is*) working overtime tonight; <u>all</u> of their time *is* (not *are*) spent complaining about work.

9. Some nouns have irregular singular and plural forms.

Singular	*Plural*
criterion	criteria
curriculum	curricula
bacterium	bacteria
phenomenon	phenomena
medium	media
datum	data

A solar eclipse is an interesting <u>phenomenon</u>; meteor showers are interesting <u>phenomena</u>.

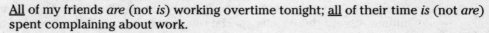

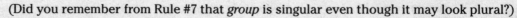

When in doubt about whether a word is singular or plural, remember that, in general (but not always), the plural form of the word ends in a vowel (data, criteria), and the singular form of the word ends in a consonant (datum, criterion).

10. The second subject in an *either/or* and *neither/nor* construction determines whether the verb is singular or plural.

Neither Kimberly nor her <u>parents</u> *are* (not *is*) on the cruise.

Neither her parents nor <u>Kimberly</u> *is* (not *are*) able to afford cruise tickets.

Neither Kimberly's friends nor her <u>parents</u> *are* (not *is*) going on a cruise vacation this year.

Many people are so concerned with the subject-verb agreement of *neither/nor* that they forget that *neither* and *nor* belong together and that *either* and *or* belong together. In other words, the constructions *neither/or* and *either/nor* are wrong. Double-check whenever you see these words.

Pronouns

1. **A pronoun (a word that takes the place of the noun) must have the same number (singular or plural) as the noun it is replacing.**

   <u>Everybody</u> is on *his* best behavior during a college interview.

   You would probably be wealthy if you had a dollar for each time you had heard someone say, "Yeah, everybody is trying *their* best." Because the construction *everybody/their* is so commonly used, it sounds correct. Consider this expression to be a red flag. Whenever you see the word *everybody,* triple-check the pronoun to make sure that it is singular.

2. **A pronoun must have the same gender (feminine, masculine, neuter) as the noun it is replacing.**

   <u>Mrs. Velez</u> is notorious for *her* difficult accounting projects.

3. **A pronoun must have clarity (that is, you must be able to tell what noun the pronoun is replacing).**

   Matthew asked Franklin to pick up *his* laundry off the floor.

   Did Matthew want Matthew's laundry picked up, or did Matthew want Franklin's laundry picked up? This reference is unclear — and thus a wrong sentence.

   An unclear pronoun reference often requires major reconstructive surgery. In this example, the entire sentence must be rewritten. Here's one possibility:

   Matthew, disgusted at seeing Franklin's laundry on the floor, asked him to pick *it* up.

   Now you know perfectly well that the pronoun *it* is referring to Franklin's heap of clothes, not Matthew's.

4. **A pronoun must be in the proper case: subjective (I, you, he, she, it, we, they); objective (me, you, him, her, it, us, them); or possessive (my, mine, your, yours, his, her, hers, its, our, ours, their, theirs).**

   A pronoun following any form of the verb *to be,* such as *is, are, was,* and *were,* is going to be in the subjective form. This form often sounds pretentious and bizarre. Following are common constructions:

It is I.	It was she who. . . .
It was he.	This is he.
It could be they.	It was they.

   I confessed <u>it</u> was *I* who insisted on including the lame jokes in this book.

Adjectives and Adverbs

1. **Place an adjective (which modifies a noun or pronoun) or an adverb (which modifies a verb, adjective, or adverb) as close as possible to the noun or pronoun it is modifying.**

   That rule is *not* followed in this sentence:

   Wrong: Nancy and Frank left the neighborhood they had lived in for ten years *reluctantly*.

   This sentence sounds as if Nancy and Frank had been reluctant to live in the neighborhood, when in fact they were reluctant to leave. Change the sentence so that *reluctantly* comes just before *left:*

   Right: Nancy and Frank *reluctantly* left the neighborhood they had lived in for ten years.

2. **An adverb (which modifies a verb, adverb, or adjective) often answers the question "How?" and may end in -ly.**

   How do I study? I study *reluctantly. Reluctantly* is an adverb.

3. **Place *not only* and *but also* in parallel positions within a sentence.**

   People often place *not only* and *but also* in the wrong positions. Following is an example of a wrong way to use these expressions:

   Wrong: Angelique *not only* was exasperated *but also* frightened when she locked herself out of the house.

   See the problem? In this wrong example, the phrase *not only* comes before the verb *was,* but the phrase *but also* comes before the adjective *frightened.*

   Right: Angelique was *not only* exasperated *but also* frightened when she locked herself out of the house.

   Not only and *but also* precede the adjectives *exasperated* and *frightened,* respectively.

Sentence Structure

1. **A run-on sentence (two or more independent clauses incorrectly joined) must be changed.**

   The following is a run-on:

   Wrong: Jessimena was furious when she went to the party on the wrong day, she went home and yelled at her boyfriend who had given her the wrong information.

   You can choose from five ways to correct a run-on.

   - **Make two separate sentences.**

     Jessimena was furious when she went to the party on the wrong day. *She* went home and yelled at her boyfriend, who had given her the wrong information.

   - **Use a semicolon to separate independent clauses.**

     Jessimena was furious when she went to the party on the wrong day; she went home and yelled at her boyfriend, who had given her the wrong information.

   - **Use a semicolon, conjunctive adverb, and comma (as in this construction: _____; *therefore,*) to separate the clauses.**

     Jessimena was furious when she went to the party on the wrong day; *therefore,* she went home and yelled at her boyfriend, who had given her the wrong information.

   - **Use a subordinating conjunction (such as *because* or *since*) with one of the clauses.**

     Because Jessimena was furious when she went to the party on the wrong day, she went home and yelled at her boyfriend, who had given her the wrong information.

   - **Use a comma and a coordinating conjunction (as in this construction: _____, *and*) between the two clauses.**

     Jessimena was furious when she went to the party on the wrong day, *and* she went home and yelled at her boyfriend, who had given her the wrong information.

2. **A sentence fragment (an incomplete sentence) must be changed to reflect a completed thought.**

   Wrong: Wendy, singing merrily to herself as she walked to class, unaware that the professor was at that very moment preparing a pop quiz.

   Right: Wendy, singing merrily to herself as she walked to class, *was* unaware that the professor was at that very moment preparing a pop quiz.

Parallelism

Parallelism (also called *parallel structure*) means that objects in a series must be in similar form.

Wrong: I spent my weekend *shopping, doing* chores around the house, and finally *got* out on Sunday evening to play a set of tennis.

Rewrite the sentence so that the verbs are in the same form:

Right: On the weekend, I *shopped, did* chores around the house, and finally *got* out on Sunday evening to play a set of tennis.

   or

Right: I spent my weekend *shopping* and *doing* chores around the house, finally *getting* out on Sunday evening to play a set of tennis.

Items in a series may be nouns, verbs, adjectives, or entire clauses. However, nonparallel verbs are the items that most commonly have errors. When a clause has more than one verb, watch out for this particular error.

Comparisons

1. **Use the *-er* form (called the *comparative* form) to compare exactly two items; use the *-est* form (called the *superlative* form) to compare more than two items.**

   I am *taller* than my brother <u>Beau</u>, but <u>Darren</u> is the *tallest* member of our family.

   A particularly difficult comparison uses the words *latter* and *last*.

   My boyfriend asked whether I would like to go to Chicago where the temperature was −5 degrees or Los Angeles where the temperature was 80 degrees; I told him I preferred to visit the *latter* (not *last*).

   Comparisons may trap you when you refer to twins. Remember that *twins* indicates two people. The following is a good example:

   Wrong: <u>Myron</u> and <u>Mayor</u> Thibadeau are identical twins, but Myron is the *oldest* by five minutes, a fact he never lets Mayor forget.

   The error is in the comparison because there are only two twins.

   Right: Myron is the *older* by five minutes.

2. **Compare only similar objects or concepts.**

Wrong: The motor skills of a toddler are more advanced than a baby.

The problem with the preceding sentence is that it compares *motor skills* to a *baby*. Its intention is to compare a toddler's motor skills to a baby's motor skills. Following are two ways to correct the error:

Right: The motor skills of a toddler are more advanced than those of a baby.

or

Right: A toddler's motor skills are more advanced than a baby's.

Diction

I like to refer to diction errors as *twosomes* because they are errors that you make when you swap two (or sometimes three) commonly confused words. Following is a list of the most commonly confused words, along with short-and-sweet definitions and examples.

*it's . . . its: **It's*** (notice the apostrophe) means *it is. It's* good to know the distinction between these two words. ***Its*** (without an apostrophe) is possessive.

assure . . . ensure: To ***assure*** means to convince. Quentin talked fast, trying to *assure* his girlfriend that the black negligee in his closet was in fact a belated birthday present for her. To ***ensure*** is to make certain. To *ensure* that his girlfriend believed him, Quentin called a friend, who pretended she was the salesgirl who had sold the item to Quentin.

lie . . . lay: To ***lie*** is to recline. I *lie* down in the afternoon for a nap to reduce stress. To ***lay*** is to place. I *lay* a cold washcloth on my head every time I get a headache from studying for the GRE.

Do you often get *lie* and *lay* confused? I have an easy way to remember them. To ***lie*** is to recline. Listen for the long *i* sound in l<u>ie</u> and the long *i* sound in rec<u>li</u>ne. When I lie down, I recline. To ***lay*** is to place. Listen for the long *a* sound in l<u>ay</u> and the long *a* sound in pl<u>a</u>ce. Now I lay me down to sleep. Now I place me down to sleep.

Few of us know how to conjugate these words correctly. <u>Memorize</u> the following:

- ✔ ***Lie, lay, have lain:*** Today I *lie* down, yesterday I *lay* down, every day I *have lain* down.
- ✔ ***Lay, laid, have laid:*** Today I *lay* my keys on the table, yesterday I *laid* my keys on the table, every day this week I *have laid* my keys on the table.

Note how confusing the past tense of *lie* is because it is the same as the present tense of *lay*. Do not use the past tense of *lie* as *lied*. The sentence "I *lied* down yesterday" is egregiously incorrect.

affect . . . effect: To ***affect*** is to influence or concern. A good GRE score will positively *affect* your chances of admission to graduate school. (It will positively *influence* your chances.) ***Effect*** means cause or result. A good GRE score will have a positive *effect* on your chances for admission (a positive *result*). A good score will *effect* (or cause) a change in which schools you consider.

Affect has another, little-known meaning. To ***affect*** also means to pretend. When I want to get out of meeting with my friends to study for the GRE, I often *affect* a headache.

imply . . . infer: To ***imply*** means to suggest. I didn't mean to *imply* that your dress is ugly when I asked you whether you bought it at an upholstery store. To ***infer*** is to conclude or deduce, to read a meaning *in*to something. Did you *infer* that I think the dress looks like a sofa covering?

who . . . whom: ***Who*** is a subject and does the action. *Who* wants to study on a weekend? ***Whom*** is an object and receives the action. I don't know *whom* to ask for help in deciding on the topic for my thesis.

eminent . . . immanent . . . imminent: Eminent is outstanding, distinguished. Dr. Regis Weiss is an *eminent* oncologist, well respected by his peers. ***Immanent*** is inherent, innate. I think that compassion probably is an *immanent* trait in a good physician; it doesn't seem possible that someone could take a course to learn how to be caring. ***Imminent*** means about to happen. When I saw Dr. Weiss shaking his head at me as I stood on the scale, I knew a lecture about weight management was *imminent*.

less . . . fewer: Less modifies a singular noun. I have *less* <u>patience</u> with problems than I should have. ***Fewer*** modifies a plural noun. I would make *fewer* careless <u>mistakes</u> in math if only I had the patience to finish each problem completely.

amount . . . number: Amount modifies a singular noun. I have a large *amount* of <u>respect</u> for the poetry of Dorothy Parker. ***Number*** modifies a plural noun. A *number* of <u>times</u> I have read her poem that contains the lines, "The lads I've met in Cupid's deadlock / were, shall we say, born out of wedlock?"

farther . . . further: Farther refers to measurable distance. I made a mistake on the test when I said that Morocco is *farther* from Egypt than it is from New York. ***Further*** refers to a figurative degree or quantity that can't be measured. Obviously, I need to study my geography *further*.

between . . . among: Between compares exactly two things. I have difficulty choosing *between* rocky-road and fudge-ripple ice cream. ***Among*** compares more than two. I go crazy when I have to choose *among* the desserts in a smorgasbord. The word *between* is often followed by *and:* I have difficulty choosing between this *and* that.

stationary . . . stationery: Stationary means unmoving. The little girl tried to remain *stationary,* hoping that the birds would come up to her and eat out of her hand. ***Stationery*** is writing paper. The little girl used her new *stationery* to write a letter telling her grandmother about the birds.

Stationary means something that *stays* and *stays.* Note the letter *a* in st<u>a</u>y and the letter *a* in station<u>a</u>ry. *Stationery* is something you write a letter on. Note the letter *e* in station<u>e</u>ry and the letter *e* in l<u>e</u>tter.

if . . . whether: If introduces a condition. *If* the teacher allows an open-book exam, I will be ecstatic. ***Whether*** compares alternatives. I don't know *whether* I could pass a normal, closed-book exam.

If usually sounds correct even when it is wrong. Personally, even though I know better, I hear myself saying, "I don't know *if* I can make it tonight," when I know I should say, "I don't know *whether* I can make it tonight." Try *whether* first. If it sounds right, it probably is right.

rise . . . raze . . . raise: To ***rise*** means to ascend. It is time to *rise* when your significant other yanks the covers off the bed. To ***raze*** means to tear down. When she threatens to *raze* the bedroom around your head, you know she means business. To ***raise*** means to lift. You wearily *raise* your body, ready to face another day.

anxious . . . eager: Anxious means worried or doubtful. Meg was *anxious* about the call from her mechanic, knowing that her car probably needed some repairs. ***Eager*** means joyously anticipating. The mechanic was *eager* to work on Meg's car, because he needed cash.

principle . . . principal: Principle means rule. The *principles* of justice upon which our country is founded apply to all. ***Principal*** means first in authority or importance. The *principal* reason democracy works, in my opinion, is that it gives everyone an equal opportunity to succeed.

Principle means rule. Note that they both end in *-le*. The English language has many uses of the word *principal,* including (for example) investment principal, the principal reason I telephoned you, and the principal of a high school.

good . . . well: Good is an adjective that modifies a noun. You're doing a *good* job learning these rules. ***Well*** is an adverb that modifies verbs, adverbs, and adjectives and usually answers the question *how?* How do you study? You study very *well.*

Well also refers to physical condition. By the time you leave the GRE, huffing, puffing, sweating, and fretting, you may not be feeling very *well.*

complement . . . compliment: Complement means to complete. The buzz haircut *complemented* the image Chan wanted to project as a no-nonsense guy. ***Compliment*** means to praise. Chan's girlfriend was eager to *compliment* him on his hot new look.

flaunt . . . flout: To ***flaunt*** means to show off. Brittany was thrilled to get her engagement ring and couldn't wait to *flaunt* it to her friends at work. To ***flout*** means to show scorn or contempt. Her fiancé was furious that Brittany had *flouted* their agreement to keep their engagement a secret for the next few months.

founder . . . flounder: To ***founder*** is to sink, fail, or collapse. Reports estimate that one of every two new businesses *founders* within the first three years. To ***flounder*** is to thrash about. A new business owner, desperate for advice, will *flounder* wildly, running from government bureau to government bureau attempting to get help.

phase . . . faze: Phase means a stage or a time period. College years are just one *phase* of your life. To ***faze*** means to upset, bother, or disconcert. Do not let the pressure of the GRE *faze* you.

everyday . . . every day: As one word, ***everyday*** means usual or customary. I wore my *everyday* clothes for a quick trip to the grocery store, little realizing that I'd run into Brad Pitt next to the kumquats. ***Every day*** as two words means each 24-hour period. From now on, I'm going to go to the store *every day* to get fresh fruit.

Miscellaneous Mistakes

Following are some of the miscellaneous grammar mistakes that many of us make every day. In the real world, we can live with these mistakes; on the GRE, they can be deadly.

In regards to . . . in regard to: The English language has no such expression as *in regards to.* Dump the *s;* the proper expression is ***in regard to.*** We need to have a heart-to-heart talk *in regard to* your making this mistake.

Hopefully: Use *hopefully* only where you could plug in the words *full of hope*. Hearing the telephone ring, Alice looked up *hopefully,* thinking that Steve might be calling her to apologize for sending her flowers on his ex-wife's birthday. Many of us incorrectly use the word *hopefully* as a substitute for "I hope." The sentence "*Hopefully* my GRE score will improve" is completely wrong. Your score won't improve unless you learn to say "I hope that my GRE score will improve."

If . . . would: Do not place *if* and *would* in the same clause. A common error is to say "*If* I *would* have studied more, I would have done better." The correct version is "*If* I *had* studied more, I would have done better" or "*Had* I studied more, I would have done better."

Where . . . that: Do not confuse *where* with *that. Where* refers to physical location only. Saying "Did you hear *where* Professor Denges ran off to Tahiti with his secretary?" is wrong. The correct structure is "Did you hear *that* Professor Denges ran off to Tahiti with his secretary?"

Hardly: Hardly is negative. Do not say "Ms. Hawker has *hardly nothing* to do this weekend after she's finished the GRE and is looking forward to vegging out in front of the TV." The correct version is "Ms. Hawker has *hardly anything* to do this weekend after she's finished the GRE and is looking forward to vegging out in front of the TV."

You get double value for your efforts in learning these rules. If there's one thing that ticks off the evaluators of the essays, it's a grammatical mistake. A glaring mistake colors an evaluator's thinking about the entire essay. If you keep nodding to yourself as you go through this grammar review, saying "Yeah, I always wondered about that rule" or "I remember every teacher since fifth grade yelling at me for that mistake," then pay special attention when you write your essays.

Index

extending the author's reasoning, reading comprehension questions, 67

extenuating circumstances, reason for repeating test, 18

extirpate, 256

eyes, relaxation techniques, 278

• F •

fact recognition, reading comprehension questions, 65–66

factoring, algebra problems, 110–111

false rumors, 269–272

fanaticism, 32

fawn, 253

fecklessness, 257

fee waivers, qualifying for, 17

ferret out, 57

fickle, 258

fidelity, 256

financial disabilities, fee waivers, 17

flamboyant, 258

flashcards, training aid, 27

fly-by-night, 256

FOIL (First, Outer, Inner, Last) method, algebra problems, 109–110, 281

foods, intermission guidelines, 14

foreign, 254

format

  antonym questions, 37

  quantitative comparisons, 141

  reading comprehension questions, 60

  sentence completion questions, 47

formulas

  area of a circle, 95

  area of a triangle, 84–85, 146

  D.I.R.T. (Distance Is Rate × Time), 115–116

  length of a circumference, 95

  one interior angle, 90–91

  probability problems, 112

  PRTI (Principal × Rate × Time = Interest), 126

  Pythagorean theorem, 85

  Pythagorean theorem (PT) ratios, 85–87

  total surface area (TSA), 92–93

  TSA of a cube, 92

  TSA of a cylinder, 92–93

  TSA of a rectangular solid, 92

  volume of a cube, 91

  volume of a cylinder, 91–92

  volume of a rectangular solid, 91

  writing down on paper before test begins, 16

fractions

  adding/subtracting, 131–132

  converting percentage to, 121

  dividing, 132

  mixed numbers, 133

  multiplying, 132

  probability problems, 112–114

frangible, 45

frank, 216

friends, problems of testing together, 275

• G •

garble, 255

general math

  absolute values, 127

  averages, 116–120

  bar graphs, 135

  circle graphs, 134

  composite numbers, 124–125

  decimals, 130–131

  D.I.R.T. (Distance Is Rate × Time) formula, 115–116

  fractions, 131–133

  graphs, 134–137

  imaginary numbers, 124

  integers, 123

  integral values, 123

  interest problems, 126

  irrational numbers, 123

  length measurement units, 128–129

  mixed numbers, 133

  mixture problems, 125–126

  number sets, 123–124

  order of operations, 128

  percentages, 120–123

  pie graphs, 134

  prime numbers, 124–125

  quantity measurement units, 128

  rational numbers, 123

  real numbers, 123–124

  statistics problems, 133–134

  three axes line graphs, 135

  time measurement units, 129

  two axes line graph, 135

  units of measurement, 128–129

  work problems, 126–127

genesis, 257

geometry problems

  acute angles, 79

  angle numbering schemes, 81–82

Notes

Notes

Notes

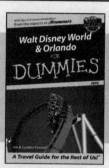

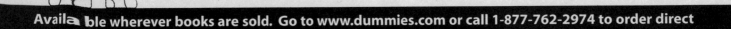

FOR DUMMIES

Helping you expand your horizons and realize your potential

GRAPHICS & WEB SITE DEVELOPMENT

0-7645-1651-5

0-7645-1643-4

0-7645-0895-4

PROGRAMMING & DATABASES

0-7645-0746-X

0-7645-1626-4

0-7645-1657-4

LINUX, NETWORKING & CERTIFICATION

0-7645-1545-4

0-7645-1760-0

0-7645-0772-9

 WILE